Gateway

Student's Book

2nd Edition

David Spencer
with Gill Holley

B2+

macmillan education

Contents B2+

1 Interact!

Reading

VOCABULARY Body idioms and human interaction

1a Match these idioms with the definitions 1–8.

be under someone's thumb • do something behind someone's back • get something off your chest • give someone the cold shoulder • lend someone a hand • pull someone's leg • see eye-to-eye with someone • stick your neck out for someone

1 treat someone in an unfriendly way
2 tell someone something that is not true, as a joke
3 help someone
4 do something without someone knowing about it
5 take a risk because you believe in someone
6 be controlled by someone
7 have the same opinion as someone
8 tell someone about something that has been worrying you

1b SPEAKING Complete these questions with the correct parts of the body. Then use the questions to interview a partner.

1 When was the last time you lent someone a ....? What did you do to help them?
2 What would you do if your friend said something mean about you behind your ....?
3 When was the last time you pulled someone's ....? What did you say or do?
4 Is there anything that you and a friend don't see ....-to-.......... about? What is it?
5 Do you think you are under anyone's ...., or that anyone is under yours? Who?
6 Who would be most likely to stick their .... out for you if you were in trouble?
7 Who do you talk to when you need to get something off your ....? Why?
8 What would you do if a friend gave you the cold ....?

2 Read four articles about experiments in human interaction. Match each article with a headline.

✔ EXAM SUCCESS

You are going to do a reading activity where you match questions or statements with different texts. In this type of activity, first underline key words in the questions. This can help you to find the relevant information in the texts.

➤ EXAM SUCCESS page 148

3 Read the texts again. For questions 1–12, choose from the four texts (A–D). The texts may be chosen more than once.

Which text describes a test that

- involved listening to what people say? 1 ....
- required people to change their normal behaviour? 2 ....
- gives a biological explanation for human relationships? 3 ....
- required participants to do two separate activities? 4 ....
- showed human relationships haven't changed? 5 ....
- took different personality types into account? 6 ....
- proves our assumptions about human behaviour are incorrect? 7 ....
- suggests group activities make people kinder? 8 ....
- confirmed what the psychologists expected? 9 .... 10 ....
- required people to record what they did every day? 11 .... 12 ....

4 CRITICAL THINKING

Think! Then compare ideas with your class.

- How effective are the research methods in the experiments?
- Do they accurately reflect human behaviour?

5 Guess the meaning of the underlined words from the context. Then use your dictionary to check.

6 SPEAKING What about *you*?

1 How important are friends to you? Do you think they influence you more than your family?
2 Is it necessary for friends to share common interests and opinions? In your opinion, what activities bond you and your friends?

1 THE REAL REASON PEOPLE LAUGH

3 IS IT REALLY SO BAD TO TALK TO STRANGERS?

2 How many friends can our brains cope with?

4 MOVING IN TIME BRINGS US CLOSER

A ☐ While most people agree that social interaction is important, we're told to keep our distance from strangers. But what if the advice is wrong?

The behavioural scientists, Nicholas Epley and Juliana Schroeder, approached commuters in Chicago who were about to get on a train. They asked one group of commuters to talk to the person next to them while they were travelling to work. Other people behaved as normal and kept to themselves. At the end of the train ride, the commuters who had talked to a stranger reported having a more positive experience than those who had been sitting alone.

In another study, psychologist Gillian Sandstrom asked people to carry two clickers, one red and one black, in their pockets all day. The people clicked the red one when they interacted with someone close to them, and the black one when they interacted with someone they didn't know well. She found that both introverts and extroverts felt happier on days when they had more social interactions. More surprisingly, interactions with strangers contributed as much to their happiness as those with family and friends.

It seems that all social interactions are important, not just with people we know well.

B ☐ Social media has revolutionised the way we relate to one another. It has allowed us to amass thousands of 'friends' online, but according to the evolutionary psychologist Robin Dunbar, certain things haven't changed.

Just over ten years ago, Dunbar began a study of the English habit of sending Christmas cards. He discovered that the average household sent about 150 cards a year. This number came as no surprise. Dunbar claims that our minds are not designed to accommodate more than a certain number of relationships – around 150, to be precise.

Over the past two decades, he and like-minded researchers have discovered groupings of 150 everywhere they looked. The average size of communities from hunter-gatherer societies up to the present day is around 150. Once a group grows larger, its members begin to lose their sense of connection.

Most of us can follow the lives and interests of about 150 friends on social media. Meanwhile, our circle of actual friends remains small. Further interviews and analysis carried out by Dunbar showed that the number of real-life friends a person can handle is 50. Our closest support group is likely to be around three.

C ☐ Researchers have long observed that humans tend to synchronise their body movements. When we walk with a friend, we often find our footsteps are in sync. The applause of a large audience tends to fall into a rhythm. What is the reason for this phenomenon in human behaviour?

Stanford psychologists Scott Wiltermuth and Chip Heath carried out a pair of tests on synchronised movements. They asked two groups of volunteers to walk around the Stanford campus. The first group was asked to walk normally, the second to walk in step.

Later, both groups were given collaborative games to play. The games were devised so that the more the participants cooperated, the more they collectively won. As Wiltermuth and Heath anticipated, the group that had walked in step cooperated better in the games. Those who had moved at their own speed and tempo were more likely to look out only for themselves.

The psychologists concluded that when people move in harmony, it helps them to feel a stronger connection to their group. It may even encourage people to act in a way that is beneficial for the community as a whole.

D ☐ Professor of psychology and neuroscience Robert Provine has been studying the roots of laughter for 20 years and has come to some surprising conclusions.

Over a ten-year period, Provine and his students recorded conversations in shopping centres and city pavements in order to discover what was happening just before people laughed. They studied 2,000 cases, and found that less than 20% of laughter followed jokes or humorous remarks. Most of the time people laughed after everyday comments such as 'Here comes Mary' or 'How did you do on the test?' Provine also found that the average speaker laughed 46% more often than the person they were speaking to.

In another experiment, 72 of Provine's students kept a record of their laughter for one week. They noted if they laughed when they were in company, or in response to the radio, TV or a book. The results showed that the students laughed about 30 times more when they were with other people than when they were alone.

Contrary to popular belief, it seems that most laughter is not about humour. It's mainly a way for people to bond with one another.

Past tenses

1a Name the tenses of the verbs in sentences 1–6.

1 They **reported** having a more positive experience than the commuters who **had been sitting** alone.
2 They asked one group to talk to the person next to them while they **were travelling** to work.
3 Social media **has revolutionised** the way we relate to one another.
4 After they **had walked** around the campus, the groups were given games to play.
5 Robert Provine **has been studying** the roots of laughter for 20 years.
6 Epley and Schroeder approached commuters in Chicago as they **were about to**/**were going to** get on a train.

1b Which tense or verb form in sentences 1–6 do we use for these situations?

a for finished actions or situations at specific times in the past
b for activities in progress at a moment in the past
c to talk about the future in the past
d for actions that happened at an unspecified moment in the past
e for actions that happened in the past before another moment or action in the past
f for actions that started in the past and are either incomplete or finished very recently, especially when the duration of the action is important
g to talk about actions that happened before another action in the past when the duration of the action is important

GRAMMAR REFERENCE ➤ PAGE 16

2 Choose the correct alternative.

1 We *have made/made* friends with some Swiss students on holiday last summer.
2 I*'ve/'d* been writing to a pen pal in Italy for the last three years. We get on really well.
3 On the way to school, we *chatted/have been chatting* to some people on the bus.
4 I know quite a lot about psychology because I've *been reading/read* six books about it.
5 My dad *has been/was* in a football team, but he stopped playing a few years ago.
6 He couldn't tell us the end of the joke because he*'d forgotten/has been forgetting* it.
7 I *had/have* been having problems with my computer for ages, so I got my brother to fix it.
8 They *left/were leaving* the cinema when they saw an old friend, so they *went/were going* back to see him.
9 She's my best friend. We *always saw/have always seen* eye-to-eye.
10 I have to go now. My train has *arrived/been arriving*.

3 Complete the sentences with the correct past form of the verbs given.

1 My friend .... (call) me at 11 o'clock last night, just as I .... (go) to bed.
2 I .... (have) a terrible headache all day – I .... (take) three headache tablets, but it won't go away.
3 When I .... (look) out of my window this morning, everything .... (be) white because it .... (snow) all night.
4 I .... (wait) to speak to the professor for over two hours, but she still hasn't arrived.
5 I find university life difficult. I .... (study) here for nine months, but I still .... (not make) any close friends.
6 I couldn't open the door because I .... (forget) to bring my key.
7 That dog is driving me mad. It .... (bark) all morning!

4 Decide if the verbs in bold are in the correct form. Rewrite the incorrect forms.

Psychologists (a) **had been interested** in discovering the key to lying for a long time, but it still doesn't seem easy to work out what makes a good liar. Once, a psychologist called Richard Wiseman (b) **has done** an interesting experiment using television. He (c) **interviewed** a famous person called Robin Day about his favourite film. In the first interview, Day (d) **told** Wiseman the truth. He (e) **described** how he loved the film *Some Like It Hot*. In the second interview, he (f) **lied**, telling the interviewer how much he liked *Gone with the Wind*, even though he really hated it. When they (g) **had been finishing** the interviews, they (h) **asked** viewers to watch the two interviews and to decide in which interview Day (i) **had been lying**. Almost 30,000 people phoned in to vote, but the votes were completely divided between the two interviews. It became clear that viewers (j) **were** simply **guessing**. Then a surprising thing happened. On the same day, the two interviews (k) **appeared** on the radio and in a newspaper. Seventy-three per cent of the radio listeners correctly (l) **guessed** when Day (m) **was lying**, and so did 64 per cent of the newspaper readers. Other recent tests (n) **have suggested** the same conclusion, that body language and facial expressions give little indication of people's sincerity. It seems to be more a question of the words we use.

5 Write one question using each of the past tenses in 1. Think of questions that help you to find out something you don't know about your partner.

6 SPEAKING **Interview your partner using your questions. Tell the class what you found out.**

Word formation – noun suffixes

1 Decide what type of noun each of these words is and then write the suffixes in the correct column.

accura**cy** • act**or** • coincid**ence** • happi**ness**
interact**ion** • move**ment** • particip**ant**
personal**ity** • psycholog**ist** • research**er**

Noun – abstract/concrete	Noun – person
-cy	

2 Add the suffixes in the table to the words below. Sometimes you can add more than one suffix. Make changes to the words if necessary.

1 science
2 argue
3 describe
4 intelligent
5 sincere
6 invent
7 similar
8 frequent
9 speak
10 lonely

3 Work with a partner. Match the suffixes with the words. Then think of at least one more word containing each suffix.

1 free
2 fail
3 import
4 safe
5 friend

a -ure
b -ance
c -dom
d -ship
e -ty

✓ EXAM SUCCESS

In this type of exercise, you should read the whole text to get a general idea of what it is about. Then read in more detail to decide if the word you need is plural, or has a negative meaning. Always read to the end of each sentence containing the gap, not just to the end of the line.

➤ EXAM SUCCESS page 148

4 Use the word given in capitals at the end of some of the lines to form a word that completes the sentence.

Recently a curious experiment was carried out in Edinburgh.
(a) .... left 240 wallets in different **RESEARCH**
parts of the city, leaving them as if their owners had accidentally dropped them. Each wallet contained a photograph, either of puppies, families, babies or an elderly couple.
The (b) .... of the experiment was **CONCLUDE**
that if you want your wallet to come back to you, you should keep a photo of a baby in it
since there was a significant (c) .... **DIFFER**
in the responses to the different photos. An unbelievable 88 per cent of the wallets with a photo of a baby were returned. The second-best result was perhaps more surprising. Fifty-three per cent of the wallets with puppy photos found their way back, whilst pictures of families and elderly couples had return rates of 48 per cent and 28 per cent respectively.
Why should the photo of a baby produce such
results? We know that (d) .... in **ACTIVE**
the section of the brain that is associated with empathy is much more responsive to baby faces than to adult faces. Perhaps our compassionate response to small children is really, deep
down, a question of (e) .... of **PROTECT**
the species.
However, there would have to be a different
(f) .... for the **EXPLAIN**
(g) .... of the puppies. **POPULAR**
All in all though, the leader of the research
teams, the (h) .... Richard **PSYCHOLOGY**
Wiseman, was pleasantly surprised to see how many wallets actually came back. It seems he
underestimated the (i) .... of **DECENT**
ordinary people.

5 Complete the words in the questions with a suffix.

1 What is your react.............. to the story about the lost wallets?
2 Why do you think people were more responsive to the appear.............. of a puppy than to elderly couples?
3 How do you account for the fail.............. to return the other wallets?
4 What would you do if you were a particip.............. in this experiment?
5 Can you give a descript.............. of your purse or wallet?
6 What do you think your purse/wallet says about your personal..............?

6 SPEAKING **Work with a partner. Discuss the questions in 5.**

EXPRESSING YOURSELF

21ST CENTURY SKILLS OBJECTIVES

- To discuss communication skills and why they're important
- To learn techniques for effective communication
- To practise and improve communication skills

KEY CONCEPTS

get across [v]: *I can generally get across my ideas and opinions so that people understand them.* **speak your mind [idiom]:** *She's not afraid to speak her mind, even if she upsets people.* **think through [phr vb]:** *If you think things through, you can organise your thoughts in a clear and thorough way.*

1 SPEAKING **Work with a partner. Discuss these questions.**

1. In what situations do you find it easy or difficult to express yourself?
2. Do you find some people easier or harder to talk to? Why do you think this is?
3. How important is it to be able to express yourself clearly?
4. Can you give an example of an occasion when someone needed to give more thought to what they said?

2 READING **Read the article. Answer these questions.**

1. What two things can lead to poor communication?
2. What are the four main tips to communicate effectively?

How to get your point across!

Imagine this situation. You're at your very first job interview. The interviewer asks you to talk about yourself. You look down, you don't know where to start and you can't think what to say. There's an awkward silence and you start to panic. Now imagine another situation. A friend makes a comment that upsets you. In the first instance you say nothing. But then you feel yourself getting angry and you explode and tell them what you really think!

Sound familiar? Well, you're not alone. We all have difficulty in expressing ourselves sometimes – we struggle to find the right words or our emotions get in the way. Yet effective communication is perhaps the most important life skill, particularly at work. Employers are often looking to hire people with strong interpersonal skills; they want people who will work well in a team and be able to communicate effectively with colleagues, customers and clients. And interpersonal skills are not just important in the workplace. Our personal and social lives can also benefit. People will good interpersonal skills are usually perceived as optimistic, calm and confident – qualities that are often appealing to others.

If we are more aware of how we interact with others, and remember to practise, we can all improve our ability to communicate. Here are our top four tips.

TIP 1 Think it through It's often difficult to come up with the right words on the spur of the moment, so give some thought to what you want to say. For instance, before an interview, think of answers to possible questions or say them out loud. Even better, try rehearsing with a friend. If you have to give an opinion, pause to organise your thoughts before you start to speak.

TIP 2 Be assertive Being assertive means expressing your ideas in a way that doesn't offend others. At the same time, it means speaking your mind without being afraid of what people might think. If you feel yourself getting angry or upset, take a deep breath and calm yourself. If necessary, take a short break from the conversation and come back to it when your head is clearer.

TIP 3 Remember to listen Too often we're so busy trying to get across our opinions that we forget to listen to what others have to say. Communication is a two-way process, which means trying to see the other person's point of view. Ask questions to help you understand, or summarise what they've just said. If you show you're prepared to listen to others, they're much more likely to listen to you.

3 **Read the article again. Explain in your own words why it's a good idea to:**

1. think before you speak.
2. pause before you give an opinion.
3. speak your mind.
4. take a deep breath and calm yourself.
5. ask questions or summarise what someone has said.
6. listen to others.
7. watch facial expressions and body language.
8. relax and smile.

4 LISTENING 01 **Two pairs of students are role-playing some situations. Watch the video or listen. Which student in each pair do you think communicates more effectively? Why?**

5 LISTENING 01 **Watch or listen again. Make notes about the ways in which the students communicate effectively, and areas to improve.**

9:30 AM

	Effective communication	Areas for improvement
Robert		
Hector		
Anna		
Aisha		

6 SPEAKING **Work with a partner. Discuss these questions.**

1. What are your areas of strengths and weaknesses in terms of communication skills?
2. What could you do to improve those skills?

A guide to effective communication

TIP 4 Watch your body language A lot of communication is non-verbal – more than 50% in fact. If someone has their arms folded, they probably feel defensive or aggressive. Facial expressions can tell us what a person is thinking, too. It's important to interpret these signals, and to be aware of your own body language. Sit calmly, keep eye contact – and remember to smile while you speak!

21ST CENTURY TASK

Work in groups of three. Taking turns, two of you are going to discuss a topic. The third person is going to observe and comment on your communication skills.

Follow this plan:

1. *Decide who will be the observer and who will discuss.*
2. *Select a topic. Then spend a few minutes thinking of your ideas.*
   - *People spend too much time on devices.*
   - *Girls are naturally better at communicating than boys.*
   - *Everyone should learn to speak at least one foreign language.*
   - *Families don't communicate as much as they should.*
3. *Discuss the topic in pairs. Remember to follow the tips from the article. As you do so, the observer will listen and observe your communication skills.*
4. *The observer will comment on your communication skills and give suggestions for improvement.*
5. *Repeat steps 1–4 with a different observer and topic of discussion. Repeat again until you have all had an opportunity to participate in a discussion.*

Flipped classroom: watch the grammar presentation video.

1 SPEAKING **Work with a partner. Discuss the questions.**

Are you now, or have you ever been, a member of a club, society or team? Give details. If not, would you like to be in one in the future? Why/Why not?

2 SPEAKING **Look at the photo. With a partner, describe what you can see. What type of group do you think they belong to?**

3 LISTENING 02 **Listen to a radio interview about fraternities and sororities in the US. What are some of the characteristics of these groups?**

4 LISTENING 02 **Listen again. Are the statements True (T), False (F) or is the information Not Given (NG)?**

1 Fraternities have a purely social purpose. T/F/NG
2 Fraternities use Greek letters as their names. T/F/NG
3 Originally, fraternities met to discuss important issues. T/F/NG
4 Sophie is a member of different clubs. T/F/NG
5 Sophie always gets good grades. T/F/NG
6 Students aren't involved in the choice about which fraternity they join. T/F/NG
7 'Hazing' is not allowed in most universities. T/F/NG
8 Students can talk about what happens in hazing rituals. T/F/NG
9 Daniel is involved in student government. T/F/NG
10 Sophie feels that her sorority has helped her with her social skills. T/F/NG

✓ EXAM SUCCESS

In True/False/Not Given listening activities, look at the statements before you listen. If you miss one answer, start listening immediately for the next one. Use the second listening to find the answers you didn't hear the first time and to check the answers you already have.

➤ EXAM SUCCESS page 148

5 SPEAKING **What about *you*?**

1 What is your opinion of fraternities and sororities?
2 Would you choose to become a member? Why/Why not?
3 Are there organisations like this in universities in your country? How are they similar or different?

Present and past habits

6 **Match the sentences with the verb forms. Then write the letter of the verb form next to the use.**

1 We're always having meetings, so it can get stressful at times.
2 They'd meet to talk about literature and politics.
3 Fraternities used to be literary societies.
4 They'll always go out of their way to help you.
5 Frats were always doing terrible things.
6 Frats often do fundraising for all sorts of charities.

a present simple (+ adverb of frequency)
b *would*
c *will*
d *used to*
e present continuous + adverb of frequency
f past continuous + adverbs of frequency

Present habit (neutral) ....
Present habit (annoying) ....
Past habit (neutral) ....
Past habit (annoying) ....

GRAMMAR REFERENCE ➤ PAGE 16

7 **Complete the sentences with an appropriate word.**

1 My brother is .... playing his music really loud. It drives me mad!
2 We .... play jokes on each other a lot when we were younger.
3 I .... to be in a chess club, but I'm not anymore.
4 We .... usually get dressed up at the weekend, but it depends where we're going.
5 As a child, I .... fall asleep in the car.
6 My sister .... always checking her phone to see if she's got a new message.
7 My dad .... always taking me to watch football with him when I was younger, even though I hated sports.
8 Marc often .... television in the evening after he's done his homework.

8 SPEAKING **Write at least five true sentences about a friend or family member, using the different forms in 7. Then discuss your sentences in pairs.**

Personal interviews

1 Look at these questions. Write the number of each question in one or more of the sections in the table. Write also *Present* or *Past*, depending on what the main focus of the question is.

1 Do you prefer studying on your own or with other people?
2 What do you do to relax?
3 What do you think is important for a successful friendship?
4 Do you prefer spending your free time alone or with others? Why?
5 How important is music in your life?
6 How long have you been studying English?
7 Who has had the greatest influence on your life?
8 How easy is it for you to meet new people and make friends?
9 Do you prefer spending your holidays with your family or friends?
10 How did you get to know your best friend?
11 What do you like to do at the weekend?
12 What has been your best holiday so far?

Language learning:
Studies: *1 (Present),*
Friends, family and relationships:
Holidays:
Free time:

2 LISTENING 03 Listen to three people answering the questions in 1. Answer the questions a–c, using the table to help you.

a Which question does each person answer?
b Does each person give just one piece of information or do they give more than one?
c Does each person create a good impression or not? How?

	Speaker 1	Speaker 2	Speaker 3
Question a			
Question b			
Question c			

3 Put these expressions from the speakers in 2 in the correct place in the Speaking bank.

1 As far as I'm concerned
2 The thing is …
3 To my mind,
4 Well,
5 For instance,

SPEAKING BANK

Useful expressions in personal interviews

Playing for time

- ……………
- Hmmm,
- ……………
- Let me think about that for a second.

Adding examples and ideas

- In fact,
- For example,
- ……………

Expressing opinions

- I think,
- Personally,
- ……………
- ……………

4 Think of answers to the questions in 1. Try to think of more than one piece of information for each question.

5 SPEAKING Work with a partner. Take it in turns to ask and answer the questions in 1. Use expressions from the Speaking bank.

6 Write two more questions for each category in the table in 1. Write a mixture of present and past questions.

7 PRACTICE MAKES PERFECT SPEAKING Work with a partner. Ask and answer your questions in 6. When you answer, give more than one piece of information.

A story

1 SPEAKING **Work with a partner. Discuss these questions.**

1 What is the last story you read? What was it about?
2 Did you like the story? Why/Why not?
3 What do you think makes a good story?

2 SPEAKING **Look at the photos and the title of the story. With a partner, discuss what the story may be about.**

3 **Read the story and check your ideas in 2.**

LOST AND FOUND AGAIN!

Greg was delighted with the gift his parents gave him for his birthday. It was a shiny new camera, just what he wanted. He hoped to become a photographer one day and would take pictures at every opportunity.

One day, he went to the park to practise his photography skills. His new camera worked like a dream and he took some of his best-ever photos. After a pleasant afternoon he returned home, only to find that he didn't have his camera. 'Oh no!' he groaned. 'I must have dropped it on the grass. How could I have been so stupid?' He immediately returned to the park to look for it, but to no avail. 'I'll never find my camera or see my photos again,' he sighed.

A few weeks later, Greg was flicking through the local newspaper when he happened to notice a photo that looked remarkably like one that he'd taken in the park. His face turned as white as a sheet. He started to read the story, and the headline leapt out at him. Did you take this photo? it said. The photo was definitely his! Greg was very surprised … as quick as a flash, he read to the end of the article and discovered that someone had been walking in the park, picked up his camera, and had handed it in to the paper. 'Mum! Dad! My photo's in the paper!' Greg yelled excitedly, before heading out of the door.

Greg rushed to the newspaper office and couldn't believe his eyes when he was given back his camera, together with the phone number of the person who had found it. He called to thank her and they arranged to meet for coffee. They looked through his photos together and they got on like a house on fire. It was only when Greg was about to leave that she revealed that she was a famous photographer! She thought his photos showed real promise and she wanted to help him with his career. Greg couldn't believe that losing his camera would turn out so well in the end.

VOCABULARY **Similes**

4a **Complete these similes from the story in 3.**

1 It worked **like** a ………………… .
2 He turned **as** white **as** a ………………… .
3 **As** quick **as** a ………………… .
4 They got on **like** a ………………… .

4b **Match 1–10 with a–j to make similes. Use your dictionary if necessary.**

1	as strong	a	as a daisy
2	as cold	b	as a feather
3	as quick	c	as ice
4	as light	d	as ABC
5	as cool	e	as a mouse
6	as quiet	f	as a flash
7	as fresh	g	as mud
8	as clear	h	as an ox
9	as easy	i	as a cucumber
10	as solid	j	as a rock

5 **Work with a partner. Invent your own similes using 1–10 in 4b.**

as strong as a ten-foot giant, as cold as winter in Alaska

6 **Compare your similes and choose the best.**

VOCABULARY Ways of talking

7a LISTENING 04 **Read the sentences and listen. Match the words in bold with the definitions 1–8. Use a dictionary if necessary.**

a 'Oh well, my team has lost again,' he **sighed**.

b 'It can't be! I thought you were dead!' she **gasped**.

c 'Stop it! Stop it this minute!' he **yelled**.

d 'But, Mum, please, I don't want to go! Please …' the girl **whined**.

e 'It's a ghost!' she **shrieked**.

f 'Don't tell Alex about the surprise party,' he **whispered**.

g 'Sorry. I didn't, I didn't really mean to do it, well, not exactly,' he **muttered**.

h 'Oh, no. Not another exam!' **groaned** the students.

1 to speak in a very loud high voice because you are so scared or angry that you cannot control yourself

2 to speak in a loud voice because you are angry, excited or in pain, or in order to make people hear you

3 to speak very quietly so that other people can't hear you

4 to speak in a way that shows you are unhappy

5 to speak breathing out slowly, making a long soft sound, especially because you are disappointed, tired, annoyed or relaxed

6 to speak while you are breathing in suddenly, for example because you are surprised, shocked or in pain

7 to complain in a way that annoys other people

8 to speak in a low voice that is difficult to hear, especially because you are annoyed, embarrassed or talking to yourself

7b **Replace *said* in these sentences with an appropriate verb in 7a.**

1 'Oh well! Better luck next time!' **said** Brian. It was the fifth time he'd failed his driving test, but he was taking it calmly.

2 'Come here right now and say you're sorry!' her mother **said**, furious at the way her daughter had just spoken to her.

3 'I want to get off!' he **said** in the middle of the roller coaster ride. He had never been more scared in his life!

4 'Sorry I'm late. It's, erm, well, the bus was late,' she **said**. Unfortunately, the teacher could hardly make out a word.

5 'It's not fair, it isn't! It's just not fair,' **said** the boy. It was the tenth time he'd made the comment and everybody was losing patience with him.

6 'My leg! I think it's broken!' he **said**, although it was hard for him to breathe because of the pain.

8 **Read the information in the Writing bank. Underline examples of each device in the story in 3.**

WRITING BANK

Useful linguistic devices in a story

Stories can be made more interesting by including:

- a variety of past tenses, including the past continuous, past perfect simple and continuous and the future in the past.
- a variety of adjectives and adverbs.
- short sections of direct speech using a variety of verbs expressing different ways of speaking.
- similes.
- linkers and expressions of time and sequence.

9 **Work with a partner. Discuss these questions.**

1 Do you like surprising people?

2 Do you like receiving surprises?

3 What's the biggest surprise you or somebody in your family has ever had?

10 PRACTICE MAKES PERFECT **Write a story of 200–250 words. Your story must end with this sentence.**

It had been the most surprising thing that had ever happened to them, and probably ever would.

WRITING BANK ➤ PAGE 154

✔ EXAM SUCCESS

When you write a narrative, allow time for planning and editing. Before you begin writing, plan the beginning, the middle and the end of the story in order to make all the main events clear. When you finish, check the number of words you have written. Cut or add details to make sure that the number is right. Don't underestimate the importance of these two stages, or the time they take.

➤ EXAM SUCCESS page 148

Grammar reference

For past simple, past continuous and present perfect simple, see page 166.

Present perfect continuous

The **present perfect continuous** is used in a similar way to the present perfect simple. However, we use the continuous when we want to emphasise the process and duration of an action.

*I've **been studying** in this school for more than five months.*

For that reason, if an action is very short, we cannot use the continuous form.

~~I've been breaking the window.~~

We also use the continuous to emphasise that an action finished very recently or is incomplete.

*I've **been washing** the dishes … and my hands are wet because I only finished a second ago/I still haven't finished.*

If we want to emphasise the completion and result of an action, or how many times an action happens, we must use the **present perfect simple**.

*I've **painted** my bedroom. (It's finished.)*

*I've **seen** that film three times.*

~~I've been seeing that film three times.~~

Past perfect simple

We use the **past perfect simple** to talk about actions that happened before another action or actions in the past. It gives importance to the completion of an activity.

*When the interview **had finished**, I left.*

Past perfect continuous

We use the **past perfect continuous** to talk about actions that happened before another action in the past. It gives importance to the duration of an activity.

*I was tired because I **had been studying** all night.*

Future activities in the past

FORM

was about to … was going to

USE

Sometimes when we are talking about the past, we want to talk about something that was in the future at that time, something which had not happened and perhaps did not actually happen in the end. To do this, we can use the past tense of the verb forms we would normally use to talk about the future, e.g. *am going to* ➡ *was going to; am about to* ➡ *was about to; will* ➡ *would*

*I **was going to** come to the cinema, but I had to babysit in the end.*

Present and past habits

To talk about present habits we can use:

1 the **present simple** with or without an adverb of frequency.

*Our lessons **start** at eight o'clock.*

2 the **present continuous** with an adverb of frequency. This usually implies that the speaker finds the habit annoying.

*She **'s always taking** my things.*

3 **will**

*My friends and I **will** usually meet and see a film on Friday evenings.*

To talk about past habits that we have stopped doing, we can use:

1 **used to**

*My dad **used to** read me stories when I was small.*

We cannot use ***used to*** to talk about single events in the past or when we give a period of time. In this case, we use the past simple.

*She **used to** work in a factory. She worked there for five years. NOT ~~She used to work in a factory for five years.~~*

The negative form of **used to** is **didn't use to**. There is no present form of **used to** – we use the present simple with an adverb of frequency.

2 **would**

We use **would** with past actions but not past states.

*He **would** come and visit us on Sundays. NOT ~~He would have a bike.~~*

We do not usually use **wouldn't** to talk about past habits.

He didn't use to give us presents. NOT ~~He wouldn't give us presents.~~

3 the **past continuous** with an adverb of frequency. This usually implies that the speaker found the habit annoying.

*My mum **was always telling** me to get up early on Sundays when I was small.*

Vocabulary

For body idioms and human interaction, noun suffixes, similes and ways of talking, see wordlist page 136.

Grammar revision

Past tenses
/ 8 points

1 Choose the correct alternative.

1 There you are! At last! I've *waited/been waiting* for you for hours.
2 That's the best festival that I *went/have been* to so far.
3 He couldn't go until he*'s/'d* finished his assignment.
4 When I'd *read/been reading* all my emails, I made myself a snack.
5 The plot in last night's film *has been/was* awful.
6 While I *was/had been* watching the match, I saw Tim in the crowd.
7 I opened the door and *stepped/had stepped* outside.
8 When he *had/had had* his shower, he dried himself.

Present and past habits
/ 6 points

2 Decide if the verbs in bold are in the correct form. Tick (✓) the correct forms and rewrite the incorrect forms.

1 My parents **will buy** me presents every week.
2 When he was five, he **would have** a bike.
3 When I lived close to the stadium, I **would go to see** matches.
4 My parents **were always insisting** that I wore gloves all winter when I was small. It was so annoying.
5 I **used to go** to Brazil once for a holiday.
6 I love films so I **use to go** to the cinema once a week.

Vocabulary revision

WORD FORMATION – NOUN SUFFIXES
/ 8 points

1 Decide if the words in bold are in the correct form. Tick (✓) the correct forms and rewrite the incorrect forms.

1 I don't understand the **import** of these events.
2 A lot of elderly people suffer from **lonely**.
3 All the **participants** win a prize.
4 My parents give me total **free** to do what I like.
5 Computers are the most significant **invent** in recent years.
6 Accidents are happening with great **frequency**.
7 Their cars have a reputation for **safe**.
8 Before we started the course, we did an **intelligent** test.

BODY IDIOMS AND HUMAN INTERACTION
/ 6 points

2 Read definitions 1–6 and complete the idioms with a part of the body.

1 do something without someone knowing about it: do something behind someone's ....
2 have complete control over someone: have someone under your ....
3 tell someone something that is not true: pull someone's ....
4 treat someone you know in an unfriendly way: give someone the cold ....
5 take a risk because you believe in someone: stick your .... out for someone
6 tell someone about something that has been worrying you: get something off your ....

SIMILES
/ 6 points

3 Complete the similes with these words. There are three extra words.

cold • easy • fresh • light • quick • quiet • solid • strong • white

1 I'm feeling as .... as a daisy.
2 I'll be over at your house as .... as a flash.
3 He sat there as .... as a mouse.
4 He's as .... as a rock.
5 His face was as .... as a sheet.
6 My hands are as .... as ice.

WAYS OF TALKING
/ 6 points

4 Answer the questions with these words.

gasp • mutter • shriek • whine • whisper • yell

How would you speak if you:
1 wanted to say something romantic to somebody, but you didn't want other people to hear?
2 were really surprised and finding it hard to breathe?
3 wanted to speak to somebody far away?
4 were really scared/angry and out of control?
5 were annoyed and were talking to yourself?
6 were continually complaining that things aren't fair?

Total: / 40 points

2 Road trips

Reading

VOCABULARY Compound nouns – cars and the road

1a Work with a partner. Match 1–10 with a–j to make compound nouns. Decide if each compound should be written as one word or two words. Use your dictionary if necessary.

1 motor	a limit
2 seat	b signs
3 driving	c jam
4 road	d ways
5 speed	e about
6 steering	f licence
7 traffic	g lights
8 traffic	h station
9 round	i belt
10 petrol	j wheel

1b SPEAKING Complete the sentences with words from 1. Then discuss the sentences with your partner. Do you agree or disagree?

1 It's compulsory to wear a .... in a car, but not everybody wears one.
2 The .... in cities is 50 kilometres an hour, but it should be 30 kilometres an hour.
3 There are often .... because too many people use their cars to travel to and from work.
4 Cars in the future will be self-driving, so they won't have a ....
5 You don't need a map when you travel by car because the .... are clear.
6 The number of accidents on .... is very high because people travel too fast.
7 Most drivers stop when the .... are red or amber.
8 The minimum age to legally obtain a .... should be 21, not 18.

2 Read the magazine article, ignoring the gaps, and answer these questions.

1 What are the legal ages for driving in New Zealand, the US and the UK?
2 According to the article, does it seem that the legal age will stay the same or rise in the future?

3 Choose from the sentences A–H the one which best fits each gap (1–8).

A Nowadays parents tend not to do this to avoid the typical family rows and shouting that sometimes follow.
B This only fully develops by the age of 25.
C They claim that it's irrelevant whether that first year is at the age of 15, 16 or 17.
D Recent findings are being used by some in the US as an argument for raising the legal age of drivers there.
E The change may well have had something to do with the fact that the fatality rate of drivers was 60 per cent higher than in neighbouring Australia.
F That may explain why ten per cent of drivers aged between 17 and 21 feel that they should not have passed their driving test.
G Plus the fact that in farming areas, many teens must learn to drive so that they can help out with the work.
H This has already contributed to saving lives, but one problem of the scheme is that parents have to enforce it, and many are not doing so.

4 Underline any reasons given in the article why young drivers have more accidents than other drivers. Can you think of any other reasons?

5 CRITICAL THINKING

Think! Then compare ideas with your class.

- What do you think is the writer's opinion of teenage drivers?
- What do you think is his/her aim in writing the article?

6 Guess the meaning of the underlined words from the context. Then use your dictionary to check.

7 SPEAKING What about *you*?

1 How important is it for you to get a driving licence? Why?
2 Do you agree that younger drivers are more dangerous than older drivers? Why/Why not?
3 What is your opinion of 'graduating licensing'?
4 What would you recommend to reduce the number of road accidents?

READY FOR THE ROAD?

What is the best age to learn to drive? This may seem like a simple question, but there is a surprising difference between the legal requirements in different countries, and a lot of disagreement on national levels.

Until just recently, in New Zealand you only had to be 15 to be able to drive. Then the New Zealand government decided to raise the legal age to 16, suggesting that they might toughen this up in the not-too-distant future.

(1) .... Unfortunately, the changes to the law have not gone down well in rural areas where there is almost no public transport and parents have to chauffeur their kids around whenever they want to go anywhere. (2) ....

Many New Zealanders who were against the raising of the legal age argued that the government shouldn't have bothered since statistically the highest number of accidents will come in a driver's first year. (3) .... However, in the US, where you can begin driving at the age of 14 in some states, there has been a lot of research done into the question of age and its influence on driving skills, and the results suggest that age makes a big difference. The research has shown that there is a part of the brain that helps to control impulsive behaviour and warn us of imminent danger. (4) .... Interestingly, there is evidence to suggest that a lot of development happens between the ages of 16 and 18, and so a new 17- or 18-year-old driver will be safer than a new 16-year-old driver. In other words, there is a scientific reason why teenagers can at times be more careless and rash, and their impetuous nature can sometimes get the better of them when they fasten their seat belts and sit behind the steering wheel.

(5) .... The statistics are frightening but clear. Sixteen-year-old drivers are more dangerous than any other teenage drivers, being involved in thousands of fatal accidents each year and being a principal cause of death amongst teenagers. One interesting discovery is that accidents are more likely when a teenage driver is accompanied than when he or she drives alone. With two or more passengers, the fatal crash risk for 16- to 19-year-old drivers is more than five times what it is when driving alone. Why? Maybe it's simply because they become distracted by the presence of other people in the car. Or maybe it's because teenagers are more likely to take risks and break speed limits when driving with their friends since they want to show off and go fast. Whatever the reason, the discovery has led to many states implementing a system known as 'graduated licensing' rules where 16-year-olds are not allowed to drive alone until they have driven a certain number of hours. (6) ....

In the UK, where you need to be 17 to get a provisional driving licence, parents are seen as contributing to the lowering of standards amongst young drivers. Traditionally, British parents used to take their kids out on practice driving lessons and these practice lessons would help the young drivers to gain confidence and experience.

(7) .... The UK Driving Standards Agency suggests that learners should have 45 hours of professional lessons, plus another 22 hours of practice. However, a recent study shows that today's young motorists only have an average of 29.9 hours of professional lessons before taking and passing their test, and 27 per cent of young drivers say they had no practice at all with their parents. (8) ....

In many countries, then, there is some debate as to what the best age is to become a driver. In general, because of the horrifying statistics, there is a growing feeling that the age should be made higher. With more and more young drivers on the road, the debate will no doubt continue.

"Sixteen-year-old drivers are more dangerous than any other teenage drivers"

Modal verbs – obligation, permission, prohibition, criticism and advice

1a Work with a partner. Explain why the words or expressions in bold are used in each sentence. Decide if they refer to the present or the past.

1 You only **had to** be 15 to be able to drive.
2 They feel they **shouldn't have** passed.
3 Sixteen-year-olds **are not allowed** to carry other teen passengers.
4 You **need to** be 17 to get a driving licence.
5 They think learners **should** have 45 hours of professional lessons.
6 Many teens **must** learn to drive so that they can help out with work.

1b How do you change each sentence in 1a from present to past, or vice versa, without changing the meaning?

GRAMMAR REFERENCE ➤ PAGE 28

2 Look at these sentences. Do they have the same meaning? If not, explain the difference.

1a I didn't need to go to school yesterday.
1b I needn't have gone to school yesterday.
2a You don't have to eat everything on the plate.
2b You mustn't eat everything on the plate.
3a We ought to leave now if we want be on time.
3b We'd better leave now if we want be on time.
4a You have to use a pencil in this part of the exam.
4b You've got to use a pencil in this part of the exam.
5a When I was small, I wasn't allowed to stay up late.
5b When I was small, I may not have stayed up late.
6a I must have worn a school uniform in primary school.
6b I had to wear a school uniform in primary school.
7a You shouldn't wake her up yet.
7b You aren't supposed to wake her up yet.
8a Must you make noise while I'm working?
8b Do you have to make noise while I'm working?

3 Complete the sentences with an appropriate modal verb and the correct form of the verbs given. There may be more than one possible answer.

1 You .... texts while you're driving. (send)
2 When I was small, we .... everywhere because we didn't have a car or a bike. (walk)
3 You .... with a red pen in the exam yesterday because the teacher gets annoyed. (write)
4 You .... early this morning because it's Sunday. Why did you do it? (get up)
5 My dad .... jeans at school. They had a special rule against it. (wear)
6 If you really want to buy a car next year, I think you .... a job and start saving. (find)

4 Complete the second sentence so that it has a similar meaning to the first sentence, using the word given. Do not change the word given. You must use between three and six words, including the word given.

1 It would have been better if I'd told you the truth.
I .... the truth. **HAVE**
2 He said we mustn't go without him.
He said we .... without him. **TO**
3 We must buy tickets from the driver.
We .... tickets from the driver. **GOT**
4 It was a bad idea for us to drive in the snow.
We .... in the snow. **HAVE**
5 It was stupid of me to worry about the exam.
I .... the exam. **NEEDN'T**
6 I'm annoyed you went to the party without me.
You .... without me. **GONE**
7 It would have been better for them to get a taxi.
They .... a taxi. **OUGHT**

5 SPEAKING Work in a group. Talk about these situations using present and past modals. Make at least four sentences for each situation.

1 Two friends, Alice and Olivia, set off on a six-month road trip together. Now, one month later, they are having terrible arguments because they each want to visit different places and do different things.
They should've decided where to go before they left.
2 Brad is riding his motorbike through Argentina during his gap year. One day, he has an accident. His bike is damaged and he's hurt his arm. He doesn't have much money and he doesn't have insurance. He doesn't speak Spanish very well.
3 Helen wants to travel in the US during the summer holidays. She's already bought a plane ticket, but now she can't persuade any of her friends to go with her. She doesn't want to go alone.
4 Dave and Ben are driving in a remote area when they run out of petrol. They haven't seen a petrol station for many kilometres and there is no coverage to make a phone call. They haven't told anyone where they're going.

6 SPEAKING Tell your partner about something you:

1 had better do today.
2 should do more frequently.
3 ought to have done last week.
4 must do next week.
5 have to do on a regular basis.
6 aren't allowed to do at home.
7 weren't allowed to do when you were young.
8 did once, but needn't have.

Collocations with *take, make* and *do*

1 Choose the correct verb to complete each of these sentences which appear in the text on page 19.

1 Teenagers are more likely to ...... risks and break speed limits when driving with their friends.
A take B make C do

2 The results suggest that age ...... a big difference.
A takes B makes C does

3 There has been a lot of research ...... into the question of age and its influence on driving skills.
A taken B made C done

2 Write these words and phrases in the correct column. Some can go in more than one column.

an apology • an attempt • business • a call • changes • a choice • a comment • a complaint • control • a course • cover • a decision • a difference • effect • harm • household chores • an improvement • an interest • a mistake • offence • place • power • research • a risk • a suggestion • a test • use of something • your best

take	make	do

3 Decide if the verbs *take, make* and *do* are used correctly. Rewrite the incorrect sentences.

1 The best way to do an apology is to be sincere.
2 It's time you took control of the situation.
3 Don't make offence, but we don't think you're the right person for the job.
4 It was a mistake to make business with them.
5 We decided to do a formal complaint.
6 Eating chocolate occasionally doesn't do any harm.

✓ EXAM SUCCESS

You are going to do a multiple-choice cloze text. To choose between different options, think about the meaning, grammar (e.g. if a verb goes with a particular preposition), and also about collocation and set phrases.

➤ EXAM SUCCESS page 148

4 Read the text and decide which answer (A, B, C or D) best fits each gap.

Driving across the US is a classic American pastime, but perhaps the first road trip **(1)** ...... place in 1903. It all started when Horatio Nelson Jackson was sitting in a club in San Francisco, discussing cars with his friends. Cars were a recent invention at the time and someone **(2)** ...... a comment that they were too unreliable to drive across the country. Jackson bet his friends $50 that he could do it.

He bought a new red car and set **(3)** ...... from San Francisco on 23rd May. He had little experience of driving and he didn't have a driver's licence because in those days you **(4)** ...... need one. There were no road signs and no petrol stations so he was **(5)** ...... a big risk. Not surprisingly, the car broke **(6)** ...... several times on the way. At one point, he had to **(7)** ...... use of a horse to pull him to the nearest town. On another occasion, he was given bad directions and got lost for 36 hours on a road that he **(8)** ...... not have taken.

In spite of all the difficulties, Jackson **(9)** ...... his best to remain optimistic. He was helped when people heard that he was **(10)** ...... an attempt to cross the country and came out to support him.

Finally, after 63 days, Jackson arrived in New York. He'd won his bet of $50, but spent $8,000 in the process.

	A	B	C	D
1	did	took	made	had
2	told	made	did	said
3	on	up	off	away
4	needn't have	mustn't have	shouldn't have	didn't need
5	taking	making	doing	having
6	up	down	away	off
7	take	do	make	have
8	must	ought	had better	should
9	did	took	made	had
10	trying	making	doing	taking

Making GOOD DECISIONS

LIFE SKILLS OBJECTIVES

- To identify what kind of decision-maker you are
- To understand how brain development influences decision-making
- To learn strategies for making good decisions

KEY CONCEPTS

a snap decision [n]: *If you make a snap decision, without thinking of the consequences, you might regret it later.* **think ahead [v]:** *The part of the brain that is associated with thinking ahead and calculating risks is located behind the forehead.* **synapse [n]:** *Chemical signals are passed from one cell in the brain to another through a structure called a synapse.*

1 SPEAKING **Work with a partner. Discuss these questions.**

1 Are you good at making decisions or are you indecisive?

2 Which of the following do you think are good ways to make decisions?

- toss a coin to see which side it lands on
- get as much information as possible and then weigh up the pros and cons
- follow your instincts
- ask for advice from an expert or friend
- make a snap decision and see what happens
- put off making a decision and hope that things work out

3 How do you usually make decisions? Have you ever used any of the ways above?

2 In your opinion, are teenagers usually good at making decisions? Why/Why not?

3 READING **Read the article. Which of the following best summarises the article?**

a Teenage decision-making is determined by brain development.

b Emotions play a big part in teenage decision-making.

c The teenage brain is not yet fully developed.

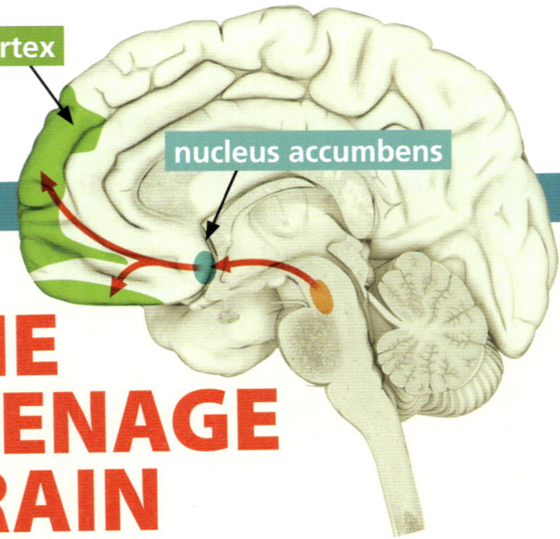

THE TEENAGE BRAIN

Why do teenagers think and act differently?

Teenagers are often accused of making poor decisions and excessive risk-taking – hence the high number of car accidents among teen drivers. But discoveries in brain science show that there is a reason for this behaviour.

For many years, scientists thought that the human brain was fully mature before the teen years. They thought that a person's brain growth was complete and the structure was more or less fixed by the age of 3. However, more recent research shows that although the brain reaches its maximum size between the ages of 12 and 14, brain development is not yet complete. In fact, certain regions of the brain continue to develop into the early 20s.

A key region of the brain that matures late is the prefrontal cortex, located just behind the forehead. This cortex acts as a control centre for thinking ahead and calculating risks. This is the area of the brain that might stop you from making a bad decision. It communicates with the other sections of the brain through connections called synapses. Scientists have found that there is a growth in synapses during adolescence. The brain automatically removes the synapses that it doesn't need in order to make the remaining ones more efficient, but because this process starts at the back of the brain and moves forward, the prefrontal cortex is reached last. As a result, teenagers rely more on the back of the brain when making decisions, whereas adults do more processing in the prefrontal cortex and so are better able to calculate risks.

Meanwhile, two other parts of the brain develop earlier, the nucleus accumbens and the limbic system.

4 Read the article again. Decide if the sentences are True (T) or False (F).

1 Brain development is complete by the age of 20. T/F
2 The area of the brain associated with risk-taking develops in the early teens. T/F
3 The number of synapses increases during the teenage years. T/F
4 The brain removes synapses that it doesn't need. T/F
5 The process of removing unwanted synapses starts in the prefrontal cortex. T/F
6 The pleasure and reward area of the brain develops early. T/F
7 The cells and connections that are used by the brain are not removed. T/F
8 The activities teenagers do has no effect on their brain development. T/F

5 Look at the model below about how to make good decisions. With reference to the article, why might it be a good idea to make a decision in this way?

10:30 AM

REMEMBER ICED

Too often we rush into decisions, and don't keep a cool head! So next time you have to decide something important, remember ICED.

- **I** – Identify what the problem or issue is
- **C** – Create possible options
- **E** – Evaluate each option – consider the possible consequences (both pros and cons) of each
- **D** – Decide on the best solution

Later, evaluate the decision you made. Was it the right choice? Why/Why not?

> "Teenagers rely more on the back of the brain when making decisions, whereas adults do more processing in the prefrontal cortex and so are better able to calculate risks."

Prefrontal cortex
A key region of the brain that matures late, located just behind the forehead. This cortex acts as a control centre for thinking ahead and calculating risks

Synapses
Communication connections between different sections of the brain

Nucleus accumbens
The region of the brain associated with pleasure and reward

The nucleus accumbens is the region of the brain associated with pleasure and reward while the limbic system plays a central role in emotional responses. The early development of these two areas explains why emotions have a much stronger influence in the decision-making process among teenagers.

Together, these factors make it easier to understand why teenagers sometimes make more impulsive choices than adults. They also suggest that important life decisions should be made later in life, or with the help of adult advice.

The good news is that teenagers do have the potential, through choice and behaviour, to shape their brain development. Scientists believe that during the time the brain is removing synapses, the cells and connections that are used survive, while the ones that are not used die away. So if a teenager is doing music, sports or academic studies, those are the cells and connections that will become part of the brain's operating system. But unfortunately, if he or she is lying on the sofa, watching TV and playing computer games, those are the brain cells that will remain into adulthood, meaning that what you do with your teenage years could have an effect on the rest of your life. Just as important is that learning how the brain develops can help teenagers be better equipped to make more intelligent choices, motivating them to take a moment before acting to consider the consequences of their actions.

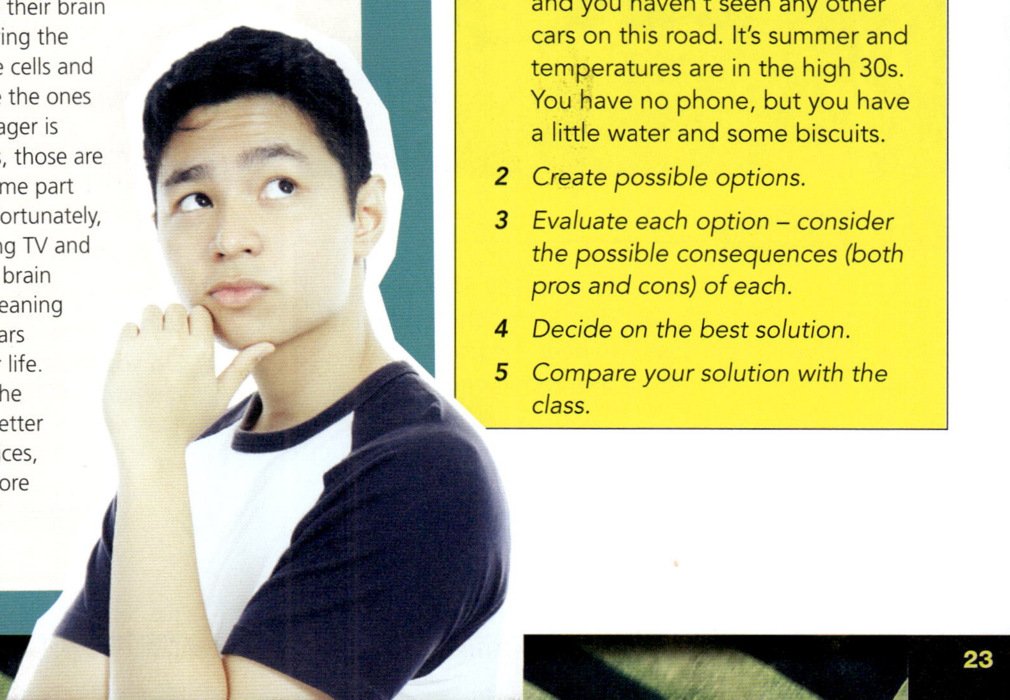

6 LISTENING 05 **A teenager called Jess is making a decision. Watch the video or listen. Does she follow the model in 5? If so, how does she do it?**

LIFE TASK

You are going to work in groups of three to make a decision.

Follow this plan:

1 *Read the situation and identify the problem.*
You have been on a school camping trip and are returning home when your group gets lost. After driving for many kilometres, the minibus breaks down. You are in a remote area so there are no houses in sight and you haven't seen any other cars on this road. It's summer and temperatures are in the high 30s. You have no phone, but you have a little water and some biscuits.

2 *Create possible options.*

3 *Evaluate each option – consider the possible consequences (both pros and cons) of each.*

4 *Decide on the best solution.*

5 *Compare your solution with the class.*

1 SPEAKING **Work with a partner. Look at the photos of 'the world's most dangerous road'. Write five questions about the road that you would like to be answered.**

✓ EXAM SUCCESS

You are going to do a multiple-choice listening activity. In this type of activity, do not choose an alternative just because you hear a word that appears in it. Think about the overall meaning of what is being said.

➤ EXAM SUCCESS page 148

2 LISTENING 06 **Listen to a podcast about the road and choose the best answers.**

1 The presenter says the road
 a is by far the most dangerous in the world.
 b is popular with sightseers.
 c may attract people because of its reputation.

2 Bill Shipman thinks
 a the locals don't understand why people go to Death Road.
 b you have to be mad to work on Death Road.
 c you can make a lot of money working for a mountain biking business.

3 The presenter thinks that the name Death Road
 a describes the road perfectly.
 b makes it sound more dangerous than it really is.
 c isn't totally accurate because in some ways it's not really a road.

4 The number of fatalities on the road per year has dropped because
 a traffic has been greatly reduced.
 b the road is exclusively for cyclists now.
 c the condition of the road has improved greatly.

5 To make the cycling journey easier, Bill and his company
 a ask for help from a local 'earth goddess'.
 b let the cyclists get accustomed to the situation progressively.
 c take the cyclists in their support vehicle for part of the journey.

6 If you fall off the road,
 a you can fall over 500 metres.
 b the biking companies are equipped to help in every situation.
 c the biking companies sometimes forget to bring suitable equipment for a rescue.

7 Most people want to ride the world's most dangerous road because they want to
 a see the spectacular scenery for themselves.
 b impress others.
 c improve their survival skills.

3 SPEAKING **Did the podcast answer all of your questions in 1? Discuss your unanswered questions and hypothesise about the answers. What could you do to find the answers?**

4 SPEAKING **What about *you*?**

1 Would you ever consider going along the world's most dangerous road by car or by bike? Why/Why not?
2 Have you ever done something dangerous?
3 Can you explain why some people like doing dangerous activities?
4 Do you think dangerous activities should be encouraged? Or banned?

Flipped classroom: watch the grammar presentation video.

Discussing photos – 1

1 Look at these photos. They show different minor accidents.

Student A: Compare and contrast two of the three pictures saying:

- how the accidents might have happened.
- how they could have been prevented.

Student B: When your partner has finished talking about the pictures, say which of them is the worst accident and why.

2 LISTENING 07 **Listen to a student doing the task in 1. Which two photos does the student talk about? Does he do all parts of Student A's task in 1?**

Modal verbs – speculation, deduction, possibility and probability

3 Work with a partner. Explain why the words or expressions in bold are used in each sentence. Decide if they refer to the present or the past.

1 The car on the right **must have** hit the other car from behind.
2 The driver on the right **could** be an inexperienced driver.
3 He **can't have** known what he was doing.
4 He **might have** been distracted by his mobile phone.
5 The accident **may well have** been easy to prevent.

GRAMMAR REFERENCE ➤ PAGE 28

4 Complete the sentences with modal verbs. Sometimes more than one can be used.

1 Surely Jamie .... have a driving licence yet – he's only 15.
2 I think they .... have left but I'm not sure.
3 I .... well take driving lessons in the summer if I have enough money.
4 She .... have taken the car because it's still here in the garage.
5 He .... have passed his driving test because I saw him driving yesterday.
6 The accident .... have happened if he had been driving more slowly.

5 Work with a partner. Apart from language of speculation and deduction, what language do you think is useful when discussing photos? Make a list, then compare it with the Speaking bank.

SPEAKING BANK

Useful language to discuss photos

- Modal verbs of speculation – *may, might, must, can't*
- Comparatives and superlatives, *(not) as … as, less … than*
- Linkers of contrast – *while, whereas, although, however*
- Expressions of opinion – *to my mind, personally*
- Prepositions and words and expressions to explain position – *in the foreground, at the back*
- Expressions such as: *Both photographs show …, One significant difference between the photos is that …, Compared with …*

✔ EXAM SUCCESS

When you discuss photos, make sure that you speak for the correct amount of time. Divide the time so that you manage to cover all the different points in the task. Remember that you have to compare and contrast the photos, not describe each one in detail.

➤ EXAM SUCCESS page 149

6 PRACTICE MAKES PERFECT SPEAKING **Work with a partner. Look at the photos on page 162 and follow these instructions.**

Student A: Compare and contrast two of the pictures saying:

- why the people may have decided to travel in this way.
- how the people might be feeling.

Student B: Do the same task with the two remaining pictures.

An opinion essay

1 SPEAKING **Work with a partner and read the statement. Do you agree with it? Why/Why not?**

The minimum legal age to obtain a driving licence in the UK should be lowered to 16.

2 **Read the essay. What is the writer's point of view? Is it similar to your opinion?**

The idea of lowering the minimum legal age to obtain a driving licence to 16 is, without doubt, a very sensitive one. Nevertheless, there are many things that 16-year-olds can already do, such as work part-time and leave home and even get married with their parents' consent. I certainly believe that the legal age to get a driving licence should be lowered and will discuss the reasons why in this essay.

Firstly, to my mind, there is no question that a driving licence is essential nowadays. Many teenagers, particularly in rural areas, need to be able to drive because public transport services are limited. Not all families have the time to chauffeur their children to places they need to go for work, studies or leisure. Without a licence, many 16-year-olds cannot take advantage of opportunities available to them.

A second major reason to lower the legal driving age is that the majority of teenagers are capable drivers. It is widely accepted that the ability to react quickly is key when driving, and young people are known to have faster reactions than older people.

Whilst it is true that the number of accidents involving young people is high, studies show that accidents usually occur in a driver's first year, regardless of age. It would be more sensible to address the issue of safety by ensuring that young drivers have plenty of driving experience. Moreover, strict testing procedures and graduated licensing rules would prevent the kinds of behaviour that lead to road accidents.

In conclusion, I am convinced that it is time to lower the legal age to obtain a driving licence. Most 16-year-olds are mature enough to make sensible decisions and act appropriately. Allowing them to drive would enable them to become more independent and develop responsibility.

3 **Look at the writer's paragraph plan. Complete it with the main points he/she makes in each paragraph.**

Paragraph 1: Introduction, including your opinion

....

....

Paragraph 2: Main point(s) in support of your opinion

....

....

Paragraph 3: Additional point(s) in support of your opinion

....

....

Paragraph 4: Point(s) in support of a different opinion and your counterargument(s)

....

....

Paragraph 5: Conclusion, restating and possibly expanding your main point

....

....

WRITING BANK

Useful expressions in opinion essays

Expressing strong opinions

- ....
- I am certain that …
- ....
- ....
- It has long been my feeling that …
- Without doubt,

Disagreeing

- There can be no justification for …
- I believe there is no evidence to support …
- I cannot agree with …

Expressing opposing views and giving counterarguments

- ....
- Despite the fact that …
- Although …, …
- Nevertheless/However,

Giving general opinions

- ....
- … is usually considered to be …
- It is often said that …
- It is generally believed that …
- On the whole, it is thought that …

4 **Put these expressions from the essay in 2 in the correct place in the Writing bank.**

1 I certainly believe that …
2 To my mind, there is no question that …
3 It is widely accepted that …
4 Whilst it is true that …, …
5 I am convinced that …

5 **Read the article section. What reasons can you think of for the initiative?**

Scotland has introduced an initiative to get more people out of their cars and onto their bikes. 'Active Travel' is designed to encourage people to think about alternative methods of travel for shorter journeys. In Scotland, a third of car journeys are less than two miles, and …

6 **Read the web pages about cycling. Which two arguments in each do you find most convincing? What other arguments can you add to the lists?**

BENEFITS OF BIKES …
WHY SHOULD I CYCLE?

- **FITNESS** – Cycling is a great way to keep fit, without going to the gym!
- **TIME** – A bicycle can be twice as fast as a car in city traffic.
- **ECONOMY** – Bicycles are cheap. There are no petrol bills, and they're easy to maintain.
- **CONVENIENCE** – You can park anywhere.
- **GOOD FOR THE ENVIRONMENT** – Bicycles produce no pollution, and they're quieter, too.
- **SAFETY** – Thousands of people are killed or injured in car accidents, but not on bicycles.
- **INDEPENDENCE** – Young people can get about without having to rely on lifts from others.

BARRIERS TO CYCLING

- **Cyclists are vulnerable – there's a danger of being hit by a car.**
- **There aren't enough bike paths – this means riding on the road or taking an indirect route.**
- **There aren't enough secure places to park (bikes are often stolen).**
- **It isn't practical if you have to carry things.**
- **What happens if it's raining?**
- **You need to take a shower when you arrive.**
- **Cycling is seen as a leisure activity, not transport.**
- **It doesn't look cool if you have to wear a helmet.**

✓ EXAM SUCCESS

You are going to write an opinion essay. In this type of essay, good organisation is vital. Plan what you want to say before you begin and organise your points into paragraphs. You can use the paragraph plan in 3.

➤ EXAM SUCCESS page 149

7 **PRACTICE MAKES PERFECT Look at this statement and write an essay giving your opinion. Use expressions from the Writing bank and advice from Exam success.**

People should be forced to travel by bicycle rather than by car for all short journeys.

WRITING BANK ➤ PAGE 155

Language checkpoint: Unit 2

Grammar reference

Modal verbs of obligation, prohibition, permission, criticism and advice – Present

We use:

- **have to** to talk about things which are obligatory or necessary. It often describes obligations imposed on us by other people and authorities.
- **don't have to** to talk about things which are not obligatory or necessary.
- **must** to talk about rules, regulations and obligations. It often describes obligations that come internally, from ourselves.
- **mustn't** to talk about prohibitions.
- **need to** to talk about things which are obligatory or necessary.
- **don't need to** or **needn't** to talk about things which are not obligatory or necessary. With **needn't** we do not use *to* before the infinitive.
- **can't** to refuse permission.
- **should**, **shouldn't**, **ought to**, **had ('d) better (not)** to give and ask for advice and recommendations. **Had better** is especially for when we think we should do something because it's a good idea. **Ought to** and **had ('d) better** are slightly less common in negative and question form.
- **be allowed to** to talk about things that we have permission to do.
- **be supposed to** when somebody is expected to behave in a particular way, especially according to someone in authority.

Modal verbs of obligation, prohibition, criticism and advice – Past

We use:

- **had to** to talk about things which were obligatory or necessary.
- **didn't have to** to talk about things which were not obligatory or necessary.
- **needed to** to talk about things which were obligatory or necessary.
- **didn't need to** to talk about things which were not obligatory or necessary, and so we didn't do them.
- **needn't have + past participle** to talk about things that were not obligatory or necessary, but we did them.
- **wasn't/weren't allowed to** to talk about past prohibitions.
- **couldn't** to talk about things that were prohibited or not possible.
- **should/ought to have**, **shouldn't have + past participle** to criticise past actions or to say that they were a mistake.

Modal verbs of speculation, deduction, possibility and probability – Present and future

We use:

- **must** when we are 90% certain that something is true.
- **may**, **might**, **could**, **may not**, **mightn't** when there is a 50% possibility that something is true (or not). We can add **well** after **may**, **might** and **could** in the affirmative to say that there is a stronger possibility.
- **can't** when we are 90% certain that something is not true.
- When we are 100% certain that something is or isn't true, we do not use modal verbs of speculation and deduction.

Modal verbs of speculation, deduction, possibility and probability – Past

We use:

- **must have** when we are 90% certain that something was true.
- **can't have** when we are 90% certain that something was not true.
- **may have**, **might have**, **could have**, **may not have**, **mightn't have** when there is a 50% possibility that something was true (or not). We can add **well** after **may**, **might** and **could** in the affirmative to say that there is a stronger possibility.

Vocabulary

For compound nouns for cars and the road and collocations with *take*, *make* and *do*, see wordlist page 137.

Grammar revision

Modal verbs – obligation, permission, prohibition, criticism and advice

/ 10 points

1 Choose the correct option.

1 I'm sorry. I *should/ought* to have asked your permission to go.
2 We *had/should* better leave the room now because somebody's waiting to use it.
3 We weren't *allowed/supposed* to write with a green pen in the exam, but there was no rule against it.
4 I *had to go/must have gone* to the hospital at the weekend because my grandfather was ill.
5 You didn't see me at the meeting because they told me that I *didn't need to go/needn't have gone*.
6 *Have we/Do we have* to sign on the dotted line?
7 I think she said that we *need/needn't* pay to get in.
8 I ran to the station but I *needn't have bothered/didn't need to bother* because the train was delayed.
9 I *didn't have to dress/needn't have dressed* up for the party but I wanted to wear my new dress.
10 You *can't park/supposed to park* here. You're blocking the entrance.

Modal verbs – speculation, deduction, possibility and probability

/ 10 points

2 Decide if the verbs in bold are in the correct form. Tick (✓) the correct forms and rewrite the incorrect forms.

1 That car **mustn't be** hers because she can't afford to buy one.
2 I wonder why he hasn't come. He **mayn't have remembered** that we have a meeting.
3 If we go now, we **may well get** there for the start of the film.
4 I don't know who lent me this pen, but I suppose it **can have been** Kay.
5 You've got the wrong answer so you **must have make** a mistake somewhere in your calculations.
6 I'm not sure when the next test is, but I suppose it **could be** next week.
7 You've had a long journey. You **must have been** tired.
8 That man has a very expensive car. He **can't earn** a lot of money.
9 I can't find my gloves anywhere. I **must have dropped** them.
10 The shop **must not have been** open today – I'll phone and check before I go.

Vocabulary revision

Collocations with *take*, *make* and *do*

/ 7 points

1 Complete the sentences with the correct form of *take*, *make* or *do*.

1 It .... no difference what I think – I want to know your opinion.
2 The actor has .... a formal apology for his behaviour.
3 He refused to continue as he .... offence at some of the interview questions.
4 It doesn't .... any harm to be polite.
5 We should .... an effort to call Ben.
6 It's difficult to get a good mark if you don't .... an interest in the subject.
7 Are you sure you've .... the right choice?

Compound nouns – cars and the road

/ 13 points

2 Use the words to make compound nouns connected with cars and the road.

about • belt • driving • licence • lights • motor • petrol
round • seat • station • steering • traffic • way • wheel

1 ....
2 ....
3 ....
4 ....
5 ....
6 ....
7 ....

3 Complete the sentences with the correct word.

1 She had to stop because the .... were red.
2 To make the car turn right, you have to turn the .... to the right.
3 The first thing you should do when you get in a car is fasten your ....
4 He got his .... after he passed the test on his first attempt.
5 You aren't allowed to drive on a .... until you've passed your driving test.
6 .... are designed to make intersections safer for drivers.

Total: / 40 points

Reading

1 Read the texts. For questions 1–9, choose from the three drivers (A–C). The drivers may be chosen more than once.

Which driver

- was the oldest when he/she started to learn to drive? 1 ....
- overcame tough physical and mental challenges by passing his/her test? 2 ....
- did not tell his/her instructor the whole truth about his/her driving experience? 3 ....
- surprised his/her instructor by surpassing the instructor's expectations? 4 ....
- is relieved not to be so dependent on others after passing? 5 ....
- discovered the secret to passing by himself/herself? 6 ....
- has used his/her driving licence as a first step to achieving another, bigger goal? 7 ....
- did not have unconditional support from his/her family for what he/she wanted to do at first? 8 ....
- made a number of mistakes just before taking the test? 9 ....

➤ TIP FOR READING EXAMS

In multiple matching activities, remember …
The information in the questions will probably be expressed with different words in the actual texts.

➤ EXAM SUCCESS page 148

A Daniel Lloyd is used to being fast, just like his hero, Formula 1 champion Lewis Hamilton. On this occasion, though, Daniel has been even faster than his idol. He's passed his driving test after just one-and-a-half hours of tuition on the very day of his 17th birthday.

Daniel, an experienced kart racer, had never actually driven on public roads before the day of his test. But he took the theory exam on the morning of his birthday and as soon as he'd passed that, he did the practical test that same afternoon.

During his one and only lesson, Daniel was far from perfect. He had to adapt from driving racing cars to driving normal ones. For a start, there's not much use for signalling in a racing car, or going in reverse for that matter, so he had to learn those from scratch.

The driving instructor thought Daniel was mad to do the test after just one lesson, since neither Daniel nor his father had mentioned the fact that he had already been racing cars for a year, worried that it might be used as an excuse to fail him. But Daniel was a quick learner, mastering road driving in just a quarter of the time that it took Hamilton.

Needless to say, Daniel's teacher couldn't quite believe that he had passed after just one lesson. And his prize? Daniel got a brand new Renault Clio for his birthday.

B Teresa Clarke was a young mother when she had her first driving lesson. Now, 27 years later, she has finally passed her test. During those 27 years, her daughters have grown up and she has had several grandchildren. She has also spent over £15,000 on lessons. Twenty different driving instructors taught her for 450 hours. She failed her test 12 times and did 50 practice tests.

A number of driving instructors got tired of trying to teach her and one even refused to carry on lessons with her. He told her that she would never learn or pass. Sixty-two-year-old Teresa is proud to have proved him wrong now. She's also glad that she no longer has to ask her husband to take her shopping.

Teresa is convinced that the key to her recent success in passing her driving test has been coffee, or rather, giving up coffee. She used to drink at least three strong coffees a day and realised that this greatly affected her concentration, the main reason why she had failed tests in the past. By not drinking coffee, she managed to improve her concentration and finally get the licence she had waited so long for. When her examiner told her the news, it took a while for it to sink in. Her dream had finally come true.

C Katie Gillard passed her driving test the first time she took it, when she was just 17. But she wasn't content with that. When the age limit for driving a lorry went down from 21 to 18 last year, she decided to take advantage. At the age of 19, she enrolled for the test, which includes demanding tasks in both theory and practice. She needn't have worried as she passed both sections in impressive fashion.

Katie is only 5ft 4 in (1.64 m) tall, but she isn't afraid of driving long distance routes around the UK. Then again, driving a lorry must be in her blood. She is going to work for her dad's transport firm, which her grandfather founded back in the 1980s. Her dad, who had been the one to suggest Katie take the exam, was very pleased for his daughter, although he hadn't always been keen on her getting into the profession. His doubts were more from the financial point of view, but Katie had always been set on lorry driving. Once her father was convinced, he encouraged her to take the test. Katie's mum couldn't be more proud either.

Katie found the two-day course stressful, especially when she had to actually sit behind the wheel. But she picked it up fast and is already planning on moving up to driving a 42-ton lorry in the future.

Use of English

➤ TIP FOR USE OF ENGLISH

In multiple-choice cloze tests, remember …
If you aren't sure which answer is right, think about why other answers are definitely wrong and eliminate them.

➤ EXAM SUCCESS page 148

2 Read the text and decide which answer (A, B, C or D) best fits each gap.

The Paris–Dakar would never have existed if French driver Thierry Sabine had not got lost in the desert. That was when he had the idea for a race that would **(1)** ………… drivers to the limit of their abilities. Little by little, the organisers have **(2)** ………… changes to the race. For example, and rather confusingly, the Paris–Dakar has not always begun in Paris and the **(3)** ………… line has not always been in Dakar. **(4)** ………… the years, the rally has had its fair share of incidents, although all the participants are clear about the risks they are **(5)** ………… by competing. Whether the vehicle is a car, truck, quad or motorbike, the challenges are extreme, and there is usually a high drop-out **(6)** ………….

(7) …………, one constant feature of the race has been the solidarity of the competitors, all willing to lend each **(8)** ………… a hand when in trouble. Meanwhile, it seems that the number of people wanting to **(9)** ………… part in the event shows no signs of falling **(10)** ………….

	A	B	C	D
1	A pull	B push	C put	D have
2	A made	B done	C had	D taken
3	A closing	B final	C finishing	D ending
4	A Through	B Over	C During	D For
5	A doing	B making	C having	D taking
6	A rate	B speed	C number	D amount
7	A Moreover	B Whereas	C While	D However
8	A one	B person	C other	D self
9	A be	B take	C have	D make
10	A out	B off	C down	D through

Listening

➤ TIP FOR LISTENING EXAMS

In multiple-choice listening activities, remember …
Read all the options before listening and underline important words.

➤ EXAM SUCCESS page 148

3 LISTENING ▶ 08 **Listen to a radio programme about international customs. For questions 1–6, choose the answer (A, B or C).**

1 Dr Elliot thinks that many social customs
   A are plainly weird and unusual.
   B make little sense within a particular group of people.
   C don't follow any logic.
2 Dr Elliot once made the mistake of
   A buying an inappropriate present.
   B giving a present when she shouldn't have.
   C giving a present in the wrong way.
3 Opening a present in front of the giver is
   A unusual in many countries.
   B considered rude in Japan.
   C a good idea, according to the presenter.
4 In China, silence is
   A better than when somebody sucks air through their teeth.
   B a sign that someone thinks what you are saying is not good.
   C better than speaking.
5 Which of these is rude when eating as a guest in China?
   A accepting more food the first time it is offered
   B accepting food the second time it is offered
   C leaving food on your plate at the end of the meal
6 When in public in Japan, you should never
   A pick your nose.
   B blow your nose.
   C cough loudly.

Writing

➤ TIP FOR WRITING EXAMS

For guidance on writing stories, see page 148.
For guidance on writing opinion essays, see page 149.

➤ EXAM SUCCESS page 148–9

4 Choose one of these two writing tasks. Write your story or essay.

1 Write a story which begins with these words:

   We had been planning the journey for several months but had no idea of the excitement that was waiting for us!

2 You have had a class discussion about travel. Your teacher has now asked you to write an essay giving your opinion on the following statement:

   Travel is the best way to broaden the mind.

3 Mind power

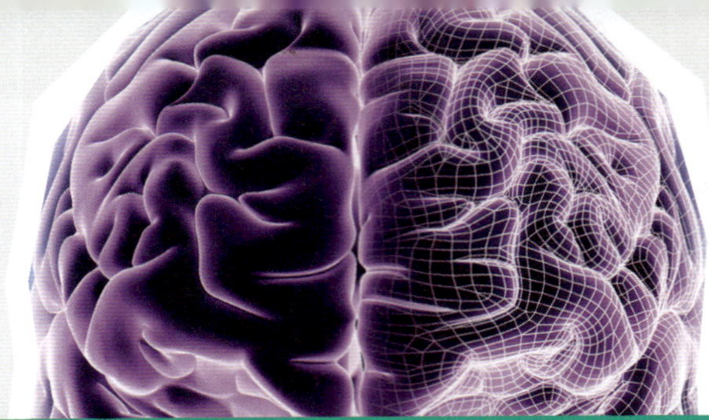

Reading

VOCABULARY The human mind

1a Check that you understand the words in bold in these sentences. Use your dictionary if necessary. Then decide if the sentences are *true* or *false* for you.

1 My mind often **wanders** when I'm doing my homework.
2 I find it easy to **memorise** numbers and dates.
3 I can **recall** things that happened to me when I was just four.
4 I'm **bewildered** by quadratic equations.
5 I **have a gift for** languages.
6 I **grasp** new concepts easily.
7 I'm not very **articulate** explaining complex ideas.
8 I don't **perceive** change as a bad thing.

1b SPEAKING Work with a partner. Discuss your answers in 1.

2 Look at the photos of savants. Savants are people with exceptional abilities. What abilities do you think these people have?

3 Read the article. What exceptional abilities are mentioned?

✓ EXAM SUCCESS

In multiple-choice reading activities, you must find information in the text to back up your answer. Underline relevant information in the text to help you.

➤ EXAM SUCCESS page 149

4 Read the article again and choose the best answers.

1 In the second mental arithmetic problem that Tammet solved in the documentary, we know that
 a his answer is more accurate than the calculator's.
 b he is not as fast as the calculator.
 c he can work out answers faster than the calculator.
 d the testers turn the calculator off when he gives them the correct answer.

2 According to the article, savants
 a have an unusual way of seeing numbers.
 b are always autistic.
 c may have an imbalance in the brain.
 d are able to express themselves well.

3 In social situations, autistic savants often
 a concentrate on non-verbal signals to help them understand people.
 b find it difficult to interpret what people say.
 c cannot imagine what it is like to be in another person's position.
 d rely on maths to understand human behaviour.

4 Ellen Boudreaux's gift for music lies in the fact that
 a she can play any musical instrument.
 b she can play music even though she is blind.
 c she isn't able to read music.
 d she has an extraordinary memory for songs.

5 George Widener and Stephen Wiltshire both
 a can remember the details of what they see.
 b rely on memory in their artwork.
 c create accurate and detailed paintings.
 d have held exhibitions all over the world.

6 Allan Snyder believes that savants
 a have a greater capacity for learning than other people.
 b are aware of how their brains calculate details.
 c have abilities that other people don't have.
 d process information differently from other people.

5 CRITICAL THINKING

Think! Then compare ideas with your class.

- Which do you think is more important, hard work or talent?
- In your opinion, is it better to have an exceptional talent or good social skills?

6 Guess the meaning of the underlined words from the context. Then use your dictionary to check.

7 SPEAKING What about *you*?

1 Which of the exceptional abilities do you find most impressive? Why?
2 What do you think life is like for a savant?
3 Have you ever met or heard of a person with unusual talents?
4 What gift would you like to have?

IS THERE A SAVANT IN ALL OF US?

Daniel Tammet

Daniel Tammet is an autistic savant. He can perform complex calculations at lightning speed, speak seven languages and he has even devised his own language. Scientists believe that his exceptional abilities may offer groundbreaking insights into how our minds work, and perhaps answer the question: do we all have these abilities deep inside our brain, but we don't know how to access them?

Daniel first came to worldwide attention in 2004 when he flawlessly recalled Pi from memory to 22,514 decimal places. It took him over five hours, and he set a European record. In a television documentary a year later, he worked out 37 x 37 x 37 in his head. The testers thought he may have memorised the cube of everything up to 100 and so asked him to divide 13 by 97. He began '0.134206 …' and continued reciting decimal points long after the calculator stopped displaying them.

He explains his fluency in numbers as the result of the way he perceives them, a phenomenon he calls synaesthesia. For him, every number up to 10,000 has a unique visual form. Different numbers have a different colour, shape and texture. The number two, for instance, is a movement, and five is a clap of thunder. 'When I multiply numbers together, I see two shapes. The image starts to change and evolve, and a third shape emerges. That's the answer,' he says.

"while autistic savants have extraordinary abilities, they often face challenges in their daily lives"

An estimated 10% of the autistic population compared to around 1% of the non-autistic population have savant abilities, but no-one knows exactly why. Scans of the brain suggest that the right hemisphere in savants, the side of the brain associated with mathematics or memory, is somehow compensating for a fault in the left hemisphere, connected with language and comprehension.

Typically, savants have a limited vocabulary, and in this respect Tammet is uncommon. He is extremely articulate and he also has an extraordinary gift for languages. During the television documentary, as another test, he was given the task of learning Icelandic in a week. The tutor assigned to him declared it to be impossible. He appeared on television seven days later and gave an interview in perfect Icelandic.

But while autistic savants have extraordinary abilities, they often face challenges in their daily lives. People with autism find basic social relationships difficult; they struggle to read non-verbal signals such as facial expressions and find it impossible to put themselves in someone else's shoes. Tammet remembers trying to use maths to predict how his mother would behave when he was younger – and being bewildered when she did something unexpected!

He has since learnt to cope with social situations, and even travels the world now as a public speaker. However, he still can't drive a car because his mind tends to wander and he has an obsessive need for order in his daily routine.

Tammet is one of an exclusive club of only about 50 savants with extraordinary abilities, the majority of whom are male. **Ellen Boudreaux**, who has a gift for music, is one of the few female savants. Ellen is able to play a piece of music perfectly after hearing it only once and she can recall and reproduce any song she has ever heard. Despite the fact that she is blind, she can also navigate her way around stationary objects without running into them, and knows exactly the hour and minute at any time of day without ever seeing a clock.

George Widener

Other savants, like **George Widener** and Stephen Wiltshire, combine a photographic memory with artistic talents. Widener has an obsession with dates, and can recall historical details, including the day of any date spanning thousands of years. He began to paint to help him relax and turned his love of numbers into paintings, which have been exhibited all over the world. **Stephen Wiltshire**, meanwhile, can draw an accurate and detailed landscape of a city after only seeing it once. On one occasion, he produced a ten-metre panoramic drawing of Tokyo after a brief helicopter ride over the city.

Some researchers attribute these extraordinary gifts to compulsive learning, but the physicist Allan Snyder claims we all have these talents locked up inside our brains. He points to the fact that we can automatically estimate an object's distance, and that the brain analyses countless details during facial recognition. Most people are not aware of these calculations, but according to Snyder, in savants the top layer of mental processing is somehow removed, leaving them with an exceptional capacity for recalling detail. He believes it may be possible one day to create technologies that will allow any non-autistic person to exploit these abilities.

Other scientists are unconvinced, but savant syndrome remains an intriguing area for future research.

Stephen Wiltshire

Verb + -ing form and infinitive

1 Can the *-ing* forms in bold be changed to a *to*-infinitive or vice versa? If so, does the meaning of the sentence change?

a He continued **reciting** decimal points.
b The calculator stopped **displaying** them.
c They struggle **to read** non-verbal signals.
d His mind tends **to wander**.
e He began **to paint** to help him to relax.
f He remembers **trying** to use maths.
g He has learnt **to cope** with social situations.

GRAMMAR REFERENCE ➤ PAGE 42

2 Put these verbs in the correct column.

admit • afford • agree • avoid • begin • bother can't stand • consider • continue • decide • deny expect • feel like • finish • help • include keep on • manage • promise • recommend refuse • risk • start • suggest • take up • volunteer

verb + -*ing* form	verb + *to*-infinitive	verb + -*ing* form or *to*-infinitive with little or no change in meaning

3 Complete the text with the correct form of the verbs.

Sheldon Cooper of *The Big Bang Theory* is perhaps the most well-known fictional savant. He has an IQ of 187, but his lack of social skills never fails to make us laugh. For example, he struggles (a) .... (understand) humour, he has never learnt (b) .... (drive) and he would never risk (c) .... (fly) in a plane. He believes he is incapable of making a mistake, and so he always denies (d) .... (do) anything wrong. He is uncomfortable with human contact and avoids (e) .... (hug). His obsession with rituals and routines includes (f) .... (knock) three times on the door when he visits someone's house, and he refuses (g) .... (sit) anywhere except on his designated seat on the sofa. He makes his flatmate Leonard agree (h) .... (sign) a flatmate agreement with numerous rules! He also has an unnatural fear of germs and would never consider (i) .... (eat) in a strange restaurant. Yet despite all his limitations, Sheldon manages (j) .... (be) endearing. He reminds us what it is to be human and it's impossible not to love him.

4 Work with a partner. Look at these pairs of sentences and discuss how the meaning changes depending on the verb form.

1a Remember to bring your dictionaries to class.
1b I remember putting the book in my bag yesterday.
2a Try to do the exercise, even if it's difficult.
2b I tried walking, but my leg still hurt.
3a As I was leaving I saw Matt and we stopped to chat.
3b After half an hour we stopped running and sat down.
4a Doing this exam means studying really hard for the next three months.
4b I didn't mean to hurt your feelings.
5a The teacher first explained the social background and then went on to talk about the economic situation.
5b The teacher went on talking for hours and hours.
6a I like to study my notes once a week.
6b I like meeting new people.

5 Decide if the sentences are correct. Rewrite the incorrect sentences.

1 On my way home from school, I stopped buying bread.
2 I like to check my emails at least once a day.
3 He went on to talk even though the teacher asked him to stop.
4 Do you realise that doing this course means paying a fee?
5 If you don't understand, try to look at the rules again.
6 I don't mean being rude, but I think you've made a mistake.
7 I stopped to buy a newspaper because all the news is available online.
8 I remember to leave my keys here, but now I can't find them.
9 We'd been working all morning so we stopped having a break.
10 I'm trying to learn Icelandic, but it's really difficult.

6 SPEAKING **Work with a partner. Talk about:**

1 something you tried to do but without success.
2 something difficult that you managed to do.
3 something that you feel like doing this weekend.
4 something you can't afford to do but wish you could.
5 a hobby or activity that you would like to take up.
6 something you'd like to keep on doing when you've left school.
7 something you can't stand doing at the weekend.
8 something you would avoid doing if you could.

Phrasal verbs – the mind

1 Read the text and match phrasal verbs 1–8 with a–h.

Everybody's mind works in a different way. You can see this in any learning situation. For example, at university, when a professor explains new concepts, some students **(1) pick** them **up** really fast, but others take a while to **(2) catch on**. Some like to analyse the new concept in smaller chunks and then gradually **(3) piece** them **together**. And some people suffer because they take longer to **(4) keep up with** the rest.

What's interesting is that some people who find it difficult to follow other people's ideas are sometimes just independent thinkers who find it easier to **(5) come up with** their own original ideas. Often they are incapable of knowing how they **(6) hit on** a solution to a problem – they are simply following their intuition. Answers just **(7) leap out at** them from nowhere. Personally, I find it useful to **(8) talk** things **through** with a friend.

a understand
b learn about something by considering all the separate bits of information you have
c learn something new
d discuss something with somebody in a detailed way
e learn at the same speed as someone else
f suddenly have an idea or discover something by chance
g be immediately obvious to someone, or immediately get their attention
h think of an idea or a plan

2 Look at these sentences. Does each phrasal verb have an object? If so, where does the object go? Does it make any difference if the object is a pronoun?

1 I've **come up with** a great idea for a new breakfast cereal.
2 How did you **come up with** it?
3 It took a while before I **hit on** the right solution.
4 It's a great solution. How did you **hit on** it?
5 He **picked up** the idea really fast.
6 You **picked** the key concept **up** straight away.
7 I think she's **picked** it **up** really fast.
8 I'm starting to **catch on**.

3 Put the phrasal verbs in 2 in the correct column.

Two-part phrasal verb (no object)	Two-part phrasal verb (inseparable)	Two-part phrasal verb (separable)	Three-part phrasal verb (inseparable)
catch on			

4 Add the phrasal verbs in the text in 1 to the correct column.

5 Read these sentences. Check that you understand the meaning of the phrasal verbs in bold, using a dictionary if necessary. Then add the verbs to the table in 3.

1 He **looks for** patterns in numbers.
2 He has three areas of expertise that **stand out**.
3 He didn't **fit in** at school.
4 At first, he finds it hard to **get on with** people.
5 He **took up** drawing at school.
6 He never **looks down on** others.
7 He was able to **work out** 37 x 37 x 37 in his head.
8 He didn't have to **write** the numbers **down**.

6 Decide if the word order is correct in each sentence. Rewrite the incorrect sentences.

1 She listened to the song just once but picked up it immediately.
2 It's a good idea to look patterns for when you learn a new language.
3 When he stopped thinking so hard about the crossword clue, suddenly the answer leapt him out at.
4 I think we should talk through it with Sarah before we make a final decision.
5 Would you say that you get on with him?
6 I think I've hit a new way on to do these equations.
7 I think I'm going to start playing chess. Do you want to take up it, too?
8 You need to go faster if you want to keep me up with.

7 SPEAKING Work with a partner. Discuss these questions.

1 What type of people do you get on with best?
2 What hobby or new activity would you like to take up?
3 When you are in a new environment, how long does it take you to fit in?
4 Does talking through your notes help you to remember them better?
5 Do you prefer to work things out in your head or to write them down?
6 Do you find it easier to pick up other people's ideas or to come up with your own?

Improving your memory

Remember!

ACADEMIC SKILLS OBJECTIVES

- To become aware of how you memorise information
- To learn about ways to improve memory
- To discuss and use memory techniques

KEY CONCEPTS

mnemonic device [n]: *Mnemonic devices are common techniques that help your brain to encode and recall information.* **chunking [n]:** *Chunking numbers instead of trying to remember each one separately makes it easier to remember them.* **rehearse [v]:** *If you rehearse what you have to remember, you're more likely to recall it later.*

1 Look at the pictures for 30 seconds and try to memorise them. Then close your book. Write down (or draw!) as many items as you can remember.

2 SPEAKING Work with a partner. Answer the questions.

1 How many items did you remember?
2 How did you remember them?
3 Do you think it's possible to improve your memory?
4 What memory techniques do you know?

3 READING Read the article about Nelson Dellis, a memory champion. According to Dellis, is it possible to improve your memory? If so, how? Does he mention any of the techniques you discussed in 2?

HEALTH JOURNAL

Bringing you the most up-to-date health news

Nelson Dellis

EXERCISE YOUR MIND!

Seven packs of cards memorised each day, 1,500 digits read aloud and years of training. How this man became a memory champion (and how you can improve yours!).

Nelson Dellis has won the US Memory Championships three times. He can recall hundreds of names and long sequences of numbers. But he says he's not special – anyone can have a memory like his.

According to Dellis, just as physical exercise has to be done regularly to keep the body fit, the mind must be exercised every day to keep it sharp. Nelson does this with a daily mental workout that involves memorising decks of cards, recalling long lists of random words, names and numbers and reciting lines of poetry.

While memorising cards or recalling the digits in Pi may not seem like something you can benefit from, enhancing your memory with a few simple tricks could really improve your day-to-day life, from remembering the names of everyone you meet to recalling phone numbers if your phone battery dies. Most importantly, improving your memory can slow or prevent brain diseases in later life.

4 Read the article again. Answer these questions.

1 What is the significance of 'eight seconds'?
2 Why is it a good idea to take regular breaks while you're studying?
3 What three mnemonic techniques does Dellis use? What does he use them for?
4 Which is better, remembering words individually or in sets? Why?
5 Why might you organise information you need to remember?
6 What is the value of saying words out loud?

5 SPEAKING Work with a partner. Answer these questions.

1 Did you use any of the techniques in the article to remember the words in 1?
2 How could you adapt these techniques to remember the words?

MONDAY, MARCH 21

TRICKS TO IMPROVE YOUR MEMORY

CONCENTRATE: First of all, to remember anything, you need to concentrate. It takes about eight seconds of intense focus to absorb information, so that means not getting distracted by TV or music! At the same time, you need to give your brain regular breaks to process what you've learnt. After about an hour and a half, nothing new can be assimilated.

USE MNEMONIC DEVICES: For Dellis, the key to remembering anything is to make it unforgettable, so he uses mnemonic devices. To remember words or names, he recommends visualisation, associating a word with an image – the more bizarre the better! So for example, if you meet someone called Elizabeth, imagine them as a queen on a throne with a crown on their head. For lists, he'd make up a story linking each item to one another. To remember numbers, he'd associate a word or picture with that number, such as James Bond for the number 7.

CHUNKING: Grouping words or numbers into sets of say three or five makes them easier to remember because it expands the short-term memory.

ORGANISE: Because we keep information stored in our memory in related groups, it helps to organise things we need to remember. This includes grouping words or facts (if necessary, in your notebook, or on a mind map*), and taking time to link new information to what we already know.

REPEAT: One of the most effective ways of remembering information is by repeating it. If you say it out loud, you're 50% more likely to remember it than if you read it over – and moving your hands or walking while you do so also helps.

PRACTICE: You need to work out your brain every day to keep it sharp so practise remembering the words to songs or your shopping list or do games like crosswords.

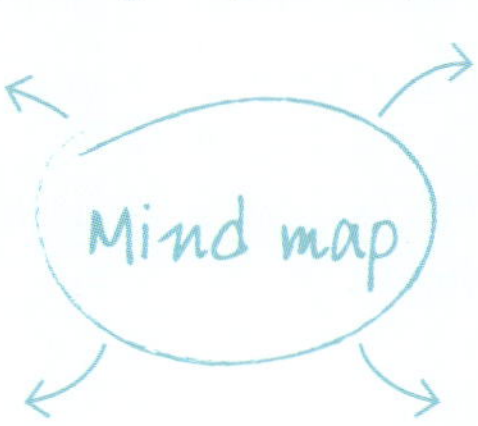

*A mind map is a visual representation of information that includes a central idea surrounded by connected branches of associated topics.

6 LISTENING 09 Some students are discussing what techniques they use to remember information. Watch the video or listen. What things do they say they find easy or difficult to remember?

7 LISTENING 09 Watch or listen again and make notes about the techniques mentioned. Look back at the article. Which of the techniques are included in the tricks to improve your memory?

8 SPEAKING Work with a partner. Discuss these questions.

1 Do you use any of the techniques when you study for a test or exam at school?
2 How do you usually remember information for a test or exam?
3 Which techniques would you like to try in the future?

ACADEMIC TASK

Work with a partner. You're going to do another memory test.

Follow this plan:

1 *Discuss how you could use techniques from the article to remember these words.*

egg • gloves • lamp • fish • bicycle
sunglasses • guitar • pencil • boat
camera • plant • rabbit • comb • cake

2 *Choose one technique that you think will work best for you.*
3 *Study the words for 30 seconds.*
4 *Close your book. Write down as many words as you can remember.*
5 *Share your results with the class. What technique did you use? Did you remember more words this time?*

Flipped classroom: watch the grammar presentation video.

1 SPEAKING **Work with a partner. Discuss these questions.**

1 What can you see in the photo?
2 Why, when and where do people do these activities?

✔ EXAM SUCCESS

When you have to match speakers with information or ideas, don't make your final decision too soon. Often a possible answer will come first, but the real answer will come later.

➤ EXAM SUCCESS page 149

2 LISTENING ▶ 10 **You are going to listen to five people talking about their journey to work. Listen and complete both tasks.**

Task 1

For questions 1–5, choose from the list (A–H) what each speaker's present occupation is. There are three extra letters which you do not need to use.

A journalist	Speaker 1	1	....
B doctor	Speaker 2	2	....
C architect	Speaker 3	3	....
D teacher	Speaker 4	4	....
E accountant	Speaker 5	5	....
F student			
G engineer			
H businessperson			

Task 2

For questions 6–10, choose from the list (A–H) how each speaker occupies his/her mind when travelling to work. There are three extra letters which you do not need to use.

A solving sudoku puzzles	Speaker 1	6	....
B doing crosswords	Speaker 2	7	....
C playing with a games console	Speaker 3	8	....
D listening to an MP3 player	Speaker 4	9	....
E reading	Speaker 5	10	....
F solving chess problems			
G observing other people			
H doing logic puzzles and brain teasers			

3 ▶ 10 **Listen again and check your answers.**

4 SPEAKING **What about *you*?**

1 Do you enjoy doing these activities? Why/Why not?
2 What are the benefits of doing puzzles for the brain?

Verb + object + -ing form and infinitive

5 **Put the verbs in bold in the correct column. Some verbs can go in more than one column.**

a Doing crosswords **helps** me keep/to keep my mind active.
b It really **makes** me wake up in the morning.
c I **ask** my husband to fill in the last words.
d I **hear** my sister complaining/complain all day.
e It **encourages** them to concentrate.
f It **allows** me to switch off and have some harmless fun.
g I just hope my sister doesn't **catch** me playing with it.
h They **teach** you to think in a different way.

verb + object + *-ing* form	verb + object + *to*-infinitive	verb + object + infinitive without *to*
	help	*help*

GRAMMAR REFERENCE ➤ PAGE 42

6 **Put these verbs in the correct columns in the table.**

advise • beg • choose • feel • find • force
inspire • invite • let • notice • order • overhear
persuade • remind • see • teach
tell • warn • watch

7 **Complete the sentences with the correct form of these pairs of verbs.**

ask/help • catch/solve • encourage/learn
feel/blow • force/read • let/rest • overhear/say
advise/do

1 If you really want to relax your mind, I .... you .... yoga.
2 She .... me .... her with the crossword because she couldn't finish it on her own.
3 At primary school, when we were tired, they .... us .... our heads on the desk.
4 I don't mean to be rude, but did I .... you .... you used to be a grand master at chess?
5 Last week the teacher .... me .... a sudoku puzzle instead of a maths equation.
6 When you .... students .... a novel, sometimes they end up hating literature.
7 Being by the sea is so relaxing, especially when you .... the sea breeze .... on your face.
8 Our school .... us .... at least one foreign language, but it's not compulsory.

Presentations – 1

1 Read the extract from a magazine article. What is Nicholas Carr's theory, and who agrees with him?

The American science writer Nicholas Carr has written a book called *The Shallows* which deplores our growing dependence on the Internet and other new media. It is altering the very architecture of our brains, he says: we can no longer concentrate like we used to. 'When we go online we enter an environment that promotes cursory reading, hurried and distracted thinking, and superficial learning. We are evolving from being cultivators of personal knowledge to being hunters and gatherers in the electronic data forest.' Carr is in good company. Sir Tom Stoppard fears the printed page is in danger of being 'swept away' on a tide of new technology, and even Barack Obama has been reproaching himself for tinkering too much with his Blackberry. 'Information becomes a distraction, a diversion, a form of entertainment, rather than a tool of empowerment,' says the president.

So, is the Internet making us shallower and less able to think deeply about things?

2 SPEAKING Work with a partner. Discuss what you think these ideas from the article mean. Which of the ideas do you agree with?

1 'When we go online, we enter an environment that promotes cursory reading, hurried and distracted thinking, and superficial learning.'
2 'We are evolving from being cultivators of personal knowledge to being hunters and gatherers in the electronic data forest.'
3 'The printed page is in danger of being swept away on a tide of new technology.'
4 'Information becomes a distraction, a diversion, a form of entertainment, rather than a tool of empowerment.'

3 LISTENING ▶ 11 Listen to a student giving a presentation about the Internet. What is her opinion? What arguments does she put forward?

4 Complete the Speaking bank with these expressions from the presentation.

1 The first thing I'd like to say is …
2 However,
3 First of all,
4 Whilst it's true that …
5 … this does not mean that …
6 Another important point to make is that …
7 Finally,
8 I accept that …
9 To sum up,

SPEAKING BANK

Useful expressions to structure a presentation

Beginning your presentation
- I'd like to begin by saying …
- ……………………

Ordering your arguments
- ……………………
- Firstly,/Secondly,
- ……………………
- Furthermore,/What's more,
- It's important to remember that …

Presenting opposing points of view
- ……………………
- You can't deny that …
- There's no denying that …
- You can't argue with the fact that …
- ……………………

Responding to opposing points of view
- ……………………
- ……………………
- Let's not forget that …
- I would still say that …
- Even so, I still believe that …
- That doesn't alter my opinion that …

Concluding your presentation
- ……………………
- ……………………
- Returning to my main point,

5 SPEAKING Work with a partner. Prepare a presentation about reading and the Internet. Follow this guide.

1 Begin by stating your opinion.
2 Make your most important point first.
3 Present one or two opposing points.
4 Give counterarguments to the opposing point(s).
5 Conclude by restating your opinion.

6 SPEAKING Practise giving your presentation to your partner. Then listen to your partner and think of constructive criticism to help him/her improve.

✓ EXAM SUCCESS

When you give a presentation you can look at your notes, but don't just read them aloud. Use the notes to help you remember what to say and to give your presentation structure. Make sure that you don't hide your face in your notes. Look up and at your audience.

➤ EXAM SUCCESS page 149

7 PRACTICE MAKES PERFECT SPEAKING Now prepare a presentation on this topic. Then give your presentation to the class.

'The best way to improve your mind is by learning a language.' Do you agree? Why/Why not?

A review

1 SPEAKING **Work with a partner. When deciding whether to watch a film, how important are these elements? Rank them 1–10 (1 = not important, 10 = very important).**

- the star and supporting actors
- the genre (comedy, science fiction, etc.)
- the plot
- the length
- the special effects and visuals
- the soundtrack
- the setting and location
- reviews and recommendations

2 SPEAKING **Compare your answers with the rest of the class. What are the most and least important elements?**

3 **Read the film review. How many stars do you think the reviewer gave the film, from one to five? Would this review make you want to see the film? Why/Why not?**

VOCABULARY Word formation – prefixes

4a **Look at these words from the review. Underline the prefix in each word and check that you understand the word. Use your dictionary if necessary.**

impenetrable • inseparable • miscast • overblown
underrated • unpredictable

4b **Match the prefixes 1–13 with their meanings a–m.**

1 *inter-*
2 *dis-/un-/im-/ir-/in-/il-*
3 *re-*
4 *ex-*
5 *under-*
6 *mis-*
7 *over-*
8 *co-*
9 *post-*
10 *pre-*
11 *sub-*
12 *super-*
13 *anti-*

a wrong, incorrect
b before
c more, bigger, better
d not enough
e too much
f between
g the opposite, not
h again
i with, together
j a position or situation that existed before, but not now
k below
l after
m against

The Theory Of Everything

12t | 123 min | James Marsh

film&music

I must admit, I had some doubts about seeing *The Theory of Everything.* As a film based on the life of the famous physicist Stephen Hawking, I expected it to be filled with scientific terms I couldn't understand, much less find entertaining. But this masterpiece by director James Marsh is one of the most moving films to hit the big screen in years.

'... the unpredictable nature of life and love ... gives this film its universal appeal'

The film stars Eddie Redmayne in the role of Stephen Hawking and follows the development of both his career and disease from his early days at Cambridge. It's here that he meets Jane Wilde, played by Felicity Jones. The two become inseparable, and when Hawking is diagnosed and told that he only has two more years to live, the couple decide to marry anyway. They go on to have three children and Hawking achieves academic acclaim in spite of his increasing disability.

While the story of Hawking's life is well known and the plot develops as we expect, the film gives us an insight into how the couple battled to overcome the difficulties that his illness created. We don't get much of a sense of Hawking's impenetrable scientific mind, but we are reminded of the unpredictable nature of life and love, which gives this film its universal appeal. As for the acting, in my opinion, Redmayne has been underrated as an actor in the past (perhaps because at times he has been miscast by directors), but here his performance is totally convincing. In fact, his portrayal of Hawking is mesmerising.

If you like overblown films full of action and special effects, then this film is definitely not for you. On the other hand, if you're looking for something thought-provoking and inspiring, you owe it to yourself to see *The Theory of Everything*.

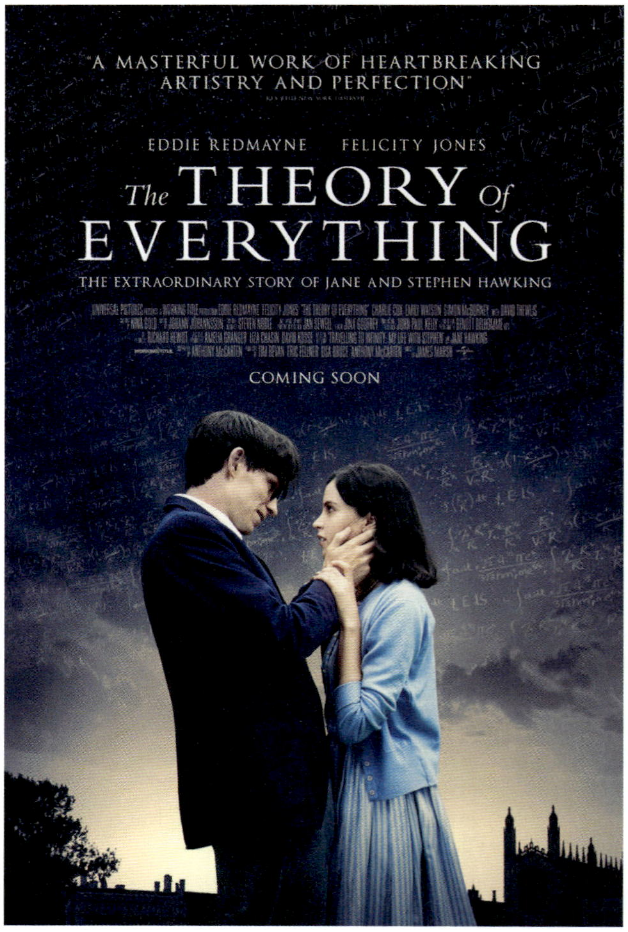

4c Complete the sentences by adding prefixes from 4b to the words in bold.

1 Jennifer Lawrence .... with Liam Hemsworth in *The Hunger Games*. **STAR**

2 Apart from the main story about organising a bank robbery, there is a romantic .... between the two main characters. **PLOT**

3 You have to be over 18 to watch the film, but experts predict that there will be a lot of .... viewers because this actor is very popular with younger spectators, too. **AGE**

4 After shooting the film, next comes the stage known as .... **PRODUCTION**

5 I'm not a big fan of .... films. I prefer historical films to fantasies. **REALISTIC**

6 I think a lot of critics have got the film wrong. They've .... what it's really about. **INTERPRETED**

7 The original film came out in 2001. This new film is just a .... **MAKE**

8 I think people have been .... of the film. OK, it isn't the best film ever, but it certainly isn't the worst, which is what some people are saying. **CRITICAL**

5 SPEAKING Work with a partner. Look at the adjectives in the Writing bank and decide if each one is generally positive, negative or neutral. What aspect(s) of a film could each one describe?

Disappointing is a negative adjective and it could describe a film in general, the special effects, or maybe the performance of one or more of the actors.

WRITING BANK

Useful words and expressions connected with films

Nouns

adaptation • box office • cliché • cliffhanger
critic • masterpiece • portrayal • script • sequel
twists and turns (of a plot)

Adjectives

disappointing • disjointed • epic • far-fetched
fast-moving • flawed • gripping • (un)inspiring
intriguing • light-hearted • low-budget
memorable • mesmerising • mind-blowing
moving • risqué • thought-provoking
up-and-coming

Expressions

(the film) bombed • (critics) panned (the film)
(the film) grossed ($10,000) • (the story) unfolds
deliver a great performance
(the film) received rave reviews
get a lukewarm reception • a box-office smash/flop
(the film) hit the big screen

6 Match words and expressions in the Writing bank with these definitions and explanations. Then check that you understand the other words. Use your dictionary if necessary.

1 likely to offend some people
2 a film that not many people pay to see at the cinema
3 did very badly
4 likely to become successful
5 continuation of an earlier film/story
6 earned
7 appeared in the cinema
8 idea that is boring because it has been used a lot
9 people wrote great things about the film
10 sudden unexpected changes in a situation
11 difficult to believe
12 film that makes you want to carry on watching to find out what happens next

7 Make notes about a film you have seen recently. Use this paragraph plan to organise your notes.

1 *General information about the film – title, genre, director, star, date it came out*
2 *The basic plot*
3 *What you liked/didn't like about the film, with examples and justifications*
4 *Your recommendation*

8 SPEAKING Work with a partner. Use your notes to talk about your film. When you describe the plot, use the present simple. Make your opinions and recommendation as clear and detailed as possible.

EXAM SUCCESS

When you write a review, have a definite idea about what you want to tell people about the thing that you are reviewing. Clarify your opinions by giving examples to justify them.

➤ EXAM SUCCESS page 150

9 PRACTICE MAKES PERFECT Write a review of the film you made notes and talked about in 7 and 8. Use words and expressions from the Writing bank and advice from Exam success.

WRITING BANK ➤ PAGE 156

Grammar reference

Verb + -ing form and infinitive

We use **verb + -ing** form after these verbs:

admit • avoid • carry on • consider • deny • face • feel like • finish
give up • include • keep (on) • practise • recommend • risk • suggest • take up

We use **verb + to-infinitive** after these verbs:

afford • agree • appear • arrange • decide • expect • fail • happen • help
hope • manage • pretend • promise • refuse • seem • volunteer • wait

We use the **gerund** or the **to-infinitive** after these verbs with little or no difference in meaning:

begin • bother • can't bear • can't stand • continue • hate • love
prefer • start

We use the **gerund** or the **to-infinitive** after these verbs, but there is an important difference in meaning:

stop to do: you stop one activity because you want or need to do another activity
stop doing: you are doing something and then you stop
remember to do: you remember you need to do something and then you do it
remember doing: you do something and then you remember it later
forget to do: you don't do something that you intended to do
forget doing: you did something, but now you don't remember it
like to do: you do something because you think it's a good idea
like doing: you do something because you enjoy doing it
try to do: you make an effort to achieve something
try doing: you do something as an experiment
mean to do: you intend to do something
mean doing: an action involves something
go on to do: you stop one activity or topic of discussion and start another, new one
go on doing: you continue doing an activity

Verb + object + -ing form and infinitive

We use the ***-ing*** form after these verbs when they are followed by an object:

catch • feel • find • hear • notice • overhear • see • watch

We use the **to-infinitive** after these verbs when they are followed by an object:

advise • allow • ask • authorise • beg • choose • encourage • force • help
hire • inspire • invite • need • order • persuade • pick • remind
send • teach • tell • want • warn

We use the **infinitive without to** after these verbs when they are followed by an object:

feel • hear • help • let • make • overhear • see • watch

For general rules on when to use the gerund or infinitive, see Unit 10.

Vocabulary

For the human mind, phrasal verbs and prefixes, see wordlist pages 137–138.

Grammar revision

Verb + -ing form and infinitive / 10 points

1 Choose the correct alternative. If both alternatives are correct, mark both.

1 How come you refused _to help/helping_ me?
2 Could you all stop _to listen/listening_ to me?
3 In some ways, being a doctor means _to dedicate/dedicating_ your life to your job.
4 As a kid, I avoided _to eat/eating_ vegetables.
5 The actor went on _to talk/talking_ for two hours.
6 When the police questioned him, he denied _to do/doing_ anything wrong.
7 We continued _to read/reading_ the book in class.
8 Please don't bother _to call/calling_ me again.
9 I forgot _to bring/bringing_ the money I owe you.
10 Let's carry on _to prepare/preparing_ our presentation.

Verb + object + -ing form and infinitive / 10 points

2 Complete the text with the correct form of the verbs given.

The film *Rain Man* (1988) was based on a man called Kim Peek who had amazing mental powers. These powers were evident when at the age of two, people noticed him **(a)** .... (read) newspapers! In 1984, scriptwriter Barry Morrow met Kim and immediately asked his father **(b)** .... (give) him permission to write a film about his life. Kim's father let him **(c)** .... (do) it. The film-makers chose Dustin Hoffman **(d)** .... (play) the part of Kim, and they invited him **(e)** .... (meet) him in person. Kim had an amazing memory for numbers and so in the film, the Rain Man's brother persuades him **(f)** .... (use) his mental powers to break the bank at the casino. However, in real life Kim refused, not because he was afraid they would catch him **(g)** .... (do) it, but because it was unethical. When Hoffman met Peek and his father, they got on well and Hoffman begged Kim's father **(h)** .... (share) Kim with the world. Kim and his father began helping people **(i)** .... (understand) more about mental disabilities. Thousands of people saw him **(j)** .... (do) his favourite trick. When somebody told Kim his date of birth, he could instantly tell them what day of the week it was.

Vocabulary revision

PHRASAL VERBS – THE MIND / 7 points

1 Choose the correct alternative.

1 I didn't understand the story at first, but eventually I pieced _it together/together it_.
2 Why don't we talk _the presentation through/through the presentation_?
3 I find that I _catch on/pick up_ new vocabulary fast.
4 The answer leapt _out at me/at me out_.
5 It took ages to come _up with/out at_ ideas.
6 You aren't keeping _on/up_ with the class.
7 It wasn't easy to think of a solution, but when they hit _it on/on it_ they were very relieved.

THE HUMAN MIND / 6 points

2 Match these words with the definitions 1–6. There are two extra words.

articulate • bewildered • grasp • have a gift for
memorise • perceive … as • recall • wander

1 learn something so that you can remember it
2 confused
3 able to express your ideas clearly and effectively
4 have a natural ability for
5 think about or understand something in a particular way
6 understand

PREFIXES / 7 points

3 Read the definitions and complete the words with the correct prefix.

1 make a mistake in calculating numbers = ...calculate
2 a temperature lower than 0 degrees = ...zero
3 not as good as some people think = ...rated
4 not earning enough money for the work you do = ...paid
5 faster than the speed of sound = ...sonic
6 a person who shares the responsibility for producing something = ...producer
7 think again about a decision to decide whether you should change it = ...consider

Total: / 40 points

4 Mad science

Reading

VOCABULARY Biology and scientific research

1a Match these words with the definitions below.

chromosome (n) • contract (a disease) (v) • enzyme (n) • genetic engineering (n) • genetically modified (adj) • parasite (n) • prevalent (adj) • resistant (adj) • species (n) • transmit (a disease) (v)

1 to pass a disease from one person to another
2 a plant or animal group whose members all have similar general features
3 a plant or animal that lives in or on another type of animal and feeds on it
4 not harmed or affected by something
5 very common in a particular place or among a particular group
6 the practice or science of adding genes to a living thing
7 to become infected with a disease
8 a structure that exists in cells, often as one of a pair
9 a natural chemical produced by animal and plant cells
10 a plant or animal that has had its genetic structure changed

1b Complete the sentences with words from 1a. Make a change to the verb or noun where necessary.

1 Females have two X .... Males have one X and one Y.
2 Some people think that .... food could reduce world hunger.
3 Animals infected with the virus can .... the disease to humans.
4 Bacteria can become .... to antibiotics.
5 He was healthy until he .... pneumonia.
6 .... has made it possible to grow plants in places they don't normally grow.
7 .... break down the food we eat so that it can be converted into energy.
8 .... such as fleas are common in cats and dogs.
9 The number of plant and animal .... at risk of extinction is growing.
10 Malaria is still .... in many countries.

2 SPEAKING Work with a partner and read the article headline opposite. What information do you expect to read in the article?

3 Read the article quickly, ignoring the gaps. How would you summarise the main points?

4 Read the article again. Six paragraphs have been removed. Choose from the paragraphs A–F the one which fits each gap (1–6).

✔ EXAM SUCCESS

In reading activities where you complete a text with paragraphs, begin with the paragraphs that you find easiest and are sure about. Cross these out so that you have fewer options for the more difficult gaps.

➤ EXAM SUCCESS page 150

5 Find the following in the article. Explain who or what they are and why they are significant.

I-PpoI • Dr Nikolai Windbichler • 627,000 • GMEP • $12 billion • Pirbright Institute

6 CRITICAL THINKING

Think! Then compare ideas with your class.

- Do you believe that humans have the right to eliminate species from the planet?
- What possible consequences can you see, both positive and negative, of this type of experiment?

7 Guess the meaning of the underlined words from the context. Then use your dictionary to check.

8 SPEAKING What about *you*?

1 Are mosquitoes a problem where you live? What are the best ways to get rid of them?
2 Would you like to work in scientific research? Why/Why not?
3 What other examples of genetic engineering in plants and animals can you think of?
4 What are the benefits and dangers of these?

MODIFYING MOSQUITOES

Genetically modified mosquitoes could help to eradicate malaria

Mosquitoes have been genetically modified so they only give birth to males in a new technique that scientists hope could help to wipe out malaria.

Scientists from Imperial College London have tested a new genetic method that changes the ratio of male to female *Anopheles gambiae* mosquitoes, the main transmitters of the malaria parasite, so that the female mosquitoes which bite and pass the disease to humans are no longer produced.

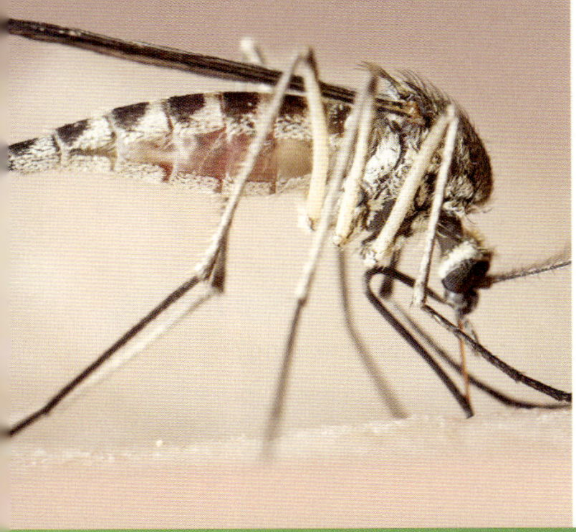

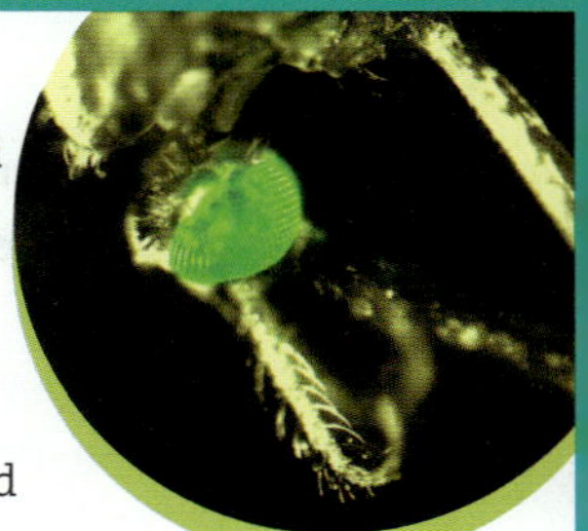

1 ____ In order to eliminate the female mosquitoes, scientists created a DNA-cutting enzyme called I-PpoI, which they inserted into a sample of *Anopheles gambiae* mosquitoes. In normal reproduction, the ratio of the X chromosome, which produces female offspring, and the Y chromosome, which produces males, is roughly equal. The enzyme used by the researchers cut the DNA of the X chromosome so that almost none could be produced. As a result, the offspring of the genetically-modified mosquitoes was almost exclusively male.

These genetically modified mosquitoes were then put into five cages containing general mosquito populations. In four of the five cages, the entire population was eliminated within six generations. The scientists hope that if they do the same thing with mosquitoes in the wild, the malaria-carrying mosquito population will ultimately die out within a few generations.

2 ____ This is the first time that scientists have been able to manipulate the ratios of male and female mosquito populations. The researchers believe the work paves the way for a pioneering approach to controlling malaria, which continues to threaten the lives of half of the global population.

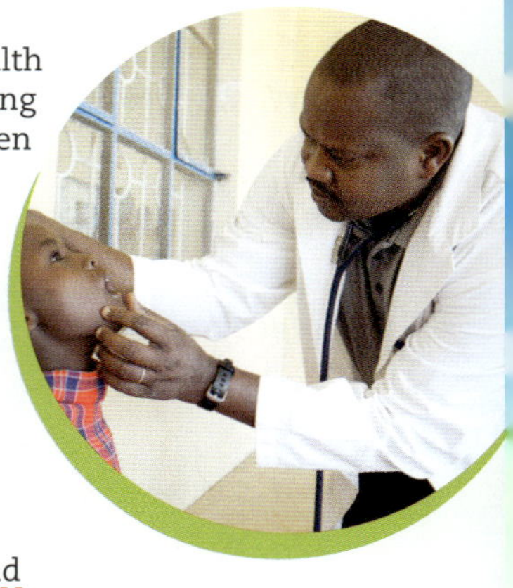

3 ____ According to the latest estimates by the World Health Organization, over 3.4 billion people are at risk of contracting the disease and an estimated 627,000 die each year. Children under the age of five are particularly vulnerable, with one child dying every 60 seconds.

4 ____ Increased prevention and control measures in recent years have reduced global mortality rates by 42 per cent, but the disease persists, especially in high-risk regions of sub-Saharan Africa. Mosquitoes have become increasingly resistant to insecticides and the malaria parasite has become resistant to drugs.

5 ____ It's likely that mosquito populations would rebound after a few years, so the genetically engineered mosquitoes would need to be reintroduced into the wild regularly in order to control them. Nevertheless, scientists are hopeful that the approach could be used to fight all types of mosquito, including the species that transmit dengue fever, which is prevalent in over a hundred countries.

6 ____ According to Britain's Pirbright Institute, mosquitoes are not a keystone species in their ecosystems. While mosquitoes can act as pollinators as well as a food source for other animals, their absence would only be a temporary setback until another species filled the niche.

The question remains, however, whether humans have the right to eliminate entire species in this way. Eradicating mosquitoes may have positive benefits in reducing disease levels, but only time will tell if this experiment will have any lasting effects on humankind.

A Concerns have been raised about the possible effect of eliminating mosquitoes on local ecosystems. After all, mosquitoes have been on the planet for about 100 million years and they represent 3,500 species worldwide. Would we miss them if they disappeared?

B As research professor Andrea Crisanti from Imperial College London said: 'Malaria is debilitating and often fatal and we need to find new ways of tackling it. We think our innovative approach is a huge step forward.'

C What's more, sub-Saharan Africa loses about $12 billion in economic productivity due to malaria infections. Eradicating the disease would have real implications for the quality of life of people in those areas. Doctors and hospitals would be able to address other health concerns and the environment would benefit from not having to use insecticides.

D Female mosquitoes use human blood to acquire the nutrients they need to create eggs. A female mosquito can lay about 200 eggs at a time and up to 3,000 eggs during her lifetime. About half of the offspring will be daughters, many of which will live long enough to produce the same number of offspring themselves. For people living in tropical and subtropical areas, these females present a very real threat.

E Dr Nikolai Windbichler, a lead researcher from the Department of Life Sciences at Imperial College London, said: 'What is most promising about our results is that they are self-sustaining. Once modified mosquitoes are introduced, males will start to produce mainly sons, and their sons will do the same, so essentially the mosquitoes carry out the work for us.'

F During the 1950s and 1960s, the Global Malaria Eradication Programme (GMEP) was successful in eliminating the disease from several parts of the world. If their efforts had continued, they would have been able to eradicate malaria completely, but a lack of funds halted progress.

Conditionals

1 Look at the sentences and answer the questions.

a The scientists hope that if they do the same thing with mosquitoes in the wild, the malaria-carrying mosquito population will die out.

b Would we miss them if they disappeared?

c If a person lives in an area with these mosquitoes, they are at risk of contracting malaria.

d If their efforts had continued, they would have been able to eradicate the disease.

1 How do we make zero, first, second and third conditionals?

2 Why do we use each one?

3 What type of conditional is each sentence a–d?

GRAMMAR REFERENCE ➤ PAGE 54

2 Complete the sentences with the correct form of the verbs given.

1 If the press hadn't found out about this story, it .... (not appear) in the newspapers.

2 If research .... (be) useful, people want to know about it.

3 If they .... (not be) scientists, they wouldn't know how to carry out these experiments.

4 If they repeat the experiment, they .... (get) the same results next time.

5 If the experiment .... (not be) successful, they wouldn't have published the results.

6 If they achieve their aim, it .... (help) a lot of people.

7 If they did experiments on some types of animal, it .... (be) illegal.

8 If it .... (not be) for past pioneers, their research wouldn't have been possible.

3 Rewrite these sentences using conditionals.

1 My brother must get good marks because he wants to study medicine next year.
If my brother gets good marks, he ...

2 I didn't know you were at home last night. I wanted to call you for help with my homework.

3 You must water plants as without water, they die.

4 It's a pity scientists don't have more funding. They need it to do more research.

5 I'm glad I read this article. I hadn't heard about this breakthrough before.

6 I think you like sci-fi so you'll enjoy this film.

7 People tend to believe stories that they read in the newspapers.

8 I'm not a scientist because I don't want to do research on animals.

Other conditional structures

4 Look at the sentences. Check that you understand how and why we use the words in bold in these sentences.

a **Supposing/Suppose** mosquitoes die out, would that affect ecosystems?

b **Provided that/Providing that/As long as** they introduce genetically modified mosquitoes into the wild, the mosquitoes won't come back.

c **Unless** scientists take action against malaria, people will continue to contract the disease.

d Scientists won't confirm that the experiment will work in the wild **in case** they are wrong.

e **If only/I wish** they had a vaccine. It would solve a lot of problems.

f **I wish/If only** they had eliminated the disease.

GRAMMAR REFERENCE ➤ PAGE 54

5 Complete the second sentence so that it has a similar meaning to the first sentence, using the word given. Do not change the word given. You must use between three and six words, including the word given.

1 I'll help you, but only if you promise to pay close attention. **THAT**
I'll help you .... pay close attention.

2 If they fail, they may lose all their funding. **UNLESS**
.... all their funding.

3 What a pity that we didn't see each other! **WISH**
.... each other.

4 If we can stop the situation, would it not be worth doing? **SUPPOSE**
................................, would it not be worth doing?

5 I'll be right here waiting for you because you might need me. **CASE**
I'll be right here waiting for you ....

6 We'll publish your research but only if you have evidence of your findings. **LONG**
We'll publish your research .... evidence of your findings.

✓ EXAM SUCCESS

In transformation activities, check that you have not changed the meaning from the original sentence or changed the form of the word given.

➤ EXAM SUCCESS page 150

6 SPEAKING Complete the sentences with your own ideas. Then discuss your ideas in pairs.

1 If I pass all my exams with outstanding marks, ...

2 If I could have any job in the world, ...

3 If I'd had more time last weekend, ...

4 If I were a politician, ...

Compound nouns and adjectives

1 Match the compound nouns 1–8 with their meanings a–h.

1	outlook	a	beginning, start
2	drawback	b	result (e.g. of a process, meeting, activity)
3	outcome	c	reduction in something (e.g. the amount of money to spend)
4	feedback	d	strong action that someone in authority takes to stop a particular activity
5	outset	e	sudden start of war, disease, violence, etc.
6	outbreak	f	disadvantage
7	cutback	g	idea of what a situation will be like in the future/your general attitude to things
8	crackdown	h	comments about how well or badly someone is doing something, intended to help them to do it better

2 Match 1–8 and a–h. Are the words compound nouns or compound adjectives? Are they written as one word, one word with a hyphen (-) or two words? Use your dictionary if necessary.

1	genetically	a	time
2	set	b	wide
3	high	c	through
4	life	d	while
5	world	e	modified
6	break	f	back
7	off	g	risk
8	worth	h	spring

3 Complete the sentences with compound nouns from 1.

1 I began reading this book yesterday and from the .... I knew I was going to love it.

2 They discussed whether they should continue with their research and the .... of the meeting was that they should.

3 Organisations which protect animal rights have made sure that there has been a .... on using animals in experiments.

4 Scientists had to work hard to find a cure when there was a sudden .... of a deadly new type of flu.

5 Because of the economic recession there was a .... in the amount of money spent on research and development.

6 I think you and I have the same .... on life.

7 The .... from potential customers about the product was generally positive.

8 There are both benefits and .... to genetic engineering when it comes to food.

4 Complete the compound nouns and adjectives in the news article.

THE END OF THE OLIVE FLY?

Scientists at a biotechnology company have made a (a) b.................... in producing (b) g.................... olive flies and are seeking permission to release them in Spain. If the plan goes ahead, male flies will first be sterilised in a laboratory and then they will be released into the environment where they will mate with wild olive fly females. Their (c) o.................... will be infertile, and the flies will eventually die out.

Although olive flies currently destroy whole harvests of olives, from the (d) o...................., the proposal has met with criticism. The main (e) d...................., critics say, is that the bodies of the flies could remain in the olives. No-one knows the effect of eating these olives over a (f) l..................... While the experiment may be (g) w.................... for farmers, for consumers it is a (h) h.................... strategy.

The organisation Friends of the Earth has called for a (i) c.................... on such experiments. Meanwhile, the company is still waiting for the (j) o.................... of their permission request.

Reading articles CRITICALLY

21ST CENTURY SKILLS OBJECTIVES	KEY CONCEPTS
▪ To question how scientific facts are interpreted in news articles ▪ To identify what to look for in science articles to decide how reliable they are ▪ To critique an article	**causation [n]:** *Correlation does not mean causation; in other words just because there is a correlation between two things, it doesn't mean that one causes the other.* **corroborate [v]:** *You need to corroborate information by looking at other research to see if it reaches the same conclusions.* **conclusive [adj]:** *Just because there is some evidence, it doesn't mean that the results of the research are conclusive.*

1 SPEAKING **Work with a partner. Look at the table. What does it show? What conclusions can you draw from this information?**

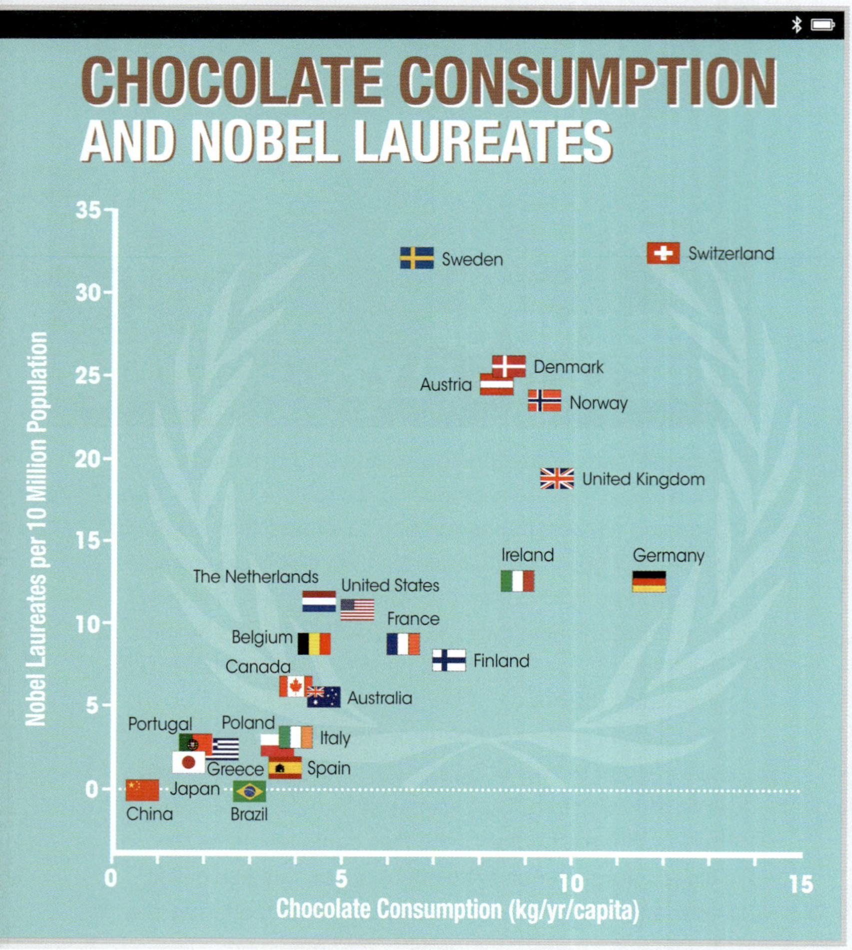

2 READING **Read the article and answer these questions.**

1 Who collected the data in the table and why?
2 What conclusion did he draw from the information?
3 How does he explain the anomaly?
4 What else supports his conclusions?

Does chocolate make you clever?

If you've ever worried about eating too much chocolate, good news is at hand. According to recent research, chocolate may actually make you more intelligent!

A cardiologist at Columbia University, Franz Messerli, decided to look into the possibility of a link between chocolate and intelligence after he had read studies stating that cocoa was beneficial for health. One study had found a connection between the consumption of cocoa and improved mental function in elderly patients. Another found that animals such as rats and even snails live longer and have better cognitive function when they eat chocolate.

Messerli decided to test his theory by comparing the number of Nobel Prize winners in a country, in proportion to the population of that country, with the nation's chocolate consumption. And the results of his study were significant.

When the two factors were compared – chocolate consumption and the number of Nobel prize winners – there was a very strong correlation. Switzerland, which has the highest consumption of chocolate per capita, has also produced the highest number of Nobel Laureates. Meanwhile, China appeared at the bottom of the table in both chocolate consumption and the number of prize winners.

The evidence suggests a clear relationship between chocolate and intelligence. The correlation found has a "P value" of 0.0001, which means there is a less than one-in-10,000 chance of getting results like these if there is no relationship between the two.

Sweden does not fit the pattern, producing a large number of Nobel laureates while eating much less chocolate. However, Messerli explains this anomaly by pointing out that Sweden is responsible for donating and evaluating the prize, so it's possible that there is a national bias. Another theory is that Swedes may have a higher sensitivity to cocoa, and a lower level of consumption would therefore be needed to produce the same effect on their intelligence.

Though it hasn't yet been proven that it is chocolate that causes the increased intelligence, it is clear from other research that chocolate, and especially dark chocolate, can be very beneficial for your health, particularly for the brain and the heart. It is known to have a high level of antioxidants, which can lower cholesterol levels and improve blood pressure. And other studies have shown that eating chocolate can reduce the chances of stroke.

So perhaps we should all eat more chocolate?

3 SPEAKING **Work in a small group. Discuss these questions.**

1. Do you agree with the conclusions in the article? Why/Why not?
2. What aspects of the article suggest that it is reliable?
3. Is there anything that makes you question the conclusions?

4 LISTENING ▶ 12 **A science journalist is discussing the article. Watch the video or listen. Do they mention any of the points you talked about in 3?**

5 LISTENING ▶ 12 **Watch or listen again. Make notes about what the science journalist says about the things to consider when reading a science article.**

- the news outlet
- the source and quotes
- the references to scientific research
- the context and purpose
- correlation and causation

6 **Look at the article again. Find further examples to support the points made by the science journalist in 5.**

21ST CENTURY TASK

Work in groups of three. You are going to read a science article and critique it.

Follow this plan:

1. *Choose one of the articles on page 162–3 or find one of your own.*
2. *Identify the different points discussed in 5.*
3. *Decide together whether you think the conclusions in the article are reliable or not and make a list of reasons why.*
4. *Prepare and present your conclusions to another group. Give reasons to defend your opinion.*

Flipped classroom: watch the grammar presentation video.

1 SPEAKING **Work with a partner. Discuss these questions.**

1 What animals do you know are in danger of extinction?
2 What animals have already become extinct?
3 Why did this happen?

2 LISTENING 13 **Listen to a podcast about bringing animals back from extinction and choose the best answers.**

1 What does Professor Rogers think about the cloning of dinosaurs?
   a No suitable DNA samples exist because dinosaurs froze too fast.
   b It's difficult because you need to have organic remains.
   c You can only clone animals using DNA samples.
2 What is the experiment at Harvard Medical School?
   a To create elephants that are hairy and woolly.
   b To insert DNA from a woolly mammoth into an elephant.
   c To engineer elephants so that they don't become extinct.
3 What is the main reason given for bringing back woolly mammoths?
   a They could graze on grass in Arctic regions.
   b Their weight would help to strengthen the ice.
   c To reduce the escape of carbon gases into the atmosphere.
4 How are scientists trying to bring back the passenger pigeon?
   a They're engineering another species of pigeon.
   b They're inserting cells into museum specimens.
   c They're using pigeons from the forests of the East Coast.
5 Why does the professor support de-extinction?
   a Humans have made a lot of mistakes in the past.
   b Animals are becoming extinct at an alarming rate.
   c It can help to restore natural habitats.
6 Which of the following does the professor believe?
   a It isn't important to spend money on saving endangered species.
   b The technology can be used for de-extinction and saving endangered species.
   c Bringing back animals from extinction is the priority.

3 SPEAKING **Work with a partner. Discuss these questions.**

1 If it were possible to bring any animal back from extinction, which would you choose? Why?
2 What are the best ways of saving endangered species?
3 In your opinion, is it better to focus on saving endangered species or bring animals back from extinction? Why?

Mixed conditionals

4 Look at the sentences and answer the questions.

a If a dinosaur had been frozen quickly, and had stayed at that temperature, then you'd have DNA samples.
b If we hadn't caused destruction in these areas, we wouldn't need to recreate species now.
c If we did more to protect endangered species, these animals wouldn't have become extinct.

1 What is the form of these conditional sentences?
2 Which sentence(s) describe an imaginary past and its present consequence?
3 Which sentence(s) describe an imaginary present situation and its past consequence?

GRAMMAR REFERENCE ➤ PAGE 54

5 Choose the correct alternative.

1 If I could bring any animal back from extinction, I'd *choose/have chosen* the dinosaur.
2 If I'd slept more last night, I wouldn't *be/have been* so tired now.
3 I'd *go/have gone* out last night if I hadn't had so much homework.
4 If I had eaten breakfast, I wouldn't *feel/have felt* hungry now.
5 I wouldn't know this city so well if I *didn't live/hadn't lived* here all my life.
6 I'd *speak/have spoken* perfect English if I'd been born in an English-speaking country.
7 If I'd finished all my homework last night, I'd *be/have been* able to go out later.
8 I'd let you borrow my mobile if I *didn't lose/hadn't lost* it.

6 SPEAKING **If you could go back in time, what three things would you change about the world? How would the world be different now?**

Talking about statistics

1 **Look at the charts and graphs. Which:**

1 is a bar chart?
2 is a pie chart?
3 is a table?
4 is a line graph?
5 show statistics which total 100 per cent?
6 shows a change or trend over a period of time?
7 shows a non-diagrammatic comparison of statistics?
8 shows a diagrammatic comparison of statistics?

2 SPEAKING **Work with a partner. Find words in the Speaking bank to talk about each chart or graph in 1. Check that you understand all the words.**

> **SPEAKING BANK**
>
> **Useful words and expressions to talk about statistics**
>
> *Numbers and proportions*
> - a half/third/quarter/fifth/sixth, etc.
> - one in two/three/five/ten, etc.
> - 5/10/15 per cent
> - the majority/minority
> - just under/over
> - approximately/roughly
> - twice/three/four/five times as many/big as
> - slightly/considerably more/fewer
> - a large/small/considerable number/proportion of (+ countable noun)
> - a large/small/considerable amount/quantity of (+ uncountable noun)
> - the (second/third/fourth) largest/biggest/highest
> - in comparison with
>
> *Trends*
> - rise/increase/grow/double/treble/rocket
> - fall/decrease/drop/decline/half/plunge/plummet
> - stay the same/change little/level off/stabilise
> - fluctuate
> - reach a high/low
> - slow(ly)/gradual(ly)/slight(ly), steady (steadily) (adj/adv)
> - significant(ly)/sharp(ly)/dramatic(ally) (adj/adv)

3 **Write a short description of each chart or graph in 1. Think carefully about which tense(s) you need to use in each case.**

4 SPEAKING **Work with a partner. What do you think about the information in the charts and graphs? Do you find it surprising, shocking, predictable, etc.? Why?**

5 LISTENING 14 **Listen to four students talking about the charts and graphs in 1. Are the speakers' descriptions and reactions similar to yours?**

THE STATE OF PUBLIC ATTITUDES TO SCIENCE 2014

A

PERCEPTIONS OF JOBS IN ENGINEERING AND SCIENCE AMONG 16–24-YEAR-OLDS

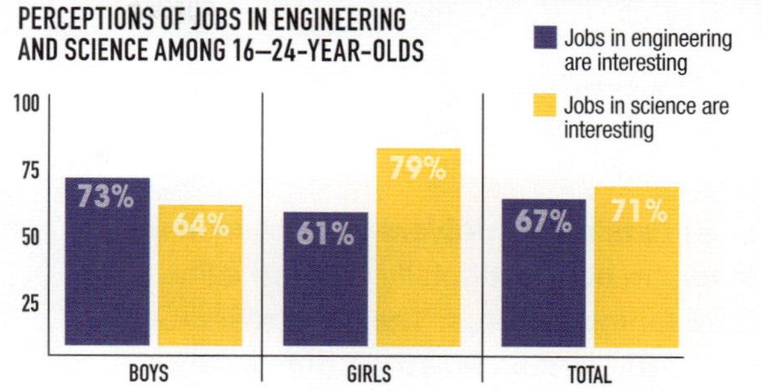

B

PERCEPTIONS OF SCIENTISTS OVER TIME

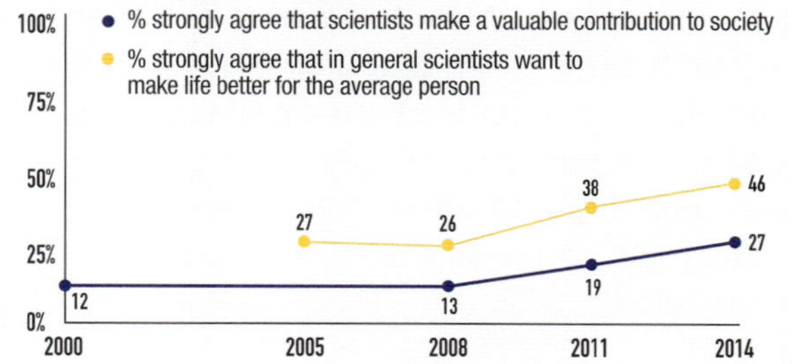

C

PECENTAGE OF 16–24-YEAR-OLDS WHO THINK THE MATHS AND SCIENCE LEARNT AT SCHOOL ARE USEFUL IN DAILY LIFE.

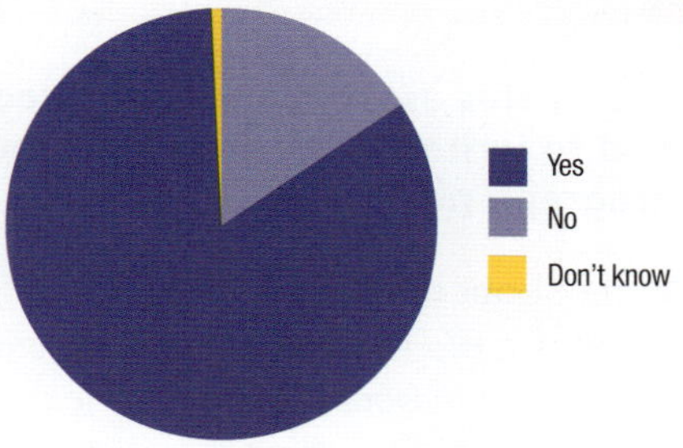

D

SOURCES OF INFORMATION ABOUT SCIENCE

	Adults 16+	16–24-year-olds
TV news	42%	34%
Other TV programmes	26%	17%
Print newspapers	23%	11%
Online newspapers or news websites	15%	24%
Family, friends and colleagues	12%	13%
Other websites	9%	10%
Radio programmes	15%	11%
Magazines	7%	6%
Social networks	6%	21%
Books	6%	10%

6 **PRACTICE MAKES PERFECT** SPEAKING **Work with a partner. Turn to page 164 and take it in turns to talk about the statistics and your reactions to them. Use words and expressions from the Speaking bank.**

> **✓ EXAM SUCCESS**
>
> In stimulus-based discussions, talk about the most important statistics; don't explain every single fact. Remember to give personal reactions to the statistics, giving reasons to justify and explain your opinion.
>
> ➤ EXAM SUCCESS page 150

Developing writing

A for-and-against essay

1 SPEAKING **Work with a partner. Read the beginning of a science article and discuss what you think the different reactions to the news have been.**

SCIENTISTS CREATE DEADLY FLU VIRUS

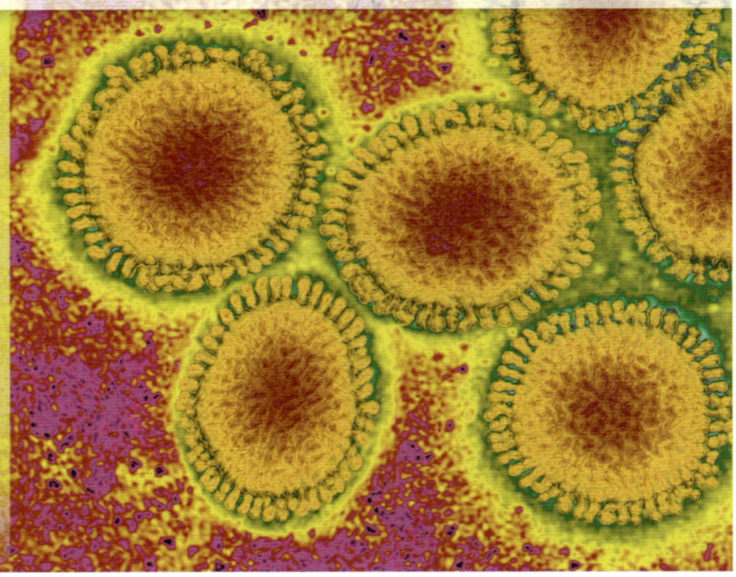

Scientists at the University of Wisconsin-Madison have artificially created a life-threatening flu virus. The virus resembles the 1918 Spanish flu strain that was responsible for the deaths of around 50 million people worldwide. Until the controversial experiment, the virus had been extinct. Scientists say that their research will help them to understand more about the health risks posed by viruses in the future. Not surprisingly, this news has been met with strong, and widely different, reactions. Some people ...

2 **Look at this essay task. What exactly do you need to write? Work with a partner and write a paragraph plan.**

> Write about the following topic:
> *Some people think that artificially creating viruses is acceptable because it could help to save lives in the future. Others think that it could have terrible consequences and put more lives in danger.*
> First discuss both these views and then give your own opinion.
> Give reasons for your answer and include any relevant examples from your own knowledge.

3 **Read the essay on the right and answer these questions.**

1. Does the essay do what the task asks for?
2. Is the organisation similar to your ideas in 2?
3. Do you agree with the writer's opinion? Why/Why not?

4a **Put these headings in the correct place (1–6) in the Writing bank.**

- Adding arguments
- Concluding
- Expressing consequences
- Making contrasts
- Expressing your and other people's opinions
- Introducing and sequencing arguments

Recent news that an extinct flu virus has been reconstructed at a laboratory in the US has given rise to a fierce debate between those who think that experiments such as this are necessary to protect people and those who believe it puts the global population in danger.

Some scientists claim that recreating viruses is essential so that governments can prepare for possible outbreaks of disease in the future. To take the example of the flu virus, they say the research will enable scientists to develop a vaccine that could save thousands of lives. Moreover, if the right precautions are taken, there should be no threat to the general public.

On the other hand, there are people who argue that it is impossible to know the full repercussions of creating a genetically-engineered virus. Despite the fact that the research is carried out in a secure laboratory, there is always the risk that the virus could escape or there is an accidental infection, which, in turn, could lead to a pandemic. A further criticism of these experiments is that there is no threat at present, and if the disease were to re-occur, scientists would be able to react quickly to deal with it. Last but not least, some people believe that the scientists who do these experiments are motivated by ambition and that there is no benefit to public health.

To sum up, this is a complex issue, but one that we cannot simply ignore. My own view is that it can be highly dangerous to play with nature unless we know the full consequences of what we are doing. Recreating viruses may solve future problems, but it is vital that measures are taken to ensure that the research is carefully controlled and that these viruses do not escape, which could have catastrophic results for our planet as a whole.

4b **Add the underlined words and expressions in the essay in 2 to the relevant sections of the Writing bank.**

WRITING BANK

Useful expressions in for-and-against essays

1 ……………………
- First and foremost,
- Secondly,
- Lastly,
- ……………………

2 ……………………
- Furthermore,
- ……………………
- What is more,
- In addition,
- not only … but also
- a further advantage of
- ……………………

3 ……………………
- On the one hand,
- ……………………
- In contrast,
- in spite of (+ noun/gerund/the fact that …)
- ……………………
- However,/Nevertheless,
- conversely
- by way of contrast

4 ……………………
- Therefore,
- and so
- as a result
- as a consequence
- consequently

5 ……………………
- In my opinion,
- Personally, I believe that
- ……………………
- As far as I'm concerned
- ……………………
- It is said that …
- ……………………

6 ……………………
- In conclusion,
- All in all
- ……………………

VOCABULARY Causes, reasons and results

5 **Choose the correct alternative. In some cases, both alternatives are possible. Check that you know what all the alternatives mean.**

1 The news has *given rise/risen* to a fierce debate.
2 People are afraid of some scientific research *since/as* they don't know what effects it might have.
3 There is always a risk of accidental infection which could, *on its way/in turn*, lead to a general pandemic.
4 We still cannot know *the full repercussions/all the negative consequences* of artificially creating viruses.
5 The *second/side* effects of some vaccines are still unknown.
6 We must be careful because playing with nature could have *disastrous/catastrophic* results.
7 The research could *bring about/lead to* changes in the way governments prepare.
8 The news about the experiment *sparked off/stemmed from* a lot of criticism.
9 I believe the research will prompt the government *change/to change* the law.
10 Some experiments are risky *due to/owing to* the lack of proper precautions.

6 **Read the beginning of another science article. Think of advantages and disadvantages of manipulating the weather.**

According to Chinese scientists, for them the words to this children's rhyme are not just wishful thinking. They say that they have the ability to control the weather. In November 2009, there was an unusual fall of snow. China claims that it prompted the snow by firing 186 chemical rockets into clouds passing over Beijing. They did this to help stop the long drought the city had been suffering. But scientists are worried that if each country unilaterally decides to use geo-engineering to manipulate the weather, the global repercussions could be catastrophic and global-warming could get worse, not better. Scientists at …

7 SPEAKING **Discuss your ideas in 6 as a whole class. Do most people think that controlling the weather would be a good thing or a bad thing?**

8 **Look at the essay task. Work with a partner and use the ideas in 6 and 7 to write a paragraph plan for the essay.**

Write about the following topic:
Some people think that having scientists manipulate the weather could be beneficial for the planet. Others think that the consequences could be very worrying.
Discuss both these views and then give your own opinion.
Give reasons for your answer and include any relevant examples from your own knowledge.

9 PRACTICE MAKES PERFECT **Write your essay for the task in 8. Use words and expressions from the Writing bank and the vocabulary section on this page, and advice from Exam success.**

WRITING BANK ➤ PAGE 157

✓ EXAM SUCCESS

Read the task very carefully to see if you should be giving your own opinion of a particular question, arguments on both sides of the question, or a mixture of both. The way that you organise your essay in each case will be different, and you will be evaluated according to how well you have completed the task.

➤ EXAM SUCCESS page 150

Language checkpoint: Unit 4

Grammar reference

For zero conditional, first conditional and second conditional, see page 166

Third conditional

FORM

If + **past perfect**, … ***would/wouldn't have*** + past participle

*If I **had studied**, I **would have** passed the exam.*

USE

We use the third conditional to talk about imaginary or impossible situations in the past and their consequences. The situations are impossible because we cannot change them now that they have happened.

Mixed conditionals

FORM

If + **past simple**, … ***would/wouldn't have*** + past participle

If + **past perfect**, … ***would/wouldn't*** + infinitive

USE

Mixed conditionals are a mixture of the second and third conditional. They can describe an imaginary present situation and its past consequence.

*If I **liked** that group I **would have gone** to see them in concert.*

Or they can describe an imaginary past situation and its present consequence.

*If I **had had** breakfast, I **wouldn't be** hungry now.*

Other conditional structures

unless = if … not, except if

*We won't be able to swim **unless** the swimming pool is open.*

as long as, provided/providing (that) = if, only if

*We'll be able to swim **as long as/provided** the swimming pool is open.*

in case = because, maybe

*We'll take our swimsuits **in case** the swimming pool is open.*

supposing/suppose = imagine …

***Supposing** he came to eat tonight, would we have enough food?*

should/were to/happened to = when something is less probable

*If it **were to/should/happened to** rain tomorrow, what would we do?*

I wish/If only + **the past** = talking about imaginary situations in the present. It expresses wishes for things to be different in the present.

*I **wish** I **was** on the beach right now.*

I wish/If only + **past perfect** = talking about past situations that we would have liked to be different. It expresses regrets.

***If only** I **hadn't spent** all my money last weekend.*

I wish/If only with **would/wouldn't + infinitive** = talking about somebody's habitual behaviour that we want to criticise and change.

*My dad smokes. I **wish** he **wouldn't** do it.*

Vocabulary

For compound nouns and adjectives, biology and scientific research and causes, reasons and results, see wordlist pages 138–139.

Grammar revision

Conditionals / 7 points

1 Complete the conditional sentences with the correct form of the verb in brackets.

1 If he had come to school yesterday, he .... (do) the exam.
2 If I .... (be) better at sport, I'd play more.
3 If I .... (not see) you tonight, I'll see you tomorrow.
4 If my sister gets a cold, I usually .... (catch) it, too.
5 If it's warm this afternoon, I .... (walk) home.
6 If I .... (see) him yesterday, I'd have given him the message.
7 If he had a part-time job, he .... (not be able) to do all his homework.

Other conditional structures / 6 points

2 Complete the sentences with these words.

case • long • only • providing • supposing • unless

1 I'll lend you my laptop as .... as you promise to return it.
2 I bought a spare pen in .... this one ran out of ink.
3 .... you won the money, how would you spend it?
4 If .... I could remember his name!
5 .... that the weather stays fine, we'll have dinner outside.
6 .... you have a passport, they won't let you into the US.

Mixed conditionals / 7 points

3 Write conditional sentences for the situations below, using the words given.

1 I'm annoyed today because you didn't help me.
If you ....
2 We couldn't go out last night because we have an exam today.
If we ....
3 I'm afraid of heights so I didn't go to the top.
If I ....
4 I don't know any French so I couldn't translate it.
If I ....
5 He didn't take his medication. That's why he's sick.
If he ....
6 They didn't let us in because we aren't old enough.
If we ....
7 She isn't happy now because she didn't get the job.
If she ....

Vocabulary revision

COMPOUND NOUNS AND ADJECTIVES / 8 points

1 Complete the compound nouns or adjectives.

1 More than 50 people have been arrested in a crack.................... on organised crime.
2 Doctors are worried because there are going to be cut.................... in health spending.
3 In the feed.................... meeting, they're going to tell me how I can improve my presentations.
4 Right from the start of the journey, from the very out...................., I knew it would be special.
5 Raising money for charity is so worth.....................
6 It took years of research before they made a break.....................
7 Nuclear power has some obvious draw.....................
8 I doubt if they'll cure malaria during my life.....................

CAUSES, REASONS AND RESULTS / 6 points

2 Write a definition or explanation for these words.

1 spark off
2 as
3 prompt
4 due to
5 in turn
6 stem from

BIOLOGY AND SCIENTIFIC RESEARCH / 6 points

3 Complete the sentences with the correct form of these words.

contract (v) • parasites • prevalent
resistant • species • transmit

1 Sleep disorders may be more .... than previously thought.
2 Some .... of birds are dying out because of the use of insecticides.
3 People who have .... the virus can now be treated successfully.
4 Scientists are concerned that the disease could be .... by air.
5 Some natural remedies, such as garlic, can remove .... from the body.
6 Infections that have become .... to drugs could cost lives.

Total: / 40 points

Reading

1 You are going to read an article about a book. Six paragraphs have been removed from the article. Choose from the paragraphs A–F the one which fits each gap (1–6).

> **➤ TIP FOR READING EXAMS**
>
> In paragraph completion activities, remember …
> When you think you have finished, read through the complete text and see if the meaning is logical. Check pronouns and linking words and look for ideas repeated from one paragraph to the next by using synonyms.
>
> ➤ EXAM SUCCESS page 150

Leonardo's Brain

He was the archetypal genius. A painter. A scientist. An inventor. An engineer. Leonardo Da Vinci was perhaps the most diversely-talented man that ever lived. In *Leonardo's Brain*, best-selling author Leonard Shlain attempts to apply modern neuroscience to understand the workings of one of history's most innovative brains.

1 ....

Yet he also excelled as a painter, and composed music and sang as well. Leonardo Da Vinci stands out in history for his talents in the fields of both art and science.

2 ....

According to Shlain, Leonardo was, in many ways, an outsider. To begin with, he was a pacifist, and he was a strict vegetarian at a time when eating meat was a symbol of wealth and power. In fact, he had such an extraordinary empathy for animals that he would stop to buy caged birds when he saw them in shops and set them free.

3 ....

What's more, he used to write with his left hand. For Shlain, this penmanship suggests that the two hemispheres of Leonardo's brain were connected in an extraordinary way.

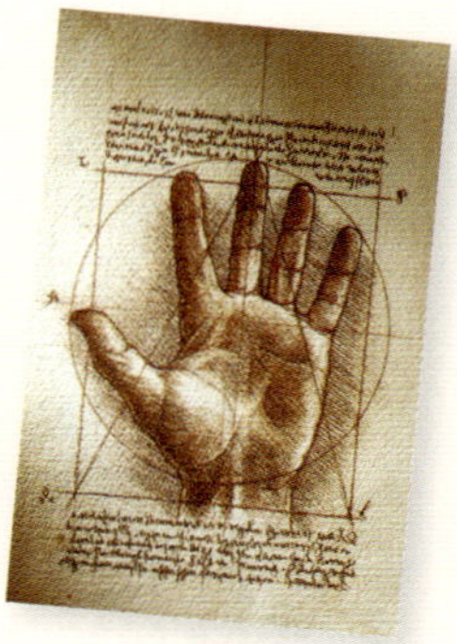

4 ....

For Shlain, creativity is a combination of courage and inventiveness. While it is impossible to say what work Leonardo would have done if he had attended university, Shlain argues that it was precisely this lack of education that allowed Leonardo to free his mind from restraints. He had what has been described as 'the gift of ignorance', which allowed him to ask new questions and look at the world in a fresh way.

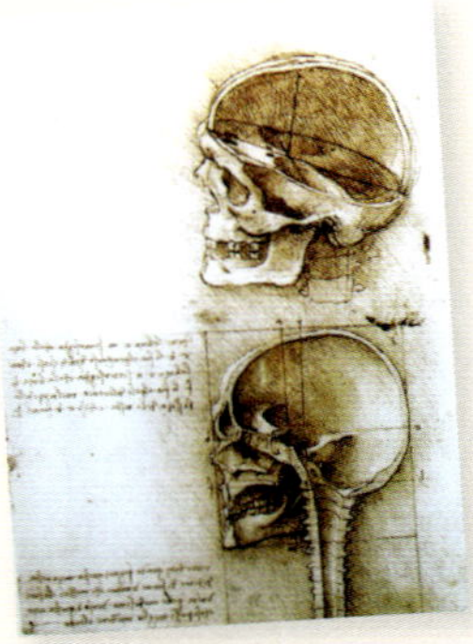

5 ....

Shlain explains that the left hemisphere, the side of the brain associated with critical thinking, is usually dominant in humans. Meanwhile, the right side of the brain, the side which processes information without rules and is usually associated with artistic talents, has less influence. For true creativity, both sides of the brain are necessary, and there must be a free connection, or exchange of ideas between the two sides of the brain.

6 ....

The question then is, did Leonardo's brain represent a jump to the future of humankind? Supposing we were able to engage both sides of the brain equally, would that lead to more creativity and innovative thinking? Shlain is optimistic. He claims that Leonardo's brain suggests what is possible for the future of our species.

A Da Vinci's childhood was also unusual and significant in his brain development. Born to a single mother, Leonardo grew up in the countryside and did not have the privilege of a formal education. Because his mother was unmarried, he was not eligible to attend the schools of the day. He didn't learn Latin or Greek, without which it was almost impossible to find out about the world. Instead, he had to rely on his own experience.

B Using information pieced together from Leonardo's notebooks and various biographical resources, Shlain sets out to explain the reasons for Da Vinci's ability to make connections between the two disciplines, and for his unparalleled creativity.

C Shlain argues that Leonardo, who is best known for painting the eternally mysterious Mona Lisa, had an exceptional scientific mind. He created visionary anatomical drawings long before medical anatomy existed, made observations of bird flight in greater detail than any previous scientist, and mastered engineering, architecture and mathematics. In fact, many of his designs for inventions were spectacularly ahead of his time and if they had actually been built, might have revolutionised the history of technology.

D Shlain believes that Leonardo's left-handedness and his mirror writing were indications that he had a non-dominant brain, and that there was an exceptional communication between the two hemispheres. As a result, Da Vinci was able to access different ways of thinking, and combine an extraordinary understanding of science with an ability to communicate that understanding through art.

E More importantly though, his lack of formal education and attentive parenting meant that he was never forced to write with his right hand, which was the practice during the Middle Ages. For Shlain, this turned out to be crucial in the anatomy of Leonardo's genius.

F He was also the only individual in recorded history who is known to write comfortably backwards, a feat known as 'mirror writing'. Instead of writing from left to right, as is the norm in all European languages, Leonardo chose to write from right to left. He would also switch sometimes in the middle of a sentence, writing some words in one direction and others in the opposite direction. Whichever way he wrote, the fluency of his writing was the same.

Speaking

> **➤ TIP FOR SPEAKING EXAMS**
>
> When giving presentations, remember …
> Don't let mistakes stop you from speaking. Correct your own mistakes if possible, or start the sentence again, but don't stop completely. Don't worry excessively about vocabulary either. When you don't know a word, explain it or use a simpler word.
>
> ➤ EXAM SUCCESS page 149

2 Read the extract about Leonardo Da Vinci's legacy. Which do you think was his most influential design?

Leonardo's legacy

Although Leonardo Da Vinci is best known for his great works of art, he was also an inspired inventor. He sketched the first so-called flying machine 400 years before one was actually made, and designed a diving suit that would allow humans to breathe under water. Ironically, given his loathing of war, he also pioneered a number of instruments of warfare. These included an armoured vehicle and a machine gun. Perhaps his most extraordinary vision was for a robot which could move its arms and mouth.

There's no doubt that Leonardo's legacy was significant and without him, the world would be a different place today.

3 Look at this topic and prepare a presentation.

> *Inventions throughout history have improved our lives in many ways, but there are some things that should never have been invented.*
> Do you agree? Why/Why not?

4 Give your presentation to the class.

Writing

> **➤ TIP FOR WRITING EXAMS**
>
> For guidance on writing reviews, see page 150.
>
> ➤ EXAM SUCCESS page 150

5 Write your review for the task below.

> You see this announcement in an English language magazine.
> **Book reviews wanted!**
> Have you read a book in which the main character impressed you?
> Write a review of the book explaining what the character did and why he/she impressed you.
> Tell us whether or not you would recommend the book.
> The best reviews will be published in this magazine.

Use of English

> **➤ TIP FOR USE OF ENGLISH**
>
> In sentence transformations, remember …
> Think about the meaning and possible uses of the word given. Think also about its grammatical function and whether it always or usually goes with another word or tense.
>
> ➤ EXAM SUCCESS page 150

6 Complete the second sentence so that it has a similar meaning to the first sentence, using the word given. Do not change the word given. You must use between three and six words, including the word given.

1 In primary school they would make us learn poetry by heart. **FORCE**
In primary school, they ………………………… poetry by heart.

2 Scientific research isn't dangerous if there are strict regulations. **PROVIDED**
Scientific research isn't dangerous ………………………… .

3 Unfortunately, we never studied anatomy at school. **WISH**
I ………………………… at school.

4 We were tired, but we worked until late. **KEPT**
We ………………………… even though we were tired.

5 In spite of the fact that I didn't like the book, I finished it. **MANAGE**
In spite of the fact that I didn't like the book, ………………………… .

6 If it were possible to travel back in time, what time would you visit? **SUPPOSING**
…………………………, what time would you visit?

7 They've been investigating this branch of science for a while. **RESEARCH**
They've been ………………………… this branch of science for a while.

8 He didn't pass his exams, so he can't find a job. **ABLE**
If he had passed his exams, he ………………………… a job.

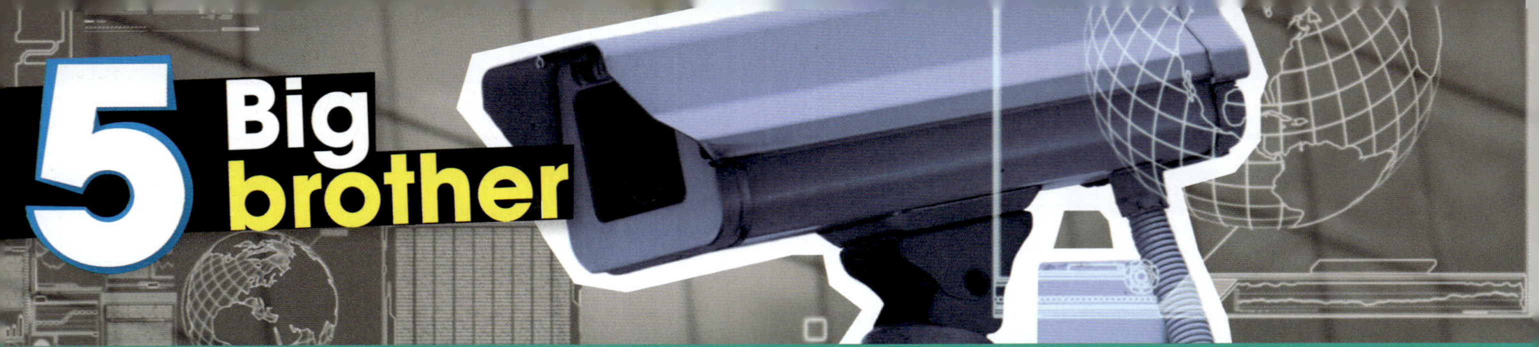

5 Big brother

Reading

VOCABULARY Minor offences and punishment

1a What would be an appropriate punishment for these minor offences 1–6? Choose from the list a–h below. Check that you understand the words in bold.

1 **Littering** in a street or park
2 Travelling on public transport without a valid ticket
3 Parking in an area **designated** for people with disabilities
4 Skateboarding in a public square
5 Putting your feet on a seat on a train
6 Smoking in a **non-designated** area

a The person should **be issued with a small fine**.
b They should pay **a heavy fine**.
c They should **be banned** from going to the place again.
d The offence should appear on the person's criminal record.
e Nothing unless a member of the public **lodges a formal complaint**.
f The person should be **prosecuted** and **judged** in court.
g They should receive a **suspended sentence**.
h They should do **community service**.

1b SPEAKING **Work with a partner. Discuss your answers in 1a.**

2 Read the three articles about minor offences. What is the offence in each case and what is the punishment? Do you agree with the punishment given? Why/Why not?

✓ EXAM SUCCESS

You are going to do a *True/False/Not Given* reading activity. In this type of activity, *False* means that the statement contradicts the facts or opinions stated in the text. *Not Given* means that the statement may or may not be true, but we have no evidence from the text to help us decide.

➤ EXAM SUCCESS page 151

3 Read the articles again. Are these statements True (T), False (F) or is the information Not Given (NG)?

1 Sian put her foot on the seat without thinking. T/F/NG
2 She was unaware that it was wrong to put her foot on the seat. T/F/NG
3 People have been convicted for putting their feet on the seat in the past. T/F/NG
4 Skateboarders in the square receive a verbal warning before they're given a fine. T/F/NG
5 Pedestrians in the square have been knocked over and injured by skateboarders. T/F/NG
6 One rider thinks the council should adopt a different policy to the sport. T/F/NG
7 People at the station were bothered by Anthony's music. T/F/NG
8 His father thinks that fines should never be given for listening to music on a mobile. T/F/NG

4 CRITICAL THINKING

Think! Then compare ideas with your class.

- How would you prove that these offences are not worth taking to court?
- What criteria would you use to judge a crime?

5 Guess the meaning of the underlined words from the context. Then use your dictionary to check.

6 SPEAKING **Read these comments that people have made about the three stories. Do you agree or disagree with each one? Why?**

1 *It's a waste of public money to take people to court for minor offences. The police and justice system should concentrate on more serious crimes.*

2 *If you don't do something about minor offences, then they only get worse. It's a crime to do nothing about them.*

3 *A fine is one thing, but for someone to get a criminal record for a minor offence is absurd.*

4 *I don't think it matters who's committed an offence. If it's an aspiring teacher or someone with a criminal record, they deserve the same treatment. An offence is an offence.*

5 *It's unfair to give a fine, or summons to appear in court, without first giving a warning.*

6 *It worries me that the train guard was wearing a CCTV camera. That's an invasion of privacy.*

Putting your feet up on the seats on public transport is seen as antisocial.

FEET-ON-SEAT PASSENGER COULD LAND IN COURT

A woman from Wrexham says she is terrified that she could get a criminal conviction for putting her feet up on a train.

SIAN JONES, 27, had been shopping with her friend in Liverpool when she took the Merseyrail service home from the city. Sian, who is getting married next year, explained what happened next.

'I raised my foot and placed it on the metal bar surrounding the seat opposite,' she said. 'I was deep in conversation about my forthcoming wedding and I didn't even realise I'd done it.'

Sian was approached by a member of the Merseyrail staff, who questioned her and asked her to sign a statement. She was advised that she would receive a court summons in the next six weeks.

'While I realise I shouldn't have done it,' she said, 'I didn't expect the repercussions to be so serious. I'm the kind of person who stands up on a crowded bus or train for an elderly person to sit down. I rarely use public transport, and I'll never go on a train again.'

Sian is one of many Merseyrail passengers who have been charged with the same offence recently. Nineteen-year-old Kathleen Jennings appeared in court after being caught with her flip flops on a seat by a guard wearing a CCTV camera on his head. Despite immediately putting her feet down and apologising, Kathleen was asked to give her details and later received a summons.

The charge was dismissed by magistrates, but Kathleen faced a criminal record if convicted, which would have ended her hopes of becoming a maths teacher and destroyed her future career prospects.

Fined for skateboarding

Skateboarders in King George Square in the centre of Brisbane have been receiving bigger fines than motorists.

More than 30 skaters, rollerbladers and cyclists have been hit with $500 fines since the square reopened as a pedestrianised area. The on-the-spot fines are larger than those given to motorists for driving over the 40 kmh speed limit, and have earned Brisbane City Council $15,000 in eight months.

Riders have slammed the penalty as excessive, but the council says that it has seven signs around the square warning riders they risk a fine.

The Chair of Community Services has justified the measures. 'People haven't been allowed to cycle or skate through King George Square for almost 40 years so this is nothing new,' she says. 'These are busy public places and we can't have cyclists or skaters careering through crowds of people and knocking them over. The best way for people to avoid a fine is to hop off their bike or board and walk it through the square, just as they would when they're crossing the road.'

One veteran skateboarder believes the fines will stop riders using the square, but says the council should do more to encourage this environmentally-friendly alternative to cars. 'Obviously, if you're wrecking public property, then it's a different story, but a lot of people use skateboarding for transport. Instead of fining people, they should be promoting the sport as a healthy activity and getting more people into it,' he said.

Skateboarding in pedestrian areas can be dangerous.

TEEN FIGHTS PENALTY FOR LOUD MUSIC

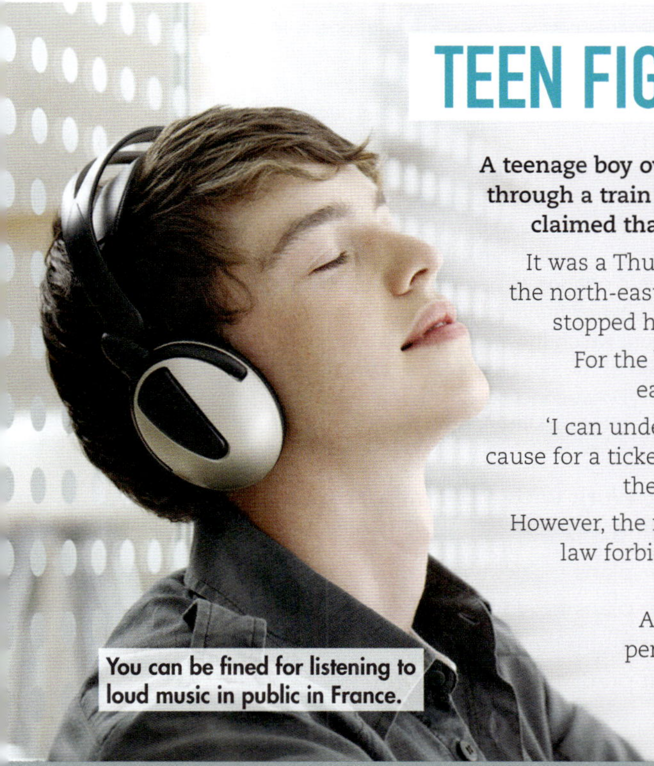

You can be fined for listening to loud music in public in France.

A teenage boy owes France's state-owned railway SNCF €375 after he was fined for walking through a train station while listening to music on his earphones. An official of the railway claimed that the music was too loud, and was causing a nuisance to other passengers.

It was a Thursday in May at around 4.50 pm when Anthony walked through the station in the north-east of Paris on his way home from school. As he was leaving the station, a guard stopped him, informed him that he was breaking the rules, and gave him a fine for €75.

For the boy's father, the idea that the music coming through the boy's mobile into his earphones could cause a disturbance in a busy train station seemed ridiculous.

'I can understand that in the train the use of a mobile phone to listen to music could be cause for a ticket,' he wrote in an appeal to SNCF. 'However, I have a hard time understanding the disruption caused on a platform at a train station on a Thursday at 4.51 pm.'

However, the railway is supporting the guard's decision to fine the boy. They say that a 1942 law forbids 'any person to use in train cars, waiting rooms, on platforms or in the train station sound-making devices or instruments.'

After the family's appeal was rejected, the original fine of €75 rose to €375 with penalties and late fees. However, the boy and his parents are still refusing to pay and say they are going to continue to fight the case.

Future forms

1 Identify the different ways to talk about the future in these sentences. Then match each sentence with the use a–f.

1 She **is getting** married next year.
2 I**'ll** never **go** on a train again.
3 Someone **is going to be** hurt by a skateboarder.
4 He believes the fines **will** stop riders using the square.
5 They **are going to** continue to fight the case.
6 The court hearing **takes place** next month.

a to make predictions based on our opinions
b for general plans and intentions
c to make decisions about the future at the time of speaking
d for schedules and timetables
e to make predictions based on present evidence
f for fixed arrangements

GRAMMAR REFERENCE ➤ PAGE 68

2 Choose the correct alternative.

1 The train to Hull *leaves/is going to leave* at 6.45.
2 We *will/are going to* go shopping on Saturday.
3 I *am meeting/will meet* Jack at the station at 6.00.
4 Perhaps we*'ll have/'re having* lunch at that new place on West Street.
5 Look at the clouds. I think it's *raining/going to rain*.
6 Jack *is going to/will* look for a present for Emily.
7 I'll be back in five minutes. I*'m going to/will* take the dog for a walk.
8 There's someone at the door. Don't worry, I*'ll/'m going to* open it.

3 Complete the sentences with the correct form of the verb. Sometimes more than one answer is possible.

1 I .... (call) you when I know the results of the exam.
2 The match .... (start) at 7.30. Don't be late.
3 .... you .... (do) anything special on Saturday?
4 Hi Mum. I'm stuck in a traffic jam. I .... (be) late for dinner.
5 We .... (visit) my brother in Holland sometime next year. We're not sure when.
6 I'm sure you .... (feel) better soon. It's only a cold.
7 I'm .... (get) my hair cut on Friday. I made an appointment last week.
8 I can't go out this evening. I .... (try) to finish the science project I have to do.

4 Read the situations and decide what you would say in each case.

1 Your computer is making a strange noise again.
Oh no! It .... (crash).
2 Your friend wants to meet this afternoon, but you have a dentist's appointment.
I'm sorry. I .... (see).
3 You're waiting for a friend at the train station, but you don't know the arrival time.
Excuse me. What time .... (get in)?
4 Your teacher asks you for your predictions about crime in your country.
I think the crime rate .... (improve).
5 A classmate suggests that you talk about some homework this evening, but you're tired.
I'm sorry. I .... (go to bed).
6 You arrive at the library, but you don't know the closing time.
What time .... (close)?
7 A friend has lost their mobile phone.
Don't worry. I .... (lend).
8 Your team isn't playing well and you have a difficult opponent in the next match.
I think we .... (lose).

5 Complete the news article with an appropriate form of the verb.

Catching litter bugs

Gravesham City Council has decided to get tough on litter bugs by introducing a new scheme. Police wearing CCTV cameras (a) .... (patrol) the streets in the hope of catching anyone who drops litter.
A spokesperson for the council said, 'If people insist on not being good community citizens and throw rubbish on the ground, they (b) .... (pay) a fine.'
However, not everyone is happy with the scheme. Some members of the police force believe that it (c) .... (cause) mistrust and damage relations with the local community. As one officer pointed out, 'Anyone seeing a police officer coming down the street (d) .... (cross) to the other side if they suspect you're wearing a CCTV.'
Residents, meanwhile, see it as an invasion of privacy and (e) .... (hold) a meeting on Saturday at the community centre to discuss the plan. The meeting, which (f) .... (start) at 9.00, is expected to consider possible options to persuade the council to rethink their plan. Several hundred people have already signed a petition, which they (g) .... (hand) in to the council. In spite of the opposition, the council is certain that the CCTV-wearing police officers (h) .... drastically .... (reduce) littering in the area.

6 SPEAKING Work with a partner. Talk about the following topics.

- Your plans for next weekend
- Your plans for your next holiday
- Your future study and career
- Your predictions for your country

Prepositional phrases

1 Complete the sentences with these words.

account • addition • aid • behalf
means • process • strength • touch

1. **In** .... **to** the prison sentence, she had to pay a heavy fine.
2. The money from the fine will go **in** .... **of** charity.
3. She received a prison sentence **on** .... **of** the seriousness of the crime.
4. They found the criminal **by** .... **of** an important publicity campaign on TV asking the public for help.
5. The police arrested him **on the** .... **of** the evidence.
6. The interviewer accused the prime minister of being **out of** .... **with** what the public really thinks.
7. I'd like to thank you **on** .... **of** all the people who work in this department.
8. The council is **in the** .... **of** changing all public signs but has not yet finished.

2a Which prepositional phrase in bold in 1 means:

1. because of?
2. using a particular method?
3. as a representative of?

2b Check that you understand the meaning of the other prepositional phrases in bold in 1.

3 Complete the sentences with a prepositional phrase from 1.

1. He lives in a tiny village in the mountains so he's .... what's happening here in the city.
2. The singer went to collect the prize .... the whole group.
3. The match has been cancelled .... the rain.
4. The house is a mess because we're .... moving.
5. The house was heated .... solar power.
6. They gave her the job just .... her interview.
7. They're going to play a concert .... the earthquake victims.
8. To visit the US you need a visa .... a valid passport.

4 Read the article below. What does it say about smoking outdoors?

It has now become the norm in many countries to ban smoking indoors. But in **(a)** .... to those laws, many cities around the world such as San Francisco and New York have already passed laws banning smoking outdoors in parks and on beaches, too. Other European cities like London and Paris are **(b)** .... the process of joining them.

The decision against smoking indoors **(c)** ...., on the **(d)** ...., been a popular one **(e)** .... account of the clear evidence of adverse health effects, with thousands of passive smokers dying each year. But whilst most people agree that the initial measures were sensible and necessary, are the risks **(f)** .... second-hand smoke so clear when people are outdoors?

Some people, smokers and non-smokers alike, believe that governments are **(g)** .... too restrictive on the freedom of the individual. They suggest that governments are **(h)** .... of touch with the values of ordinary people. And they also claim that an enormous amount of money will have to be spent **(i)** .... putting up signs in parks and on beaches telling people that they can't smoke, as **(j)** .... as signs informing them of specially designated areas where smoking is permitted.

On the other hand, organisations campaigning **(k)** .... smoking in outdoor places argue that some children are becoming smokers just as a result **(l)** .... the bad influence of seeing adults smoking in public. In the UK, for example, school pupils are more likely to say that smoking is unacceptable since the ban **(m)** .... smoking indoors came into force.

Whichever side you are on, one of the positive benefits of banning smoking outdoors will be a decrease **(n)** .... the amount of litter caused by cigarette ends being thrown away. This was part of the **(o)** .... for the ban on outdoor-smoking in California in the first place. Even if there is no significant threat to others by smoking outdoors, the ban can do no harm and may even do some good.

5 Complete the article by putting one word in each gap.

✓ EXAM SUCCESS

In this type of activity, read the text once quite quickly to get a general idea of what it is about. Then look closely at the words that come just before and after each space to decide what type of word you need. Many missing words will be prepositions, auxiliary verbs, articles, pronouns and conjunctions, but some may be nouns or verbs.

➤ EXAM SUCCESS page 151

6 SPEAKING **Work with a partner. Should smoking be banned in parks, on beaches or in other outdoor public places? Why/Why not?**

Understanding netiquette

21ST CENTURY SKILLS OBJECTIVES

- To understand the importance of netiquette
- To learn the rules of netiquette
- To evaluate your netiquette and consider ways to improve

KEY CONCEPTS

flaming [n]: *Flaming, or expressing opinions in a strong way to be provocative, is really bad netiquette.* **trolling [n]:** *Trolling is disruptive in online discussions – these comments are meant to be annoying.* **recipient [n]:** *You need to consider the recipient of any message you send.*

1 SPEAKING **Work with a partner. How often, and in what situations do you:**

- send and receive text messages?
- send and receive emails?
- post messages on discussion boards?
- write or comment on blogs?

2 SPEAKING **Assess your online behaviour. Choose the option that best applies to you. Then compare your answers with a partner. What reasons can you think of for doing each of these things?**

	ALWAYS	SOMETIMES	NEVER
1 I consider the feelings of the people who read my messages.			
2 I re-read my messages before sending them.			
3 I avoid posting any personal information.			
4 I use correct grammar, spelling and punctuation.			
5 I write in lowercase letters.			
6 I try not to provoke others by posting strong opinions.			

3 READING **Read the article. What reasons are given for the rules of netiquette in 2?**

How good is

Online communication is an integral part of everyday life and many academic courses. Whether we are meeting someone for the first time, or are just having a chat with someone we know, when we talk to someone in person we have clues such as body language, facial expressions and tone of voice that that can help us understand the other person and in return be understood in the way we want. When communicating online, however, we don't have these non-verbal clues to help us convey meaning. The typed word is all we have to communicate with and we can easily give the wrong impression. It's therefore very important to be aware of the conventions of behaviour, known as 'netiquette', or 'Internet etiquette'.

Be aware of your reader

When you communicate online, all you see is a computer screen. It's easy to forget that real people will read your messages. Be sensitive to your audience, and adapt your style accordingly. If you are writing to a friend or family member, emoticons and abbreviations such as textspeak are acceptable, but for more formal correspondence in an academic or professional situation, accurate spelling, grammar and punctuation are vital to create a good impression. You don't want to offend your reader and you want to make sure they understand what you are saying.

Common courtesies

When sending an email or message, make sure your subject heading reflects the content. Then open with a friendly and appropriate greeting and if necessary, introduce yourself first. Be polite by saying 'please', 'thank you', or 'sorry', and remember to sign off at the end.

- Avoid expressing yourself in a way that could offend the recipient. 'Flaming', for example, can spoil the atmosphere of an online group.
- 'Trolling' is also a nuisance and disrupts discussion threads.

your netiquette?

Be aware of your tone

Because you don't have the benefit of non-verbal clues when communicating online, the reader relies on the written message alone, so misunderstandings can occur. Read everything carefully before sending to make sure your meaning is clear.

- Be wary of using irony or sarcasm.
- **DON'T SHOUT!** Using all capital letters is the same as shouting at someone who is right next to you. To emphasise a point, use **bold**, *italics* or underline.

The written word is permanent

Messages can come across more strongly when written down, especially if they're brief. If you feel angry, wait before pressing the send button. Consider electronic communications as permanent – you don't want to say anything that you'll regret later.

- Don't share any personal information online as there is no expectation of privacy.
- Never forward an email or other correspondence without the author's permission.

Reasonable expectations

Always respond to an email, even if it's just to say thank you. Be aware that when you send an email though, the recipient may be busy and unable to reply as quickly as you expect.

- Avoid sending repeat emails or other communications in order to provoke a response.
- Unless it's essential for other people to read a message, you may waste their time by copying them in.

4 Read the article again. Answer these questions.

1. What example is given of adapting your style to your audience?
2. Why is it important to be aware of your tone when you write?
3. What advice is given about the heading of a message?
4. What shouldn't you do with another person's emails?
5. In what situations is it inappropriate to send repeat emails? Why?
6. Is it always necessary to include others when you send an email? Why/Why not?

5 SPEAKING **Discuss these questions with a partner.**

1. Have you ever had an experience of 'bad netiquette'? What was it?
2. Which rules of netiquette do you follow? Which behaviour could you improve?
3. Are there any other rules of netiquette you would like people to use?
4. What do you think are the three most important rules?

6 You're going to watch students talking about the rules of netiquette. What do you think are the three most important rules?

7 LISTENING 15 **Watch the video or listen. Do they mention the rules you discussed in 6? Did they include rules you didn't expect?**

8 LISTENING 15 **Watch or listen again. Make notes about the students' answers to the questions in 5.**

21ST CENTURY TASK

Work in groups of three. You are going to make a video or a slide presentation about netiquette.

Follow these steps:

1. *Choose either one aspect of netiquette or three 'golden' rules to include in your presentation.*
2. *Prepare your presentation. Think about how you can illustrate the rules.*
3. *Practise your presentation/make your video. Make sure that each person in the group is included.*
4. *Present your video or slide presentation to the class.*

Flipped classroom: watch the grammar presentation video.

1 SPEAKING **With a partner, discuss these questions.**

1 Do you have apps on your phone? How many? What do they do?
2 What are some advantages and disadvantages of apps?
3 What do you know about tracking apps?

2 LISTENING 16 **Listen to a radio programme about teen tracking apps. Answer the questions using a maximum of four words for each one. Listen twice.**

1 In location apps, what do the dots represent?
2 How can these apps analyse behaviour?
3 Why do the app companies license the technology?
4 According to the psychologist, what do these apps suggest to teenagers?
5 What does she say teenagers need to do?
6 When Steve has to pick his children up, what does the app do?
7 What is the general reason Steve installed the apps?
8 How do Steve's children feel about the apps?
9 Which two groups of people can use the data from apps?
10 What should you do to protect your privacy?

3 SPEAKING **What about *you*?**

1 What ideas support the use of tracking apps?
2 What arguments are there against the apps?
3 On balance, are you in favour or against them? Why?
4 What predictions can you make about the use of tracking apps in the future?

Advanced future forms

4 Look at the sentences and answer the questions.

a We **are on the verge/point of** putting spy-cameras into phones.
b By the time they leave home, they**'ll have learnt** what's right and what's wrong.
c They**'ll be collecting** data for marketing purposes.
d By the time they're older, these companies **will have been collecting** data for several years.

Which sentence:

1 uses the future continuous to talk about an activity in progress at a moment in the future?
2 uses the future perfect simple to talk about an activity completed before a particular time in the future?
3 uses the future perfect continuous to emphasise the duration of an activity that continues up to a particular time in the future?
4 talks about something that is going to happen very soon?

GRAMMAR REFERENCE ➤ PAGE 68

5 Choose the correct alternative.

1 Are you on the verge of *finish/finishing* your school studies?
2 By the end of this year, how long will you *be/have been* studying English?
3 What will you *be doing/have done* next summer?
4 Will you *work/have started work* by the time you're 25?
5 Do you feel as if you're on the point *to start/of starting* a new period in your life?
6 If you stay in your home for one more year, how long will you *be/have been* living there?
7 Do you reckon you'll *be getting/have got* married by the time you're 30?
8 Do you think you'll *be living/have lived* in the same city in ten years' time?

6 SPEAKING **Use the questions in 5 to interview your partner.**

Role-plays

1 SPEAKING **Work with a partner. Look at the pictures and describe what is happening in each one.**

2 SPEAKING **With a partner, discuss what issues you might face at large outdoor events, such as carnivals or concerts. Give reasons.**

3 SPEAKING **Work with a partner. Read this task and follow the instructions.**

A British friend is going to a two-day music festival in your country. He/She asks you to give him/her some details and advice about personal safety and precautions. Discuss the following issues:

- types of crime to watch out for
- advice for looking after your money and valuables
- best places to stay
- what to do if you have any problems

Student A: You are the British friend. Write questions to ask.

Student B: Make notes with advice to give your British friend.

Both: Look at the Speaking bank for ideas about what language to use.

SPEAKING BANK

Useful words and expressions to give advice

Asking for advice

- Do you think I should …?
- Should I …?
- If you were me, would you …?
- What do you reckon I should do if …?
- What about …?

Giving advice

- If I were you, I'd …
- Have you thought about …?
- Why don't you …?
- You might want to …
- You ought to/had better …

Responding to advice/Asking for clarification

- That's a good idea.
- That sounds sensible/helpful/ideal.
- But what about …?
- The (only) problem with that is …
- Don't you think it'd be better to …?
- Do you mean …?
- Are you saying that …?

✔ EXAM SUCCESS

In role-plays, whether you are working with another student or with the teacher/examiner, remember to listen to the other person and to respond to what they say. If you are allowed to make notes before the role-play, use the notes to remind you of ideas, but never just read the notes out.

➤ EXAM SUCCESS page 151

4 PRACTICE MAKES PERFECT SPEAKING **Work with a partner. Do the task below, using expressions from the Speaking bank.**

A British friend wants advice about places to see while he/she is staying in your city or town. Discuss the following issues:

- the best places to go during the day and in the evening
- the best ways of getting around
- opening and closing times
- dress code and suggestions

Student A: You are going to give the advice.

Student B: You are going to ask for advice. Ask for more detail at different moments in the conversation, and disagree politely with the advice once or twice to get your partner to give you more ideas.

A letter of complaint

1 Read the article about the use of slang in schools and answer the questions.

1 What reasons does the school give for implementing the ban?

2 What has the general response been to the ban?

In an effort to improve language skills, a school in London has decided to ban the use of slang by its students. The school has placed a series of posters around the school premises with lists of words that students are no longer permitted to use. The school's spokeswoman explained at a press conference that 'in addition to giving students the teaching they need to thrive academically, we want them to develop the soft skills they will need to compete for jobs and university places.'

The school has received strong support for the ban. Many people have praised the action, including the local MP, who said: 'Speaking slang is fine in a social setting ... but a school should be a professional, educational environment, and if part of that means banning slang then that's fine by me.' His comments have sparked concern that the ban will now be extended to other schools.

2 SPEAKING Work with a partner. Are you in favour of or against a ban on the use of slang in schools? Think of arguments to support your opinion.

3 Read the letter. What is the writer's opinion about banning the use of slang in schools and what arguments does she give to support her view? Do you agree with them?

Dear Sir/Madam,

I am writing to protest about the possible enforcement of a ban on the use of slang in schools. I believe that this measure would not only be unpopular but would also be completely ineffective.

Although I agree that a number of young people use slang when they are talking to their peers, the vast majority of students are able to distinguish between when it is appropriate to use slang and when it is not, and are able to express themselves perfectly in more formal situations. The fact is that by trying to control the language that students use, schools will merely encourage the use of slang, since it is a well-known fact that banning something only serves to make it more interesting.

To make matters worse, I believe that the measure will prove to be ineffective as the only way to enforce the ban is by means of supervising conversations between students. On the one hand, this could be highly expensive as it would involve installing more CCTV cameras or recruiting staff to listen to students during break times. On the other hand, if teachers are required to enforce the ban, this would surely take their attention away from the more important business of teaching.

In conclusion, I should like to draw your attention to the fact that there are more important issues that the school should be concerned with than the use of slang. On behalf of the numerous students who are hoping to attend university in the future, might I suggest that you concentrate on providing the best possible education and facilities, not on enforcing a ban that will simply alienate many students?

Yours faithfully,

Louisa James

Louisa James

4 SPEAKING Read the letter again and look at the underlined words and phrases. Work with a partner and discuss why and how the words and phrases are used.

VOCABULARY Formal register

5a Find the more formal synonyms for these words in the letter in 3.

1 some (paragraph 2)
2 most (paragraph 2)
3 just, only (paragraph 2)
4 very (paragraph 3)
5 many (paragraph 4)
6 offering, giving (paragraph 4)

5b Use the correct form of the formal words in 5a to rewrite these sentences.

1 It's very inappropriate to use offensive language when talking to teachers.
2 Many schools have CCTV cameras in classrooms and corridors.
3 There have been some complaints from parents.
4 Most students disagree with the policy.
5 This is just another way to control students.
6 The school gives students clear guidelines about how they should behave.

6 Tick (✓) the expressions in the Writing bank that appear in the letter in 3.

WRITING BANK

Useful expressions in letters of complaint

- I am writing to complain/protest about …
- I am writing on behalf of …
- I should like to draw your attention to …
- My second/next/main complaint concerns …
- To make matters worse,
- I urge you to …
- I demand that you …
- I would ask you to …
- Might I suggest you …?
- The fact/truth/problem is that …
- What annoys/surprises/amazes me is …
- Yours faithfully (after Dear Sir/Madam)
- Yours sincerely (after Dear Mr/Mrs/Ms)

7 SPEAKING Work with a partner. Look at the letter again and identify features of the letter that are typical of a formal register.

more formal vocabulary, e.g. numerous instead of many

8 SPEAKING Read this newspaper article and answer the questions. Ignore the notes at the side of the text.

1 What happened at the cinema?
2 Do you think Michelle and her mother are right to be angry?
3 Do you think the story is an example of 'teenage discrimination'?

Last Saturday local girl Michelle Richards had an unpleasant experience at the North Woods Multiplex Cinema. Michelle, 17, had gone to see the latest Johnny Depp film with three friends aged between 15 and 17. The film had begun at 3.45 pm. When the film finished, Michelle and her friends went to the cinema lobby to wait indoors for her mother to come and pick them up. After five or six minutes, the manager of the multiplex came and asked them if they had tickets. Michelle told the manager that they had just come out of seeing a film and that they were waiting for their parents. The manager then told them that they couldn't wait in the lobby and that they would have to leave. When Michelle asked why, the manager said that she had seen them in the lobby on many previous occasions and that she was sick and tired of the problems that they caused. The manager threatened to call the police if they didn't leave immediately and so Michelle and her friends had to wait outside. When Michelle's mother arrived, she was shocked to see her daughter out in the cold and dark, in an area that was unfamiliar to her. Michelle and her mother say that they are not simply going to forget the incident. They are going to make a formal complaint to the cinema so that this type of 'teenage discrimination' which put the girls at risk does not happen to others. The director of the North Woods Multiplex Cinema refused to comment.

We didn't make any noise or interfere with people waiting in the queues.

It was really cold and pouring down with rain that day!

It was the first time we'd ever been to that cinema because we live on the other side of town.

Would they have done the same if we'd been 25 or 30 years old?

✓ EXAM SUCCESS

You are going to write a letter of complaint. When writing letters, make sure the style and register are appropriate to the situation and the person you are writing to. As many marks may be given to appropriate style as to grammatical accuracy. Letters of complaint are more formal, so you should not use contractions, but do use words, phrases and linkers that are more typical of formal register.

➤ EXAM SUCCESS page 151

9 PRACTICE MAKES PERFECT Imagine that you are one of the friends who were with Michelle that day. Use the notes and any other ideas to write a letter of complaint to the director of the cinema. Use the information in the Writing bank and in Exam success to help you.

WRITING BANK ➤ PAGE 158

Grammar reference

be going to

1 We use *be going to* to talk about plans and intentions for the future. We use it for things that we have already decided to do in the future.
*I've decided that next year **I'm going to** do more exercise.*

2 We can also use *be going to* to make predictions about the future, particularly when we have evidence for the prediction.
*All the evidence suggests the situation **is going to** get worse.*

will/won't

1 We use *will* and *won't* to make general predictions about the future. We often use *think*, *hope*, *expect*, *imagine*, etc. with *will* and *won't* to show that our prediction is based on thoughts, opinions and expectations.
*I believe that one day we **will** live on Mars.*

2 We also use *will* and *won't* when we decide to do something at the moment of speaking.
*It's cold. **I'll** close the window now.*

Present continuous for future

We use the present continuous to talk about future arrangements; plans that have been confirmed.
*Experts from around the world **are meeting** next month.*

Present simple for future

We use the present simple to talk about the future when the action is part of a timetable or routine.
*My train **leaves** at 9 pm tomorrow.*

Future continuous

We use the future continuous to talk about activities in progress at a particular time in the future. The activities are in progress and so they are unfinished.
*At this time tomorrow, **he'll be flying** to the US.*

Future perfect simple

We use the future perfect to talk about activities that will be finished by a certain time in the future.
*I **will have gone** to bed by midnight.*
We often use the preposition *by* with the future perfect. It means 'some time before'.

Future perfect continuous

We use the future perfect continuous to talk about how long an activity will be in progress before a particular moment in the future.
*By 8 pm **I'll have been revising** history for five hours!*

be on the verge/point of

We use *be on the verge/point of* to talk about something that is going to happen very soon.
*They are **on the verge of** inventing something really revolutionary.*

Summary of future tenses

Tense	Use	Example
be going to	1 For plans and intentions	***I'm going to** study physics at university.*
	2 For predictions based on current evidence	***It's going to** rain soon – look at the clouds.*
will/won't	1 For general predictions	*I think Spain **will** win the World Cup.*
	2 For decisions made at the time of speaking	*Wait there, **I'll** answer the door.*
Present continuous	For arrangements	***I'm meeting** my friends at 6 pm tonight.*
Present simple	For timetables or routines	*The train **leaves** at 9 am tomorrow.*
Future continuous	For activities in progress at a particular time	*Don't call me at 8 pm because **I'll be having** dinner.*
Future perfect simple	For activities that will be finished by a certain time	***I'll have finished** my project by Friday when we have to hand it in.*
Future perfect continuous	To talk about how long an activity will be in progress before a certain time	*My family **will have been living** abroad for five years this September.*
be on the verge/point of	To talk about something that is going to happen very soon	*Scientists **are on the verge of** a breakthrough in their research.*

Vocabulary

For prepositional phrases, minor offences and punishment and formal register, see wordlist pages 139–140.

Grammar revision

Future forms
/ 6 points

1 Choose the correct alternative.

1 Be careful! The train *will/is going to* leave.
2 Can I change my appointment to this afternoon because I*'ll leave/'m leaving* tomorrow.
3 I've checked the school timetable and the exams *end/are ending* in June.
4 I *go/'ll go* to the shops as soon as they open.
5 We*'ll go/'re going* to see a film at the cinema tonight, so don't call then.
6 The prime minister predicts that inflation *is falling/will fall* next year.

Advanced future forms
/ 14 points

2 Complete the sentences with the correct form of the verbs given. In 2–7, use the future continuous, future perfect or future perfect continuous.

1 The final whistle is about to go and the team are on the verge of .... (make) history!
2 Next month, my dad .... (work) at the same company for 30 years.
3 Don't call me at 6 pm because I .... (have) my driving lesson.
4 Mum will have her car back by the weekend because the mechanic .... (fix) it by then.
5 By 2 pm, he .... (run) for over six hours!
6 This time next month we .... (lie) next to the pool on holiday.
7 My parents are celebrating next month because by then, they .... (marry) for 20 years.

3 Decide if the sentences are correct or incorrect. Tick (✓) the correct sentences and rewrite the incorrect sentences.

1 When your plane arrives, a representative from the company will wait for you to take you to your hotel.
2 It's a pity that they're going to close the gym. This time next month, I'll have gone there for six years.
3 It'll take too long to drive to Manchester so we're going to take the train.
4 Once I've finished this book, I'll have been reading all of the novels by this author.
5 Look at those clouds! I don't think we should go out now because it'll rain.
6 I'm having lunch with Sam today. There are some things we need to discuss.
7 Do you think you'll still have been living in London in five years' time?

Vocabulary revision

PREPOSITIONAL PHRASES
/ 7 points

1 Complete the sentences with the correct preposition.

1 They brought in the new law .... account of the number of accidents.
2 He's a very bright politician. In addition .... that, he's charismatic.
3 I am writing to you .... behalf of a friend.
4 We are .... the process of improving our system.
5 They did it .... means of new technology.
6 You're out of touch .... today's music.
7 We're putting this concert on in aid .... charity.

MINOR OFFENCES AND PUNISHMENT
/ 7 points

2 Complete the sentences with these words. There are two extra words.

banned • community • criminal • issued • judge • lodge • non- • prosecute • suspended

1 The police officer .... him with a fine for parking in a .... designated area.
2 I wish to .... a formal complaint.
3 He only got a .... sentence.
4 The .... ordered them to do three months' .... service.
5 He was .... from driving for 12 months.

FORMAL REGISTER
/ 6 points

3 Rewrite these sentences in a less formal register.

1 I have numerous friends.
2 A number of students are absent.
3 The vast majority of his fans like his new look.
4 This manoeuvre can be highly dangerous.
5 The hotel will provide us with a hot meal.
6 This is merely a joke.

Total: / 40 points

6 Moving home

Reading

VOCABULARY Finding a place to live

1a Match the words with the definitons 1–10.

do up (a property) • flat-/house-hunt • flat/house share • fully-furnished • landlord/landlady • lodger • move in • put down a deposit • squatter • tenant

1 a person who owns a house or flat that people can rent
2 start living in a house or flat
3 a person who rents a house or flat
4 look for a house or flat to live in
5 repair, paint and improve an older property
6 a house or flat that you rent with all furniture already in it
7 pay money when you start to rent, returned when you stop renting
8 a flat or house where friends live together
9 a person who lives in a place without paying rent to the owner
10 someone who pays to live in a house or flat with the person who owns it

1b SPEAKING Work with a partner. Answer the questions.

1 What are the most common types of accommodation for students where you live?
2 How easy or difficult is it for students to find accommodation? Why?

2 Read the page from a student accommodation website. Where do the four students live? Why?

3 Read the web page again. For questions 1–13, choose from the four people (A–D). The people may be chosen more than once.

Which person

- doesn't pay rent to the owner? 1 .... 2 ....
- has additional monthly expenses? 3 ....
- sometimes has to deal with differences of opinion? 4 ....
- doesn't have to travel far to get anywhere? 5 ....
- didn't want to spend a long time looking for somewhere to live? 6 ....
- lives with a lot of other people? 7 ....
- has decorated his/her home? 8 ....
- found the living situation unusual at first? 9 ....
- was worried about security? 10 ....
- wanted to live in a specific area? 11 ....
- followed a friend's advice? 12 ....
- doesn't object to the inconveniences? 13 ....

4 CRITICAL THINKING

Think! Then compare ideas with your class.

- How would you prioritise what to look for in a home?

5 Guess the meaning of the underlined words from the context. Then use your dictionary to check.

6 SPEAKING What about *you*?

1 Which of the four living situations would you prefer? Why?
2 What are the advantages and disadvantages of living alone and with other people? Which would you prefer? Why?

STUDENT ACCOMMODATION: WHAT ARE THE OPTIONS?

HOME | GETTING STARTED | PLANNING | LOOKING | FEEDBACK | SEARCH

- Halls of residence
- Studio flats
- Shared student houses/flats
- Renting a room as a lodger
- Host families
- Alternative living situations

A HELP AN OLDER PERSON

Homestay is a charity that places students, or professionals, in the homes of elderly people. It may not sound like the typical student lifestyle, but if you're looking for a valuable experience and affordable accommodation, I recommend it.
I've been living with Edith for three years now. She had an extra room but needed someone to help her around the house. I pay a small monthly fee to the charity to help with running costs, and then do ten hours a week of cooking or light cleaning. There are some ground rules – I had to promise that I would stay for a minimum of six months, and I'm not allowed to have guests. I admit it's not like living with people my own age, and it was a bit intimidating at first to move into someone else's home. You're not family and you're not a lodger and so you have to work out where the lines are drawn. But it's quieter and more comfortable than other student accommodation.
We do have our disagreements, but having said that, Edith has always been very welcoming and we've become good friends.

Belinda, 24

B DO SPEED FLATSHARING

I lived in a hall of residence for my first year and then moved into a house with some friends. I think we rushed into signing the contract because the landlord was a bit of a nightmare. He used to turn up unannounced to inspect the property, and when we complained, he simply denied doing it. At one point the boiler broke down and he refused to repair it.
After this experience, I wanted to try something different for my third year and a friend suggested that I try speed flatsharing. It's essentially a social event where people with a room available, and others who are looking, go to meet. You simply wear a sticker saying which you are and mingle.
I was quite nervous about going, but once I got there, I realised that everyone was in the same boat. I met some people who had a room in the area I wanted and two weeks later, I moved in. It beats trawling through online ads and travelling all over the city. I met a lot of really nice people and I would definitely do it again.

Adam, 21

C BECOME A PROPERTY GUARDIAN

There are hundreds of properties all over the city that lie empty for one reason or another.
Some need funds before they can be renovated, while others are waiting for new owners. With accommodation in short supply, it makes sense to use these properties.
I find my homes through a company called Ad Hoc, which liaises with the owners. For them, the advantage is that the property is protected from becoming derelict or occupied by squatters. For me, it's a chance to live in a central location at an affordable rent.
I've lived in four places so far. At the moment, I'm living in a former hospital with 14 other guardians, but you could find yourself anywhere from a church to an old sports hall. You have to be handy with DIY because the owners aren't particularly diligent about maintenance. And these are short-term rentals. Some people accuse Ad Hoc of not allowing tenants their usual rights, but they warn you that they can give you four weeks' notice before you move in.
You meet some great people, apart from the savings and convenience. For me, it's worth the hassle.

Daniel, 22

D LIVE ON A BARGE

When I heard that I'd been accepted onto my music course, the first thing I did was start looking into accommodation options. Everything seemed so expensive. My parents had a friend who lived on a barge and wondered if I would like to do the same. Buying a boat would cost the same as my rent over three years, and at the end of the day, I still had the boat.
We found one and spent the summer refurbishing it. It has two bedrooms, a dining room and a living room with a sofa bed. The kitchen has all the mod cons, and there's even a washing machine and a power shower.
At first I was worried I wouldn't feel safe in the dark, but now I feel like it's my home. I could look for someone to share the boat to make some extra cash, but for now I prefer to be alone.
You need to budget for the mooring costs, but it's better than living in a pokey studio flat in a dodgy area. It might seem a bit unusual, but it makes sense to me.

Lucy, 19

Reporting structures

1a Look at the sentences. How could you rewrite them using direct speech?

a He simply **denied** doing it.
b A friend **suggested** that I try speed flatsharing.
c He **refused** to repair it.
d They **wondered** if I would like to live on a boat.

1b Put each verb in bold in 1a in the correct category.

1 verb + (*that*) + sentence in reported speech, e.g. *add, admit, claim, confess, promise, reply, say*
2 verb + object + (*that*) + sentence in reported speech, e.g. *inform, tell, remind, warn*
3 verb + question word/*if* + sentence in reported speech, e.g. *ask, want to know,* ....
4 verb + (*not*) *to*-infinitive, e.g. *agree, claim, offer, threaten,* ....
5 verb + object + *to*-infinitive, e.g. *advise, invite, order, remind*
6 verb + gerund, e.g. *admit, recommend, regret,* ....
7 verb + (object) + preposition + gerund, e.g. *accuse of, apologise for, blame somebody for, confess to*
8 verb + (*that*) + object + (*should*) + infinitive without *to*, e.g. *demand, insist, recommend,* ....

GRAMMAR REFERENCE ➤ PAGE 80

2 A number of reporting verbs can go with more than one structure. Look at the sentences and add the verbs in bold to another category in 1b.

a I **promised** to stay for a minimum of six months.
b They **warned** me not to damage the property.
c He **denied** that he had done it.
d She **suggested** going to a speed flatsharing event.

3 Complete the sentences with these words. Then rewrite the sentences using direct speech.

criticised • ~~insisted~~ • offered • reminded wanted to know

1 My flatmate *insisted* that I would love her cat.
'You'll love my cat!' my flatmate insisted.
2 He .... us for leaving the house in a mess.
....
3 My landlady .... me to take my keys.
....
4 I .... to cook dinner for Edith.
....
5 We .... if we had to pay a deposit.
....

4 Choose the correct alternative. In each sentence one, two or all alternatives may be correct.

1 My friend insisted *that I try/on me trying/to try* speed flatsharing.
2 They claimed *to have/having/that they had* a suitable room in the area.
3 The landlord denied *to go/going/that he had gone* into the house without our permission.
4 He refused *paying/to pay/he pays* back the deposit.
5 My parents suggested *looking/I look/that I should look* for someone to share the boat.
6 They promised *to visit/visiting/they would visit*.

5 Complete the second sentence so that it has a similar meaning to the first sentence, using the word given. Do not change the word given. You must use between three and six words, including the word given.

1 'You did a great job of painting your room,' Jim told Cathy. CONGRATULATED
Jim ....
2 'I'll call your parents,' the old lady told us. THREATENED
The old lady ....
3 'Are you doing anything at the weekend?' Oliver said to Anita. ASKED
Oliver .... anything at the weekend.
4 'You're always making excuses,' Wayne told Sandra. ACCUSED
Wayne ....
5 'You must pay the bill,' the landlord said to Sarah. ORDERED
The landlord ....
6 'Try speaking to your flatmate first,' Tamara told Matt. SUGGESTED
Tamara .... flatmate first.

6 Think about occasions when:

1 somebody congratulated you on doing something.
2 somebody suggested that you do something.
3 somebody apologised to you for doing something.
4 you admitted doing something wrong.
5 you criticised someone for doing something.
6 somebody asked you to do him/her a big favour.

7 SPEAKING Work with a partner. Discuss the occasions in 6. Ask and answer questions about what happened.

Idiomatic expressions with *home*

1 SPEAKING **Look at these sentences. With a partner, discuss what you think the expressions in bold mean.**

1. I once worked at a summer camp so I**'m at home with** children.
2. I know that **home truths** hurt, but I have to tell you that we aren't happy with your behaviour recently.
3. We're winning 5-0 and there are only five minutes of the match left. We**'re home and dry**!
4. I was really disappointed by his new book. It **wasn't anything to write home about**.
5. When temperatures reach 45° C it really **brings it home to you** that climate change is real.
6. I'm from New York so for me a big city like London is **home from home**.
7. Can I ask how much you **take home** a month?
8. She **homed in** on the shoes she saw in the sales.

2 Match the expressions in 1 with the definitions a–h. How many did you guess correctly?

a be comfortable and relaxed with
b to move quickly towards something
c a place where you feel as relaxed as in your own home
d having achieved victory, or certain to achieve it
e make you realise something (often unpleasant) or understand it better than before
f earn
g unpleasant facts or opinions about you that someone tells you
h not be anything special

3 Complete these dialogues with idiomatic expressions from 1.

1. **A:** What was the film like?
   B: It was OK, I suppose, but …
2. **A:** This hotel makes you feel really welcome.
   B: I agree. It's …
3. **A:** Wow! Those pizzas are all gone!
   B: I know. As soon as the kids saw them they …
4. **A:** It's going to be difficult to find a place to live.
   B: I know. Looking at the flat share adverts really …
5. **A:** Is your mum comfortable using the Internet?
   B: She wasn't at first but now she …
6. **A:** It's time he heard what we really think of him.
   B: I agree. Let's tell him some …
7. **A:** So far we've got all the quiz questions right.
   B: I know, but don't get too excited. We aren't …

✔ EXAM SUCCESS

In multiple-choice cloze activities, if you aren't sure which option is right, think about why others are definitely wrong and eliminate them.

➤ EXAM SUCCESS page 151

4 Read the text and decide which answer (A, B, C or D) best fits each gap.

A recent report claims that a **(1)** .... number of people in the UK are living at home longer. They clearly prefer not to have to do the shopping, washing and ironing. And, let's **(2)** .... it, Mum's cooking is usually difficult to beat. But one thing that is curious is that more men stay at home than women. We wondered **(3)** .... and so we asked Elizabeth Marsh, a sociologist, to suggest some reasons. She **(4)** .... that girls tend to have a wider network of friends with whom they can share a flat. They are also more at home **(5)** .... household chores and are ready to do them as soon as they move **(6)** .... Ms Marsh accused other family members **(7)** .... taking advantage of this. If young women stay at home, they end up doing chores for other family members. So all those factors **(8)** .... may explain why so many young women prefer to move out of the parental home at the first **(9)** .... Of course, another factor to consider is that young people can't live alone **(10)** .... account of the fact that they don't **(11)** .... home enough to be able to pay the rent or take **(12)** .... a mortgage.

	A	B	C	D
1	A bigger	B growing	C increasing	D steady
2	A say	B accept	C face	D add
3	A why	B what	C if	D how
4	A informed	B told	C reminded	D explained
5	A on	B with	C for	D in
6	A on	B in	C into	D home
7	A for	B with	C that	D of
8	A mixed	B altogether	C joined	D combined
9	A occasion	B event	C opportunity	D moment
10	A on	B in	C for	D with
11	A make	B go	C write	D take
12	A out	B up	C on	D to

5 SPEAKING **Work with a partner. Discuss these questions.**

1. Do young people tend to live at home or live independently in your country? Why is this?
2. What are some advantages and disadvantages of continuing to live at home?
3. Do you agree that girls have better skills for living independently than boys?

Negotiating in situations of CONFLICT

LIFE SKILLS OBJECTIVES

- To understand why conflicts arise when sharing accommodation
- To identify appropriate ways of resolving conflicts
- To practise resolving a conflict in a flatmate situation

KEY CONCEPTS

respectful [adj]: *Most conflicts can be resolved with a mature and respectful conversation.* **lose your temper [v]:** *Try not to lose your temper. If you get angry, it will only make matters worse.* **a compromise [n]:** *A solution will probably involve a compromise, with each person giving something and getting something.*

1 SPEAKING **Work with a partner. Look at the photos. What is the possible cause of conflict between flatmates in each photo? What other problems can you think of?**

2 What do you think is the best way to deal with each problem?

3 READING **Read the information at a student accommodation website. Does it suggest the solutions you discussed in 2?**

THE ESSENTIAL GUIDE TO FLAT SHARING

Living with flatmates isn't always easy. In fact, conflicts are bound to occur from time to time – sharing a living space can be stressful and sometimes situations that work when you first move in together become more difficult as time goes on. People are always growing and changing, which can impact even the healthiest of relationships.

Some of the most common issues that might cause conflict are cleaning and noise levels. Different people have different values and lifestyles and it's normal for these to collide. For example, one flatmate may feel quite comfortable having frequent visitors to the flat while the other wants the flat to be a quiet place away from social interaction. Whatever the issue, however, most differences of opinion can be resolved with a mature and respectful conversation. Conflict can often arise when one or both flatmates do not have the confidence or communication skills to confront the problem.

Recognise the signs

If you start to notice that your flatmate doesn't want to talk with you, gets annoyed with you over little things, or leaves the room when you're there, you should recognise these as signs of a potential problem.

Approach your flatmate in private

- Make sure that this is a good time for both of you to talk. If one of you feels rushed, the conversation is less likely to be effective.
- Be direct. Say clearly what is annoying you, but refer to the behaviour rather than your flatmate's personality. That way, he or she won't get defensive.
- Be patient. Once you have stated the problem, listen to what your flatmate has to say. Remember there are two sides to every story.
- Be respectful. Presume that your flatmate has the best of intentions and wants to resolve the conflict, too.
- Evaluate both of your needs. Discuss different ways that you can resolve the problem before deciding on a solution. Make sure that it is acceptable to both of you.
- Remember that a solution will probably involve a compromise, with each person giving something and getting something. The solution may not be your ideal scenario, but it will be an improvement on the current situation.

Mediation

If you are unable to resolve the conflict, it may be helpful to have an unbiased third party to help mediate the discussion.

Things to avoid

1 Talking about the problem with other people behind your flatmate's back. This will cause mistrust.

2 Leaving notes or post-its. A common way of communicating between flatmates, but the message is easily misunderstood.

3 Responding with emotions. However annoyed you may feel, try not to get angry. Losing your temper will allow the other person to do the same. If necessary, ask for a bit of time to cool off (for example, go for a short walk).

4 According to the web page, what would you say to a friend who makes these comments about their flatmate?

1 I don't understand why we have so many arguments. It isn't normal.
2 I had no idea that there was a problem.
3 I try to talk to her, but she's always busy or in a hurry.
4 When I accused him of being untidy, he just got defensive.
5 We came up with a solution to the problem, but I'm still not happy.
6 Everybody agrees with me that my flatmate is annoying.
7 I leave lots of messages, but it doesn't make any difference.
8 We had a big argument and both ended up shouting at each other.

5 LISTENING 17 **A family are talking about situations that cause conflict in their house. Watch the video or listen. What problem does each person describe?**

Mark ....
Clare ....
Asha ....
Ethan ....

6 LISTENING 17 **Watch or listen again. How effective were the family at resolving the conflict? What did they do right or wrong, according to the information you read in 3?**

LIFE TASK

Imagine that you have a problem with your flatmate. You're going to have a conversation with him/her to try to resolve the conflict.

Follow this plan:

1 *Work in groups of three. Choose two people to have a conversation and one person to observe.*
2 *Select a problem from the options below.*
   - Your flatmate is always taking your food without asking.
   - Your flatmate never does the washing-up after cooking and always leaves the kitchen in a mess.
   - Your flatmate always plays music very loudly and late at night. It disturbs you when you want to study or sleep.
3 *Have a conversation in pairs to resolve the conflict. Remember to follow the tips from the web page. As you do so, the observer will listen.*
4 *The observer comments on how effectively you were able to resolve the conflict.*
5 *Repeat steps 1–4 with a different observer and problem. Repeat again.*

Flipped classroom: watch the grammar presentation video.

1 SPEAKING **This photo shows the home of one of the richest men in the world. Work with a partner. Discuss these questions.**

1 Where do you think the house is? Why?
2 How would you describe the house? (the building, the interior) What special features does it have?
3 How many people do you think live there?

2 LISTENING 18 **Listen to a podcast about the house. Does it have any of the features you predicted?**

✔ EXAM SUCCESS

In sentence completion activities, before you listen, read the sentences and think about what type of words may come in the space. When you listen, don't write down the first word you hear that could fit as there may be another possible answer later on.

➤ EXAM SUCCESS page 151–2

3 LISTENING 18 **Listen again and complete the sentences. Write no more than three words and/or numbers for each answer.**

- The house is currently thought to be worth (1) ....
- There are (2) .... floors.
- The name that Mukesh has given the house comes from (3) ....
- At the top of the house there are (4) ....
- The house has one floor dedicated to (5) .... his cars.
- Mukesh Ambani is in charge of a big (6) .... and retail company.
- Architecturally speaking, some people are shocked by the building's (7) ....
- Some are unhappy that there is such a rich house in Mumbai where (8) .... million people live in poor conditions.
- Mukesh has built his house using (9) ....

4 SPEAKING **What about *you*?**

1 What do you think of the house? Would you like to live there?
2 Do you agree with the opinion that criticisms of Mr Ambani are not justified? Why/Why not?

Impersonal reporting structures

5a Look at the sentences. Why do you think the passive form of the reporting verb is used in each sentence?

a Mukesh Ambani **is said to be** worth £18 billion.
b The building **is reported to have gone up** in value.
c At the time, **it was claimed that** Ambani had spent £44 million on his home.
d Mumbai **is known to have** lots of traffic.
e **It is thought that** 600 servants or staff are needed to run the house.
f **It has been suggested that** he has spent so much on his home because he is a private person.

5b There are two different impersonal reporting structures. Which sentences above follow pattern A? Which follow pattern B?

A *It* + reporting verb + *that* + subject + verb ......, ..., ...
B Subject + reporting verb + *to* + present/past infinitive ......, ..., ...

5c In which sentences:

1 is the reporting in the present? ......, ..., ..., ...
2 is the reporting in the past? ......, ...
3 is the action being reported in the present? ......, ..., ...
4 is the action being reported in the past? ......, ..., ...

GRAMMAR REFERENCE ➤ PAGE 80

6 Rewrite the sentences following the example.

They say that an Englishman's home is his castle.
It is said *that an Englishman's home is his castle*.

1 They suggested that the house took years to build.
It ....
2 They estimate that the house is worth 15 times more.
It ....
3 They know that the house has three helicopter pads.
The house ....
4 They have reported that he is living in New York now.
It ....
5 They believe that the house has been updated.
The house ....

7 Rewrite the sentences using the word given.

1 They say that the house has a lot of space. HAVE
2 They have reported that the gardens are indoors. BE
3 They have suggested that there's a yoga room. IT
4 They know that celebrities have visited. TO
5 They say they are building another house. BEING

Discussing photos – 2

1 SPEAKING **Work with a partner. Describe what you can see in the photo.**

2 LISTENING 19 **Listen to a student discussing the photo in an exam. What four questions does the examiner ask? Does the student answer all four questions?**

✓ EXAM SUCCESS

When we discuss photos in speaking exams, describing the photo is just one part of the task. We usually have to answer questions which take us from the photo itself to the general theme and our own experience of it. When you look at the photo for the first time, start thinking of possible questions connected to the situation and theme that the examiner might ask you.

➤ EXAM SUCCESS page 149

3 LISTENING 19 **Look at the information in the Speaking bank and listen again. Tick (✓) the adverbs and adverbials you hear. Where do they usually come: at the start of the sentence or in the middle?**

SPEAKING BANK

Using comment adverbs and adverbials

We can use adverbs and adverbials to:

1 show our attitude or opinion about what we are saying:
frankly, generally speaking, honestly, interestingly, luckily, personally, sadly, to be honest, unfortunately

2 say how certain we think something is:
apparently, clearly, definitely, maybe, obviously, presumably, probably, undoubtedly

3 say what we think of someone else's actions:
carelessly, cleverly, foolishly, kindly, rightly, stupidly, wrongly

4 Rewrite the sentences. Replace the underlined phrases with an adverb or adverbial from the Speaking bank.

1 To tell you the truth, I don't like her bedroom.
2 They say that she's got two brothers.
3 To give you my opinion, I would tidy the room up straight away.
4 Everyone can see that it's a mistake.
5 It seems that she doesn't have a computer in her bedroom.
6 He agreed to help, but that was a silly thing to do.
7 That is, without question, a great idea.
8 This is a pity, but not everyone lives in a nice house.

PRACTICE MAKES PERFECT

5a SPEAKING **Work with a partner. Student A, look at photo 1 and prepare three questions to ask your partner about it. Student B, do the same with photo 2.**

1

2

5b Ask your partner to describe your photo. After approximately one minute, begin to ask your three questions. Allow your partner time to give full answers.

An article – describing a place

1 SPEAKING **Work with a partner. Discuss these questions.**

1 Look at the three cities in the photos. Which would you prefer to live in and why?
2 What factors do you think decide the quality of life in a city?
3 Which cities in the world do you imagine offer the best quality of life? Choose five and discuss the reasons for your choice.

2 Read this information. How many of your five choices in 1 appear in the list? Are you surprised by the top ten? Why/Why not?

Each year a consulting company called Mercer ranks cities around the world according to the quality of living of the inhabitants. The living conditions are analysed according to different factors grouped into these ten categories:

1 political and social environment
2 economic environment
3 socio-cultural environment
4 health and sanitation
5 schools and education
6 public services and transportation
7 recreation
8 consumer goods
9 housing
10 natural environment

The results in 2014 were as follows:

1 Vienna, Austria
2 Zurich, Switzerland
3 Auckland, New Zealand
4 Munich, Germany
5 Vancouver, Canada
6 Düsseldorf, Germany
7 Frankfurt, Germany
8 Geneva, Switzerland
9 Copenhagen, Denmark
10 Bern, Switzerland

3 SPEAKING **Read the task. With a partner, brainstorm what you could say about your home town/city. Make notes.**

You read the following announcement in a travel magazine.
Following a recently published ranking of the world's best cities to live in, we would like readers to send in articles nominating their home town or city to be included in the table next year. Tell us why your home town or city is special and why it should be nominated.

4 Read this article written by a student. Does it make you want to live in this city? Why/Why not?

Looking for quality of life?
Look no further!

VOCABULARY Describing cities and towns

5a Match these words with the definitions 1–8. For 5 there are two possible answers. There are extra words.

atmospheric • bustling • cosmopolitan • crowded
filthy • hilly • historic • industrial • isolated
magnificent • picturesque • quaint • renowned for
run-down • shabby • spotless • sprawling
steeped in • thriving • touristy • vibrant
welcoming • well-connected • well-off

1 interesting or attractive with a slightly strange and old-fashioned quality
2 full of noise and activity in a pleasant and interesting way
3 friendly and pleasant, especially to someone who has just arrived at a place
4 built over a wide area in a way that is not carefully planned, and maybe ugly
5 in bad condition because no-one has spent money on repairs
6 where people from many different countries and cultures live
7 having a lot of a particular quality or thing
8 famous/well-known for

Imagine a city that's steeped in history. Now think of a city that is vibrant and modern. Maybe you think no city can be both, but you'd be wrong. Istanbul, the most well-known city in Turkey, manages to combine both ancient traditions with a lively, contemporary feel.

The only city in the world that is situated on two continents, Istanbul is clearly something special. On the legendary Silk Route that once linked Asia and Europe and the capital of many different civilisations in the past, Istanbul has a cultural diversity that few cities can offer. It remains to this day a welcoming place for the thousands of people that come to visit it each year.

Before you start thinking the city is touristy, Istanbul has more than just historic monuments. Alongside its fabulous mosques and palaces, you can find cool art galleries and trendy cafés. In fact, there is so much variety you can always find something that suits your mood. If shopping is more your scene, you can head to the Grand Bazaar with its thousands of stalls, or visit the many shopping centres and fashion stores. At night the streets are bustling with life and you're spoilt for choice for places to eat and drink.

Being on two continents, Istanbul is well-connected. You can easily reach many European cities by road, and the public transport system in Turkey is as good as you'll find anywhere.

Quite frankly, Istanbul should be on any list of the world's most liveable cities for its unique beauty and character. But don't just take my word for it. Come and see for yourself. You might just end up staying, like many have before!

5b SPEAKING Work with a partner. Check that you know what the other words in 5 mean and answer these questions.

1 Is each word generally positive or negative?
2 Which are used to describe Istanbul?
3 Which could you use to describe your home town or city?

✓ EXAM SUCCESS

Remember that your writing is judged, amongst other things, on the range of vocabulary you use. In articles in particular, you need to make your writing more appealing to the reader by going beyond basic vocabulary and using more precise and complex words and expressions. By using varied vocabulary and more complex synonyms, you should also avoid repeating words.

➤ EXAM SUCCESS page 152

6 Read the information in the Writing bank. Which of the expressions or ideas are used in the article in 4?

WRITING BANK

Ways to involve the reader

- Think of a title that grabs the reader's attention.
- Use *you, your* or *we, our.*
- Use expressions such as:
  If you're into …,
  If … is what you're looking for,
  For those seeking …,
  If … is more your scene,
  Imagine …/Just think …
- Use direct questions.
- Use comment adverbials (see page 77) to make your own opinion clear.

7 SPEAKING You are going to do the task in 3. Choose a city or town in your country which you think has a good quality of life. With a partner, make notes. Then make a plan, organising the notes into paragraphs.

8 PRACTICE MAKES PERFECT Write your article for the task in 3. Use vocabulary from 5 and expressions from the Writing bank.

WRITING BANK ➤ PAGE 159

Grammar reference

For reported statements, see page 167.

Reported speech – Questions

FORM

The same changes occur with tenses, pronouns and other words as with reported statements.

We do not use the auxiliary verb **do**.

'Do you like rap?' ➤ She asked me if I liked rap.

There is no inversion of subject and verb.

'Where are you?' ➤ He asked me where I was.

Reported questions are not real questions so they do not need question marks.

~~*She asked me what I needed?*~~

When there is no question word (*who, what, how, why,* etc.), we use *if* or *whether*.

*'Can you do it?' ➤ They asked me **if** I could do it.*

Reported speech – Different types of reporting structures

1 verb + (*that*) + sentence in reported speech, e.g. *say, reply, add, admit, agree, announce, claim, complain, explain, promise, deny*

*He **promised that** he would help me.*

2 verb + object + (*that*) + sentence in reported speech, e.g. *tell, remind, warn, inform*

*She **informed us that** she was running late.*

3 verb + question word/*if* + sentence in reported speech, e.g. *ask, wonder, want to know*

*She **wanted to know** if I would go to the party that night.*

4 verb + (*not*) to-infinitive, e.g. *agree, offer, claim, threaten, promise, refuse, demand*

*I **offered to** help my mum.*

5 verb + object + (*not*) to-infinitive, e.g. *tell, advise, forbid, ask, instruct, tell, order, warn, invite, remind*

*The teacher **instructed us to** do the activity.*

6 verb + gerund, e.g. *deny, admit, suggest, recommend, admit, regret*

*The waiter **recommended trying** the fish.*

7 verb + (object) + preposition + gerund, e.g. *insist on, accuse somebody of, confess to, congratulate somebody on, criticise somebody for, warn somebody against, apologise for, blame somebody for, object to*

*Police **accused him of** the crime.*

8 verb + (*that*) + object + (*should*) + infinitive without *to*, e.g. *suggest, recommend, insist, demand*

*They **suggested that we should** go to the museum.*

Reported speech – Impersonal reporting structures

FORM

1 *It* + *be* + past participle of *believe, know, think, say, expect, claim, report* + *that*

***It is said that** dolphins can communicate.*

***It was claimed that** the president knew about it.*

2 Subject + *be* + past participle of *believe, know, think, say, expect, claim, report* + *to* + infinitive/*have* + past participle

*Dolphins **are said to** be able to communicate.*

*The president **was claimed to** have known about it.*

USE

We use this structure to talk about what people in general say, think or believe about something.

Vocabulary

For idiomatic expressions with *home*, finding a place to live and describing cities and towns, see wordlist pages 140–141.

Grammar revision

Reporting structures / 10 points

1 Decide if the sentences are correct. Tick (✓) the correct sentences and rewrite the incorrect sentences.

1 They accused me that I'd stolen the laptop.
2 She claimed to know the director personally.
3 My friend denied to have done anything wrong.
4 The police wanted to know what had the group of teenagers been doing in the street.
5 The authorities advised to not drive in the snow.
6 Ed suggested me to learn to play the guitar.
7 They promised not to play loud music that night.
8 Ben apologised that he had woken everybody up.
9 She insisted to pay for the meal, even though she didn't have much money.
10 The neighbours threatened with calling the police.

Impersonal reporting structures / 8 points

2 Rewrite the structures.

1 People claimed that nobody could build such a tall building. It ....
2 They knew Johnson was at the scene of the crime. Johnson ....
3 They believe that the houses are unsafe. The houses ....
4 At first, people said that the telephone was a useless invention. At first, it ....
5 They thought that the burglar knew exactly what he was looking for. The burglar ....
6 They believed the car was his. The car ....
7 They say that home is where the heart is. It ....
8 People have suggested that the family owns three houses elsewhere. It ....

Vocabulary revision

IDIOMATIC EXPRESSIONS WITH *HOME* / 7 points

1 Complete the idiomatic expressions.

1 Staying with my aunt is like home .... home because I'm so comfortable there.
2 You might not like what I'm going to say, but you need to hear some home ....
3 She'd worked hard on her assignment, but she knew she wasn't home and .... yet.
4 Personally, I don't think the food there is .... to write home about.
5 When I heard about his accident, it really .... home to me how important he is to me.
6 The lions immediately homed .... on the sleeping zebra.
7 I don't know exactly how much he earns, but I know he .... home a good salary.

FINDING A PLACE TO LIVE / 8 points

2 Complete the sentences.

1 They agreed to rent the house and put down a .... to close the deal.
2 He's our .... We pay him the rent each month because the flat belongs to him.
3 The house is ours! Next month we can .... in.
4 The new flat is .... so we don't have to take our horrible old sofa and table.
5 She can't afford to buy a flat so she's looking for a flat or house .... while she's a student.
6 Personally, I think that .... have a right to occupy a property if it's empty.
7 The house was in a terrible state so we spent a lot of time .... it up. Now it looks fantastic!
8 When renting, ... don't need to pay for repairs. It's the owner's responsibility.

DESCRIBING CITIES AND TOWNS / 7 points

3 Tick (✓) the pairs of words that have a similar meaning. Explain the difference for the other pairs.

1 bustling/thriving
2 well-connected/well-off
3 shabby/run-down
4 renowned for/famous for
5 hilly/sprawling
6 lively/vibrant
7 quaint/picturesque

Total: / 40 points

Listening

➤ TIP FOR LISTENING EXAMS

In sentence- or text-completion activities, remember …
Check that you know how many words and/or numbers you can write in each space. Usually you are expected to write the words that you actually hear. Be careful to spell them correctly.

➤ EXAM SUCCESS page 151–2

1 LISTENING ▶ 20 **Listen and complete the sentences. Write no more than three words and/or a number in each space.**

- The first British document similar to a passport was written in (1) ....
- The only person who doesn't need a passport in Britain is (2) ....
- The origin of the word *passport* could come from (3) .... for a word meaning *door* or *gate*.
- After 1858, the message in British passports was written in (4) .... and ....
- At the start of the 20th century, British passports had a (5) .... cover.
- The (6) .... that accompanied the photo in these old passports was often disliked.
- Since 1858, British passports have been valid as travel documents, but also as (7) ....
- People began to need passports for foreign travel during the (8) ....
- British passports changed colour in (9) ....
- Microchips should help (10) .... go faster.
- Unlike passports in many other countries, (11) .... are not obligatory for British passports.
- The Nicaraguan passport includes watermarks and (12) .... among its 89 different safety features.
- Ian Fleming named his house (13) ....
- His special passport was sold for (14) ....

Use of English

➤ TIP FOR USE OF ENGLISH

In open cloze tests, remember …
When you think you have finished, read the whole text again with your answers in the gaps. Often you will need to read a larger section of the text to know what word is correct.

➤ EXAM SUCCESS page 151

2 **Read the text and think of the word which best fits each gap.**

Be careful with your rubbish. That's the message from the police (a) .... the strength of recent research, which has shown that criminals are going through bins looking for documents which they then use to steal identities. Identity theft and identity fraud are considered to (b) .... amongst the most serious and widespread crimes today. One British criminologist has calculated that there is one case of identity theft (c) .... four minutes. The (d) .... is that we make it easy for the criminals. It is (e) .... that around 77 per cent of household rubbish contains one or more items which can help criminals steal an identity. Researchers took a typical sample of rubbish and found papers that contained credit card numbers and documents with bank account numbers (f) .... addition to complete signatures, (g) .... criminals could then copy. (h) .... people don't realise is that, with all this information, identity thieves can make purchases in their name, take out bank loans or even empty their bank account. Usually identity theft is protected by banks and credit card companies, but it can take up to 300 hours of phone calls and visits to banks to clear up the situation. The process can be not (i) .... stressful but also highly depressing. Indeed, a survey found that around 40 per cent of the population are more afraid of identity theft (j) .... pickpocketing, mugging or burglary.

So what can you do to prevent identity theft? Firstly, never give out any personal information (k) .... unidentified individuals or organisations, either in person, on the phone, by mail or online. You (l) .... also recommended to check your accounts regularly for any unusual transactions. If you do suspect something, contact your bank (m) .... the police as soon as possible. And last (n) .... not least, when you throw documents away, always destroy them first, either using a paper-shredding machine or simply tearing them up by hand. An old letter from the bank (o) .... well seem like rubbish to you, but to an identity thief it could end up being pure gold.

Speaking

➤ TIP FOR SPEAKING EXAMS

When discussing photos, remember …
Practise your timing so that you don't finish too early or run out of time. The more you practise, the easier it will be.

➤ EXAM SUCCESS page 149

3 SPEAKING **Work with a partner. Take it in turns to compare two of the photos and say what type of accommodation they show. Who do you think lives in these places? What are the good and bad points of each place? Speak for about a minute.**

Writing

➤ TIP FOR WRITING EXAMS

For guidance on writing letters of complaint, see page 151.
For guidance on writing articles, see page 152.

➤ EXAM SUCCESS page 151–2

4 Choose one of these two writing tasks. Then write your answer.

1 You recently stayed in student accommodation while taking an English course in the UK. However, the accommodation was not as advertised.

Read the advertisement and the notes you made. Then write a letter of complaint to the school.

ACCOMMODATION PROVIDED!

- Simple but comfortable rooms available in hall of residence.
- Single and twin rooms available with en suite bathroom.
- Well-equipped kitchen and fridge.
- Free room cleaning.
- Friendly and helpful staff.
- Only two minutes' walking distance from the school.

Apply: Accommodation Officer, English Exchange, 40 West Grove, Brighton

- Asked for a single room but had to share!
- No microwave!
- Room not cleaned in two weeks
- No-one available to help
- Walked for at least ten minutes!
- Ask for a refund of 50%

2 An English-speaking friend is doing research into living situations of young people around the world and has asked you to write a contribution.

Write an article explaining:

- what living situations are available (e.g. with parents, shared flat).
- which is most common and why.
- what you think should be done to improve options for young people.

7 Marketing campaign

Reading

VOCABULARY **Advertising and selling**

1a Read these statements about how companies advertise and sell their products. With a partner, discuss the meaning of the words and expressions in bold.

1 They **launch a marketing campaign** on TV.
2 They give away **freebies**.
3 They make **cold calls**.
4 They get a celebrity to **endorse** their product.
5 They change the **brand name** or logo.
6 They put posters on **billboards** in streets.
7 They use **word-of-mouth publicity**.
8 They use **banners** and online videos.

1b Match the words in bold in 1 with the definitions a–h.

a the name that a company chooses for its particular product or group of products
b an advertisement on a website
c things given to you that you don't have to pay for
d people talking to each other about and recommending a product
e unexpected phone calls or visits by someone trying to sell you something
f say in public or in an ad that you like a product
g large boards used for advertisements in an outside public place
h make public a series of things such as adverts or commercials that try to persuade a person to buy a product

2 SPEAKING **Work with a partner. Which three methods of advertising products do you think are the most effective? Which one do you think is the least effective? Give reasons and examples of advertisements you have seen.**

3 Read the article and explain what the photos represent in terms of advertising.

✓ EXAM SUCCESS

In multiple-choice reading activities, begin by taking away options that in your opinion are definitely not correct. Then read the other options and the relevant section of the text in greater detail.

➤ EXAM SUCCESS page 149

4 Read the article again and choose the best answers.

1 Marketing companies have had to change their tactics because
  a people don't notice traditional adverts.
  b customers weren't buying enough products.
  c traditional ads don't give enough information.
  d how people find out about products has changed.
2 People prefer influencers to celebrities because
  a their recommendations are more credible.
  b they give more information about products.
  c a lot of people follow them.
  d they don't get paid to promote brands.
3 According to the article, vloggers
  a have more fans than sports, TV and music stars.
  b are always employed by marketing companies.
  c are better known than celebrities.
  d have a lot of influence over young people.
4 The Pepsi Max campaign
  a used online stars to promote their product.
  b gave prizes for talking about the product.
  c used a competition to promote their product.
  d offered a trip if people visited their website.
5 In the Samsung campaign
  a fans could buy the new phone before it appeared in the shops.
  b fans could buy the phone more quickly if they promoted it.
  c people recorded videos of queues.
  d over 70,000 people joined an online queue.
6 The shop and pizza restaurant campaigns
  a required people to post photos online.
  b asked people to tweet the company's name.
  c offered to reduce prices in return for publicity.
  d involved giving people freebies.

5 **CRITICAL THINKING**

Think! Then compare ideas with your class.

- Successful advertising causes a failure of critical thinking. How far do you agree?

6 Guess the meaning of the underlined words from the context. Then use your dictionary to check.

7 SPEAKING **What about *you*?**

Which of these marketing campaigns seems most effective? Why?

WHAT'S NEXT FOR MARKETING? YOU!

> 'People like being informed about products by people they know, and they want to get involved.'

They say that the average person is exposed to thousands of advertisements every day. They're on billboards, banners, TV and increasingly on our mobiles, too. Not surprisingly, people have grown tired of advertising and cynical about the claims that adverts make. Marketers are having to find innovative ways to reach potential customers and they're turning to social media to do so.

People nowadays want to be informed about products, and get opinions from people they trust. According to a recent survey, nearly three-quarters of consumers turn to social networks to help them to make a decision about what to buy. A recommendation from a friend or someone they know has more credibility than any advertisement or product review. So marketers have realised that they need to encourage people to talk about their products online.

One way they're doing this is through so-called online 'influencers'. An influencer can be anyone who has an influence over other people's purchasing decisions. Traditionally, these have been celebrities, who are used by marketing companies to endorse brands. But savvy consumers are becoming wise to this kind of advertising. Celebrities are known to have representatives who dictate much of their lives and decisions, and they're also paid huge sums of money for endorsement deals.

So, more recently, bloggers and video bloggers have taken over as the ones with the real power.

Bloggers and vloggers are seen as more authentic and relatable than celebrities, and when they recommend a product, viewers are much more likely to trust their advice. They often have large and loyal followings. They also tend to focus on one particular area, such as fashion, fitness or technology.

Tanya Burr and Zoe Sugg, also known as Zoella, are two beauty vloggers. They record videos in their homes, covering everything from make-up tutorials to best buys. With millions of followers, they now work with companies who pay them to promote their brands. The gamer Felix Kjellberg, or PewDiePie, who records himself playing video games, has done little brand promotion to date, but sales of games increase dramatically after appearing on his channel.

Video bloggers hold particular sway when it comes to young people. In one study, 1,500 teenagers were asked questions to compare celebrity and online influencers. With 20 well-known personalities to choose from, half of them from the world of sports, TV and music and half online stars, the teens ranked the online stars as more popular. The online influencers also came out on top in terms of approachability, authenticity and other criteria.

Marketing companies are also encouraging ordinary people to create a buzz about their products online. Pepsi Max, for example, launched a campaign in which they challenged fans to perform a series of social media tasks, including tweeting why they liked the drink more than a rival brand. Prizes such as a TV or a year's supply of Pepsi were offered in return for completing the tasks quickly, and the most successful fans went on to compete for a prize trip. The brand had over 7,000 entries and more than 50,000 people visited the competition website.

Samsung turned to fans to create excitement before the launch of a new Galaxy smartphone. Instead of allowing people to wait in line to buy the phone, Samsung created a virtual queue. People could sign up and create a profile and then they could move up the queue by talking about the product online. The more likes, tweets and comments they generated about the phone, the closer they got to the front of the queue. The results of the campaign were impressive – 12,000 people got involved and they shared 74,000 stories about the product.

These marketing strategies have been adopted by small companies on a local level. One little-known South African retailer created a campaign in which visitors to their shop were offered a $10 coupon if they took a selfie of themselves trying on some clothes and tweeted it using the company's name in the hashtag. They managed to get more people into the store, trying on clothes and sharing images of their outfits. A pizza company had another inspired idea when they offered to reduce the price of the main pizza of the day according to how many people tweeted a particular hashtag before lunchtime. The result was half-price pizzas and a lot of word-of-mouth publicity.

It seems that social media is breaking down the barriers between advertisers and potential buyers. People like being informed about products by people they know, and they want to get involved. So what does that mean for the future of marketing? Perhaps that products will be promoted more and more by the people who really use them.

Flipped classroom: watch the grammar presentation video.

Passives, passive infinitives and passive gerunds

1 Look at the sentences and answer the questions.

a People nowadays want **to be informed** about products.
b Prizes **were offered** in return for completing the tasks quickly.
c Perhaps products **will be promoted** by the people who use them.
d These marketing strategies **have been adopted** by small companies.
e They like **being informed** about products by people they know.

1 Which sentence contains a passive infinitive?
2 Which contains a passive gerund?
3 What tenses are the passive verbs in the other sentences?
4 In sentence b, in the context of the article on page 85, which is more important – the action or the agent (the person who did it)?
5 Do you always need to state the agent in passive sentences? Why/Why not?

GRAMMAR REFERENCE ➤ PAGE 94

2 Complete the text with the correct passive form of these verbs. Use each verb only once.

analyse • ask • brainwash • expose
read • show • use

Neuromarketing is a new procedure where scientists use functional Magnetic Resonance Imaging to investigate how our brains react when they (a) .... to publicity. First, you get inside a long white tube, which is in fact the scanner. Then, while images of products (b) .... on a screen in front of you, you (c) .... to imagine yourself using the product. When you finish, the results (d) .... by experts in the human brain. Basically, when a certain part of the brain is active, it means that we are interested in the product. In this way, advertisers can test out their products and adverts on a number of people before 'going public'. The concept of *neuromarketing* appeared for the first time in 2002. Since then, the procedure (e) .... by many companies because the answer to the question 'Do you like this product?' is not at all reliable. Meanwhile, though, the idea that our minds can (f) .... by scientists worries some people. Nobody likes the idea of (g) ...., and maybe companies will use neuroscience to do precisely this in the future.

Passives with verbs with two objects

3 Look at the sentences and answer the questions.

1a They pay celebrities huge sums of money.
1b Huge sums of money are paid to celebrities.
1c Celebrities are paid huge sums of money.
2a They offered visitors to the shop a $10 coupon.
2b A $10 coupon was offered to visitors to the shop.
2c Visitors to the shop were offered a $10 coupon.

1 How many objects follow the verbs in 1a and 2a?
2 Which do you think is more common – to use the thing or the person as the subject in this type of passive sentence?

GRAMMAR REFERENCE ➤ PAGE 94

4 Rewrite the sentences using the person or people as the subject. All your sentences must use the passive.

1 They sell us a load of things we don't really need.
2 A present was bought for me by my friends.
3 They are going to offer you a refund.
4 They taught him some new marketing strategies.
5 My sister showed me a great new advert on the Net.
6 They may promise you a free gift.

Causatives

5 Look at the sentences and answer the question.

a Suzie had/got her photo taken by a friend.
b Suzie got a friend to take her photo.
c Suzie had a friend take her photo.

Did Suzie take the photo herself in any of the sentences above?

GRAMMAR REFERENCE ➤ PAGE 94

6 SPEAKING Complete the questions with the correct form of the verbs given. Then ask your partner the questions.

1 When was the last time you had your eyesight .... (test)?
2 Do you usually get somebody .... (give) you lifts? Who?
3 Have you ever had somebody .... (fix) your computer? Who?
4 Have you ever got somebody .... (do) your homework for you? When and why?
5 Have you ever had clothes .... (make) for you? What was it? Why?

Word formation

1 Read the sentences with adjectives. What is the suffix in each adjective?

1 Bloggers are more **authentic** than celebrities.
2 A recommendation is seen as **credible**.
3 People have grown **cynical** about adverts.
4 Social media has become more **important**.
5 Marketers are having to find **innovative** ways to reach potential customers.
6 Some vloggers are **lucky** and earn money.
7 Marketers need to make **memorable** ads.
8 Many people think ads are **pointless**.
9 The campaign was hugely **successful**.
10 Teens are not influenced by **childish** ads.

2 Add a suffix to each of these words to create an adjective. In some cases, more than one suffix is possible. Make any changes to the word that are necessary.

effect • fun • help • optimist • origin
predict • resist • sense • thought • young

3 Which words in 2 can you change to an adverb by adding *-ly*?

4 Look at these sentences and decide what difference the suffix *-ish* makes to a word.

1 I should be home about eightish.
2 I wouldn't say I'm tall, but I'm tallish.
3 My hair is straightish.

5 SPEAKING Write down at least five adjectives to describe yourself. Each adjective must contain a suffix (one or two can contain *-ish*). Compare adjectives in pairs.

6 SPEAKING Work with a partner. Look at these words and answer the questions.

autograph • collectable • creative
criticism • endorsement • famous
imagination • instantaneous • intensify
likelihood • modernise • multi-purpose
officially • originality • post-concert
powerful • pre-concert • readiness

1 Underline the prefix or suffix in each word.
2 Decide either a) what meaning each prefix adds to the root word, or b) what type of word the suffixes create.

7 Work with a partner. How many new words can you make from the words below by adding prefixes and/or suffixes? Use the list of prefixes and suffixes on pages 145–146 to help you.

1 nation
2 able
3 produce
4 act
5 cook

✓ EXAM SUCCESS

In word-formation cloze tests, remember that the spelling of some root words changes when we add a suffix or a prefix. Also, for some words you may need to add a prefix and a suffix. Lastly, check whether any words need to be plural.

➤ EXAM SUCCESS page 148

8 Read the text. Use the word given in capitals at the end of some of the lines to form a word that fits in the gap in the same line.

Shopping in supermarkets used to be simple, but over the past twenty years it has become **(a)** .... more sophisticated. In fact, **INCREASE** it has become so complicated that a whole new profession has come into **(b)** .... – **EXIST** the retail anthropologist. Retail anthropologists study shoppers in the supermarket, for example. They use a **(c)** .... of techniques **VARY** to analyse how many products each shopper touches, which labels they read, how long they spend in each aisle. Their **(d)** .... **ATTEND** to detail certainly pays off. Although the way we shop may seem totally **(e)** ...., retail **PREDICT** anthropologists can find important trends that help shop owners to design their supermarkets. The location is important for a start. **(f)** .... if your supermarket is next **FORTUNE** to a bank, it won't do very good business since it has been found that banks remind people of how much money they owe and this stops them from going in and spending more. Amongst the other **(g)** .... made is the **DISCOVER** importance of mirrors. When we see a mirror, we tend to slow down, and so you can sell a product more **(h)** .... if it is close to one. **EFFECT** This leads designers to **(i)** .... their **STANDARD** designs, and one supermarket looks very similar to another. On the other hand, supermarkets are far more **(j)** .... to disabled people **ACCESS** than they used to be.

Understanding the GLOBAL ECONOMY

21ST CENTURY SKILLS OBJECTIVES

- To consider the advantages and disadvantages of globalisation
- To learn about implications of globalisation on jobs in the future
- To investigate where and how things we use every day are made

KEY CONCEPTS

interdependent [adj]: *Countries no longer operate independently of each other. They are interdependent.* **developing countries [n]:** *Companies move production to developing countries to reduce costs.* **economic growth [n]:** *One of the main benefits of globalisation is economic growth, especially in industrialised countries.*

1 SPEAKING **Work with a partner. Talk about the clothes you're wearing and the things you're carrying with you. Do you know where they were made?**

2 Answer these questions.

1 What do you think of when you hear the word 'globalisation'?
2 What are some good things and bad things about it?
3 What effect do you think it will have on jobs in the future?

3 READING **Read the article about the global economy and answer these questions.**

1 On balance, does the article suggest there are more advantages or disadvantages to globalisation?
2 What is the main implication for young people?

GLOBALISATION
Are you prepared for it?

"Knowledge and awareness of the world are more important than academic qualifications."

Your shirt was made in China and your mobile comes from Japan. You can eat at McDonald's in Moscow and watch an American film in Rome. Advances in technology such as mobile phones, aeroplanes, telephones and the Internet have made the growth of transport and communication networks possible. Amongst other things, this means that people and countries can exchange information and goods more quickly and in a less complicated way in a process called globalisation. But what are the downsides of the global market? And how will it affect jobs in the future?

Globalisation means we have access to more goods and at more affordable prices, but it comes at a cost. When a company moves production to an economically disadvantaged country because of the lower costs involved, people in industrialised nations lose their jobs. Meanwhile, workers in places such as Bangladesh and China earn low salaries and their working conditions are often poor. Big fashion companies, for example, sell well-known brands at a sizeable profit, but the people who make the clothes earn only a fraction of the price at which they're sold.

Interdependency also means that if there is a problem in one country, it can have far-reaching effects elsewhere. Many multinational corporations obtain raw materials in one country, manufacture their products in another and sell all over the world. If these materials aren't available, there can be economic repercussions across the globe.

What's more, globalisation causes ecological problems. The number of planes, ships and lorries that are used to transport goods from one country to another is constantly on the increase, which means more carbon dioxide is released into the atmosphere. That in turn, leads to global warming.

The good news is that consumers are becoming more aware of the issues, especially when it comes to how products are made. Increasingly, companies are being pressurised to improve ethical standards. Levi's, the iconic jeans maker, recently announced a plan to offer financial incentives to businesses in developing countries if they improve conditions for their employees and their environmental performance.

4 Read the article again. Make notes on the advantages and disadvantages of globalisation. Add any other ideas that are not mentioned.

	Advantages	Disadvantages
For industrialised countries		
For developing countries		

5 SPEAKING **Work with a partner. Discuss these questions.**

1 Are you surprised by the results of the survey? Why/Why not?

2 How would you evaluate your awareness and knowledge of the world?

3 What are some ways to gain a better understanding of global issues?

6 LISTENING 21 **Three people are talking about how globalisation affects their workplace. Watch the video or listen. Make notes of the following:**

1 Their job

2 The positive effects of globalisation

3 The negative effects of globalisation

4 The methods of communication they use

5 The skills needed in the global workplace

21ST CENTURY TASK

You're going to research a product that you use regularly and make a presentation about where and how it is made.

Follow this plan:

1 *Choose a product, e.g. a food product, clothing, sports shoes, a drink.*

2 *Find out how and where it is made using books or the Internet.*

3 *Prepare a presentation.*

4 *Give your opinion about what your research shows about the effects of globalisation.*

5 *Give your presentation to the class.*

Raw materials are gathered from one country and sold around the world

So while globalisation encourages economic growth, especially in developed countries, it also presents new challenges. Which is why companies are beginning to consider the skills that young people will need to become the business leaders of the future. It seems that it may no longer be enough to get the best exam results to succeed in the global workplace. In a recent survey of executives and directors, 79% said that knowledge and awareness of the wider world were more important to them than academic qualifications. In particular, they valued the ability to think critically about global issues, to understand different perspectives and to interact well with people from diverse countries, and many were concerned that young people were not aware of the importance of global thinking.

1 SPEAKING **Work with a partner. Look at the pictures and answer the questions.**

1 Where would you expect to see these logos?
2 Are there many products in your country which claim to be 'green'? Which types of product?
3 What do you think the term 'greenwashing' might mean?

2 LISTENING 22 **Listen to an interview with a consultant for a consumer protection organisation and choose the best answers.**

1 An American marketing firm
   a found 1,018 environmentally friendly products.
   b found 1,017 environmentally friendly products.
   c investigated 1,018 different products.
   d were astonished that they couldn't find even just one environmentally friendly product.
2 The problem with one shampoo manufacturer was that it said
   a the shampoo was organic, but when it was tested, it evidently wasn't.
   b it had proof that the shampoo was organic, but the proof didn't exist.
   c it had proof that the shampoo was organic, but the proof was falsified.
   d something that was only partially true.
3 The consultant says
   a all natural products are good.
   b all products are essentially natural.
   c knowing a product is natural is not good enough.
   d companies should list all the natural ingredients in a product.
4 The consultant tells us
   a to buy products that claim they are CFC-free.
   b not to buy products that claim they are CFC-free.
   c any product that says it's CFC-free is lying.
   d CFC-free products are the best for protecting the ozone layer.
5 The consultant tells us that one of the keys to buying products that help the environment is
   a to read all the information and then check that the information is true.
   b to disbelieve the ecological claims that companies make.
   c not to believe that all products with an EcoLogo or Green Seal are good for the environment.
   d not to reject a product if the manufacturer mentions something negative about it.

3 SPEAKING **What about *you*?**

1 What would you propose to stop companies making false claims about green products?
2 What reasons are there for people not buying green products?
3 What could be done to encourage people to buy more?
4 What other things can people do to be 'green' in their daily lives?

Developing speaking

Collaborative tasks – 1

1 SPEAKING **Work with a partner. Which of the advertisements (a–e) do you like and why?**

a

b

c

d

e

2 LISTENING 23 **Read the instructions for the speaking task and then listen to two people doing the task. Which advertisement do they choose and why? Do you agree with their decision?**

> Here are some advertisements that have recently appeared in magazines. First, talk to each other about what messages you think the adverts are giving about the products that they are trying to sell. Then decide which advert you think is the most effective at selling the product.

3 Answer these questions.

1. Did the students do both parts of the task?
2. Did they always agree?
3. Did they reach a decision at the end?
4. Did both students speak for more or less the same amount of time?

✓ EXAM SUCCESS

In collaborative tasks, you must interact with your partner. This means asking them questions, making suggestions, expressing opinions and above all listening and responding to what your partner says.

➤ EXAM SUCCESS page 152

4 Look at the expressions in the Speaking bank. With a partner, add as many expressions of your own as possible to each category.

SPEAKING BANK

Useful expressions to negotiate and collaborate

Asking your partner's opinion

- What do you think about (the first ad)?
- What about you?
- So what shall we (choose)?
- Don't you think so?
- ....
- ....

Making suggestions

- Why don't we choose (this one)?
- Let's …
- ....
- ....

Agreeing with your partner

- Yes, you're right.
- I see what you mean.
- Absolutely.
- ....
- ....

Partially agreeing with your partner

- I see what you mean, but …
- I suppose so, but …
- ....
- ....

5 SPEAKING **Work with a partner and practise doing the task in 2. Give your own opinions.**

6 PRACTICE MAKES PERFECT SPEAKING **Work with a partner and do this task. Use expressions from the Speaking bank.**

> The things below have a strong influence on people in their daily lives. First, talk to each other about the ways these things influence us. Then decide which you think has the biggest impact on the world today.

the Internet | television | advertising

THINGS THAT INFLUENCE US

smartphones | newspapers | social media

A report

1 SPEAKING **Work with a partner. Discuss these questions.**

1 Do you think that advertising generally has a positive or a negative effect on society? Why?
2 Do you think young people are more at risk from advertising? Why/Why not?
3 Do you think there is too much or not enough control on advertising? Why?

2 Read this task and report. Decide what title you could give to each section of the report.

You see this announcement in an international newspaper.

A large multinational company is interested in knowing how young people feel about advertising in your country. Please help us by writing a report which should:

- outline what media are most commonly used for advertising to young people
- describe the main positive and negative aspects of advertising in your country
- suggest what could be done to improve the approach to advertising in your country.

A report on the relationship between advertising and teenagers in my country

Introduction

The purpose of this report is to outline the most common media used for advertising to teenagers in my country and detail the major positive and negative aspects of advertising. I will also suggest ways of improving advertising here.

1 ……………

Advertising aimed at teenagers has traditionally been in the form of TV commercials. Nowadays, a considerable number of teenagers watch TV online, on mobile devices, or pre-recorded on digital video recorders, which means that they can avoid seeing commercials. Consequently, it will come as no surprise that many companies are changing their strategy and now place their products directly in TV programmes or in video games.

Social marketing is also common. Most teenagers, if not all, use social media and advertisements appear on these sites, although in reality few pay attention to them. At the same time, mobile phone advertising is increasing.

2 ……………

While many teenagers have become resistant to advertising, some adverts still grab our attention by being funny or original. Advertisements which provide information, or which show us products that we are genuinely interested in, are considered useful. However, a major criticism of adverts is that they produce unreal expectations in young people. Every advertisment shows a slim and attractive person. Moreover, each of the situations they appear in suggests that the way you look is important. This leads teenagers to become obssessed with their weight or appearance.

3 ……………

To avoid the negative impact of advertising on teenagers, I strongly recommend that advertisers include more normal, everyday teengers in their ads. This would help stop teenagers trying to achieve an unnatural perfection, something which can easily lead to depression.

Determiners and quantifiers

3 Read sentences a–h and decide if statements 1–7 are True (T) or False (F).

a **Every** actor is always slim and beautiful.
b **Each of** the situations shown gives the impression that appearance is everything.
c **A** considerable **number of** teenagers watch two or more hours of TV a day.
d That will come as **no** surprise.
e **Most** adverts grab our attention by being funny.
f Not **all of** the ads are good.
g **None** show normal teenagers.
h **None of** the actors look like you or me.

1 *Every* and *each* are used with singular countable nouns. T / F
2 *Each of* and *every one of* go with plural countable nouns. T / F
3 *A number of* goes with singular countable nouns. T / F
4 *No* can go with uncountable, singular countable or plural countable nouns. T / F
5 *All, all of, most, most of* can go with uncountable, singular countable or plural countable nouns. T / F
6 *None* is a pronoun and so does not go with a noun. T / F
7 *None of* can go with uncountable or plural countable nouns. T / F

GRAMMAR REFERENCE ➤ PAGE 94

4 Decide if the sentences are correct. Rewrite the incorrect sentences.

1 I always remember each adverts I see on TV.
2 None of the models in the photo are overweight.
3 There are lots of pop-ups on this website, but none are very effective.
4 All adverts showing people smoking are banned.
5 Most of my friends watch hours and hours of television all days.
6 Every one of the actors have beautiful shining teeth.
7 I have not interest in the world of advertising.
8 A number of people I know has worked as models.

5 SPEAKING **Read the report in 2 again and discuss these questions with a partner. When you finish, read Exam success and the Writing bank.**

1 Who is the report written for?
2 Is the style more formal or informal?
3 Are contractions used?
4 Why do you think the passive or impersonal reporting structures are used on several occasions in the report?
5 Which linkers are to be found in the report? What do they add to the report?

✓ EXAM SUCCESS

The style in which a report is written is of great importance. Often reports are written for organisations, companies or people in positions of responsibility. In this case, the report needs to be formal. Sometimes reports are written for a group of your own peers. Here the style will be a little less formal, but will still be informative.

➤ EXAM SUCCESS page 152

WRITING BANK

Useful language and expressions in more formal reports

- Use passive and impersonal structures to convey a more serious, formal style.
- Do not use contractions.
- Use linkers of addition, contrast, consequence, etc. to structure your arguments.
- Use determiners and quantifiers to say how general your findings and comments are.

Beginning the report

- *The aim/purpose of this report is to outline/ describe/present the findings …*
- *This report is intended to …*
- *This report is based on …*

Ending the report

- *As I/we have previously mentioned,*
- *I/we (would) suggest/recommend …*
- *My/our main recommendation/suggestion is …*
- *Having taken everything into consideration,*
- *All things considered,*
- *All in all,*
- *To sum up/conclude,*

VOCABULARY Describing clothes and fashions

6a Match some of these words with the definitions 1–6. Several words may be possible for some definitions. With a partner, check that you understand the other words.

60s/70s/80s-style • adventurous • baggy • casual
check • chic • classic • flowery • glamorous
loose • old-fashioned • plain • scruffy • smart
sophisticated • stripy • tight • trendy

1 fashionable, stylish and attractive
2 untidy or dirty
3 fitting very close to your body
4 very large, not fitting next to your body
5 simple in design, with no particular decoration
6 with a pattern of squares

6b SPEAKING Work with a partner. Describe the outfits and accessories in the photos.

6c SPEAKING Check that you understand the words in bold. Then answer the questions.

1 Do you think the clothes **match**?
2 Do you think they **fit** the people wearing them?
3 In your opinion, do they **suit** the people wearing them?
4 Do you think they would **suit** you? Why/Why not?
5 Are there any items of clothing or accessories in the photos that you **wouldn't be seen dead in**? Which?
6 Are any of the clothes in style at the moment? Do you think they could **set a trend** in the future?

PRACTICE MAKES PERFECT

7 Read the writing task and follow these steps.

1 Identify who you are writing the report for and the key information that you need to include in it.
2 Decide how many sections you will need in your report and give each one a heading.
3 Make notes with ideas for each section.
4 Write your report.

An international research company wants to know more about teenage fashion in your country. Help them by writing a report. This should:

- outline styles or items of clothing that are in fashion at the moment.
- explain how important (or not) you think fashion is for teenagers.
- recommend any improvements to the fashion industry in terms of products, models, prices and marketing.

WRITING BANK ➤ PAGE 160

Grammar reference

For the passive, see page 167.

Passive infinitives and gerunds

FORM

We make passive infinitives with *to be* + past participle.
We make passive gerunds with *being* + past participle.

USE

The decision whether to use an infinitive or gerund depends on the preceding verb, preposition or structure.

*I love **being** spoilt.*

*I want **to be** respected.*

The passive: verbs with two objects

FORM

Some verbs are followed by two objects, one usually a **thing** and the other a **person**. When this happens, we can make two different passive sentences.

*I was given **a surprise**.*

*A **surprise** was given **to me**.*

It is more common to make passive sentences with the **person or people** as the subject.

These common verbs are followed by two objects: *give, send, tell, show, lend, pay, promise, refuse, offer, teach, bring, buy, owe*

Causatives

FORM

Subject + *have* or *get* + object + past participle (*by* + agent)

Subject + *have* + agent + infinitive without *to*

Subject + *get* + agent + *to*-infinitive

USE

We use these structures to talk about actions people do for us; often for payment. *Get* is slightly more informal.

With these structures we make different tenses by changing the tense of *have* or *get*.

*He **got** his friend **to fix** his computer.*

*He's **having** a friend **fix** his computer.*

With the structure subject + *have* or *get* + object + past participle, we can use the preposition *by* to introduce the agent. If it is not important who does the action we do not put anything.

*He **had** his computer **fixed by** a friend.*

Determiners and quantifiers

FORM

a (large/small) number of (+ plural countable nouns)
all, all of (+ singular, plural and uncountable nouns)
most, most of (+ singular, plural and uncountable nouns)
each, every (+ singular countable nouns)
each of, every one of (+ plural countable nouns)
no (+ singular, plural and uncountable nouns)
none (without *of*, cannot go with another noun)
none of (+ plural countable and uncountable nouns)

USE

Each and *every* are followed by singular verbs.

__Each__ one is different. __Every__ day is different.

None of can be followed by a singular or plural verb if it refers to a plural countable noun.

__None of__ us like/likes that film.

Some and *most* can be followed directly by a noun if there is no other determiner.

__Some__ people, __most__ children

We must use *some of* and *most of* if we use another determiner.

__Some of__ the people who came were angry. __Most of__ the chocolate disappeared.

All does not have to go with *of* if there is another determiner.

__All (of)__ the people here are friends of mine.

Vocabulary

For noun, adjective and adverb suffixes, prefixes, advertising and selling and describing clothes and fashions, see wordlist page 141.

Grammar revision

Passive structures — / 7 points

1 Decide if the sentences are correct. Tick (✓) the correct sentences and rewrite the incorrect sentences.

1. A prize was given to the director.
2. Don't worry, the money has received.
3. After be seen by the doctor, she left the hospital.
4. The truth was told to me.
5. This is the apartment that is being stayed in by us.
6. The packages are been sent by airmail next week.
7. I'm meeting by two friends at the airport.

Causatives — / 7 points

2 Rewrite the sentences using the word given.

1. Tanya always cuts his hair for him. **HAS**
   He always .... by Tanya.
2. Her mum picked her up. **BY**
   She got ....
3. Decorators are decorating their house. **GETTING**
   They ....
4. They'd delivered the pizza for us. **DELIVER**
   We'd had .... the pizza.
5. They thought that the burglar knew exactly what he was looking for. **THOUGHT**
   The burglar ....
6. I got the shop assistant to wrap the present. **WRAPPED**
   I .... the shop assistant.
7. I want them to print it out for me. **HAVE**
   I'm going to .... it out for me.

Determiners and quantifiers — / 6 points

3 Complete the sentences with these words. There are three extra words.

all • each • has • have • no • none • not • number • one

1. Life is surprising – .... day is different.
2. Money, riches, fame. .... of them interest me.
3. Who's eaten my cake? .... of it has gone!
4. There is .... doubt he is wrong.
5. I've read every .... of the books on that shelf.
6. Each of these actors .... endorsed a product.

Vocabulary revision

WORD FORMATION — / 7 points

1 Complete the sentences with the correct form of the words given.

1. Let's think .... (sense) about this.
2. There has been a .... (understand). I didn't order this.
3. It was .... (point) queuing for a ticket when they had already sold out.
4. The fashion designer was praised for the .... (origin) of her latest collection.
5. No-one knows who is going to win. The result is .... (predict).
6. People are becoming .... (increase) tired of commercials on TV.
7. She expected me to respond to her email .... (immediate).

ADVERTISING AND SELLING — / 7 points

2 Read the definitions and complete the expressions.

1. give away a ....: when a company gives you something you don't have to pay for
2. .... a product: say in public you like a product
3. make cold ....: unexpected telephone calls or visits by someone trying to sell something
4. launch a marketing ....: make public a series of adverts to persuade people to buy a product
5. .... publicity: when people talk to each other about a product or recommend it to each other
6. a .... name: the name that a company gives to its particular product or group of products
7. ....: a large board used for advertisements in an outside public place

DESCRIBING CLOTHES AND FASHIONS — / 6 points

3 Write a simple definition for the words and expressions.

1. casual
2. set a trend
3. wouldn't be seen dead in
4. match
5. loose
6. stripy

Total: / 40 points

8 One life, live it

Reading

VOCABULARY Compound adjectives – parts of the body

1a Work with a partner. Match 1–10 with a–j to make compound adjectives. Then match them with the definitions i–x. Check your answers in a dictionary.

1 soul-	a blowing	i making you feel happy, usually because other people are being kind
2 heart-	b raising	ii attractive or unusual and therefore noticed
3 heart	c warming	iii used to describe a situation that makes you very unhappy because you think it will never improve
4 hair-	d biting	iv used to describe a situation that makes you very excited, worried or tense
5 break	e stopping	v extremely impressive, exciting or shocking (informal)
6 ear-	f destroying	vi very frightening
7 eye-	g opening	vii very frightening, but often exciting at the same time
8 eye-	h catching	viii very fast, at .... *speed*
9 nail-	i splitting	ix used to describe a situation that shows you something surprising that you didn't know before
10 mind-	j neck	x very loud

1b Complete the questions with the correct parts of the body.

1 Have you ever travelled at break............ speed? When?
2 Have you ever witnessed a ....warming scene? What happened?
3 What's the most ....-splitting sound you've heard?
4 What's the most ....-raising thing you've done?
5 What's the most ....-blowing film you've seen?
6 What's the most ....-biting sports event that you've seen?

1c SPEAKING Work with a partner. Discuss the questions in 1b.

2 You are going to read an article about a bungee jumping accident. Six paragraphs have been removed from the article. Choose from the paragraphs A–F the one which fits each gap (1–6).

3 Read the article again and answer the questions.

1 What problems and what dangers did Erin face?
2 What factors contributed to her survival?

4 CRITICAL THINKING

Think! Then compare ideas with your class.

- How do you think an experience like this would change your outlook on life?

5 Match the underlined words in the text with these explanations and definitions.

1 holding tightly
2 not clearly visible, usually when moving very fast
3 a deep valley with high sides where a river has cut through rock
4 held together with a narrow piece of material
5 move very fast and with great energy
6 fix in a small space between two objects
7 a sudden violent movement
8 feeling of sudden, intense excitement
9 try something
10 hit, usually with the palm of the hand

6 SPEAKING What about *you*?

1 Have you ever done an extreme or dangerous sport? Would you like to one day? Why/Why not?
2 What would you choose to do as a 'big adventure'?
3 Why do you think people do dangerous sports? Do you think they are brave or irresponsible?
4 Do you know any other cases where people have survived in extreme circumstances?

AUSTRALIAN SURVIVES FALL AS BUNGEE JUMP ROPE SNAPS OVER RIVER

Erin Langworthy, a 22-year-old student from Australia, miraculously survived when her bungee cord snapped and she fell into a crocodile-infested river.

The thrill seeker from Perth had never done a bungee jump before, but decided to give it a go while travelling in Zambia. Having just finished university, she wanted a big adventure, so she'd set off for Africa. She was travelling alone but joined a tour group when she heard they were heading to Victoria Falls to go bungee jumping. Known as the adrenalin capital of Africa, Victoria Falls is the ultimate destination for extreme sports enthusiasts looking for mind-blowing experiences. The idea of jumping from a 111 metre-high bridge over the gorge with the thunder of the falls behind sounded too good to miss.

1 ....

She remembers the spectacular views as she looked out over the Zambezi River. Then she spread her arms and fell forward. 'Everything sped by in a blue-green blur,' she says. 'The rush was amazing.'

2 ....

On the platform above, Erin's friend Rebecca Johnson filmed the heart-stopping moment. 'She was supposed to come right back out and she never did,' Rebecca said. 'Everybody on the bridge just panicked.'

3 ....

Feeling as though she had been slapped all over, and hardly able to breathe, Erin floated along with the sound of the falls roaring in her ears. Tied to her bungee cord and with her ankles still strapped together, she was pulled downriver and underwater into whirlpools. At one point, the cord got caught and she was dragged beneath the surface. Running out of air, and with her vision starting to fade, she managed to dive down and free the rope. Eventually, she was able to wedge her arm between two rocks on the side of the river. All she could think about was clinging on.

4 ....

Although she'd jumped at 5.30 in the afternoon, Erin didn't get to hospital until 11 pm. The paramedics got lost on the way and she'd ended up on the Zimbabwean side of the river without a passport, so she was essentially an illegal immigrant.

5 ....

Erin was visited in hospital by the people from the bungee company, who were astounded that she was still alive. Friends she had met while travelling helped her to get her belongings and passport and she was then flown to South Africa for medical treatment. Two weeks later, she travelled home to Australia.

6 ....

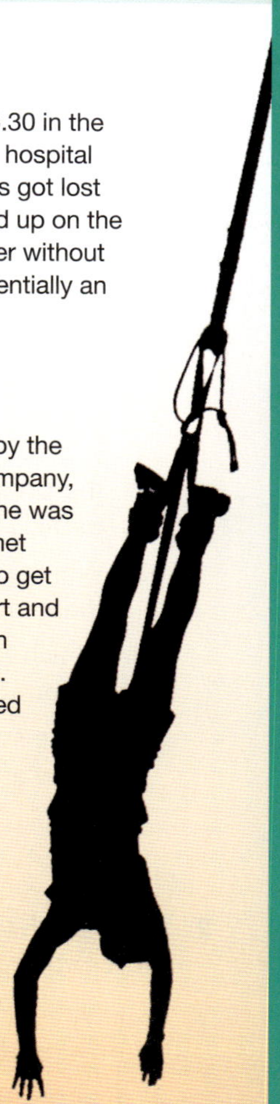

A Erin was in the water for 40 minutes before one of the men from the bungee company reached her. He grabbed her harness, pulled her out of the water and laid her on her back. Worried that he didn't have first aid training, Erin moved herself into the recovery position. Then she started coughing up water from her lungs. Her body was purple with bruises from the impact, she felt exhausted and she was struggling to come to terms with what had happened.

B Erin admits to feeling nervous as she waited for her jump, but didn't think for a moment that anything could go wrong. A hundred and four people had already made the jump that day – she was the 105th. As she stood on the platform with her ankles strapped together, she was most worried that the straps would become loose and her feet would slip out. She was assured that was the last thing that would happen.

C Being a positive person, Erin says she has never felt angry about what happened to her. 'Around 50,000 people jump from that spot every year, so it was pure chance that the rope snapped on me,' she said. Before doing the jump, Erin had sent her mother a postcard saying: 'I'm doing a bungee jump tomorrow, so I'll say goodbye … only joking!' Her mother is adamant that she'll never do another jump, but Erin hasn't ruled out the possibility.

D Erin zoomed towards the river, but instead of recoiling back up as planned, the cord snapped, sending her head first into the river rapids. She recalls a jolt, then the wind rushing past her ears. Instinctively, she brought her arms up to protect her head, which prevented her from blacking out as she hit the water.

E Erin fell for four seconds at breakneck speed after the rope snapped, for a distance of 40 metres. If she'd been over land, she would have died. Luckily, it had rained the day before, so the river was turbulent and full. But that morning, she'd seen crocodiles in the water.

F When she arrived at the hospital, she was put on a ventilator, given an ultrasound and taken to see a lung specialist. The doctors were most concerned about how much dirty water from the river she'd ingested and gave her a large dose of antibiotics. The X-rays showed no broken bones, though her lungs had partially collapsed.

Participle clauses

1 Look at the sentences and answer the questions.

a <u>Known as the adrenalin capital of Africa</u>, Victoria Falls is the ultimate destination for extreme sports enthusiasts.

b <u>Having just finished university</u>, she wanted a big adventure.

c <u>Feeling as though she had been slapped all over and hardly able to breathe</u>, Erin floated along.

d <u>Running out of air, and with her vision starting to fade</u>, she managed to free the rope.

e <u>Tied to her bungee cord and with her ankles still strapped together</u>, she was pulled downriver.

f <u>Being a positive person</u>, Erin says she has never felt angry about what happened to her.

1 Which of the <u>underlined</u> participle clauses use the present participle and which use the past participle?

2 Which of the two types of participle clause gives a meaning similar to the passive?

3 Which tense do we use when one action happens before the other, *doing* or *having done*?

4 Is the subject of the participle clause usually the same as in the other half of the sentence?

GRAMMAR REFERENCE ➤ PAGE 106

2 Choose the correct alternative. In one case, both alternatives are possible.

1 Damaged by the storm, *the sailors/the boat* managed to get back safely to the port.

2 *Being/Been* a good swimmer, she managed to get to the shore.

3 *After meeting/Having met* her, I wasn't surprised she managed to survive.

4 When *climbing/having climbed*, you must pay complete attention.

5 Written in true style, *I really enjoyed this story/this story is one of my favourites*.

6 *Blaming/Blamed* for the accident, the workers lost their jobs.

3 Complete the sentences with the correct form of the verbs given.

1 .... (walk) to work, I saw an accident.

2 After .... (learn) to dive, we went on holiday to the Red Sea.

3 .... (teach) to sail when she was a child, she crossed the Atlantic single-handed at the age of 20.

4 .... (learn) to ride a motorbike first, he started to drive a car soon after.

5 Since .... (qualify) as a doctor, she has gained lots of experience at this hospital.

6 .... (catch) in the storm, they took shelter.

✔ EXAM SUCCESS

In sentence transformation activities, do not add or change words unless you have to. They may change the meaning of the sentence or make you write too many words.

➤ EXAM SUCCESS page 150

4 Complete the second sentence so that it has a similar meaning to the first sentence, using the word given. Do not change the word given. You must use between three and six words, including the word given.

1 Because he knew little about animals, he had no idea about how to look after the dog.
Not ...., he had no idea about how to look after the dog. **MUCH**

2 When they had checked the weather forecast, they set out on their journey.
After .... the weather would be OK, they set off on their journey. **MAKING**

3 The car hit the skateboarder and they had to rush him to hospital.
...................., the skateboarder had to be rushed to hospital. **BY**

4 The singer performed the song for the first time in 2005, but he wrote it in 2001.
The song, first ...., was written by the singer in 2001. **IN**

5 Being totally fearless, she loves extreme sports.
She loves extreme sports .... **SINCE**

6 His coach thought he would not be able to compete again because he thought there was no solution.
His coach, ..., thought he would not be able to compete again. **FEARING**

7 She couldn't drive fast because she couldn't see where she was going.
.... she was going, she couldn't drive fast. **BEING**

8 They offered Alex the chance to play and he said yes straight away.
Alex, ..., said yes straight away. **GIVEN**

5 Write questions using participle clauses.

1 Having done your homework, *what do you usually do to unwind?*

2 Having studied English for many years now, …

3 After doing sport, …

4 Being a student, …

5 When made to wait, …

6 Hanging out with friends, …

7 When ignored, …

8 Not being able to vote yet, …

Words with more than one meaning

1 SPEAKING **Work with a partner. Discuss the different meanings of the words in bold in these pairs of sentences.**

1a It became **clear** to them that the cord had snapped.
1b The sky was **clear** that day – not a cloud to be seen.
2a The weather was **fair**, though it had rained the day before.
2b It might not seem **fair** that others had made the jump before without any problems.
3a The rescuer tried to **cover** her with his jacket because she was wet.
3b The hikers set off to **cover** as much distance as possible before lunch.
4a As she fell, she **picked up** speed.
4b The ambulance **picked** her **up** several hours later.
5a She had been travelling **since** she left university.
5b She couldn't swim **since** her ankles were strapped together.

2 Look at how the word *point* is used in these sentences. Match each use with a definition a–g.

1 I don't agree with you on that **point**.
2 What is the **point** of doing that?
3 At this **point** I'd like to thank Joe for coming here today.
4 Let's meet at a **point** that's close to the cinema.
5 This team has got six **points** and the other has only one.
6 The **point** of the knife caught the light.
7 Don't **point** at her. It's rude.

a a particular moment in time
b show something by holding out your finger or a long thin object
c the sharp end of something
d a particular place
e an idea or opinion among a number of others
f the reason for something
g a unit for counting the score in a game or sport

3 SPEAKING **Read these sentences containing phrases with the word *point*. With a partner, discuss what you think each phrase means. Check your answers in a dictionary.**

1 I **see your point**.
2 Can you please **get to the point**?
3 All right, you've **proved your point**.
4 I think you've **missed the point**.
5 She was **on the point of** giving up hope.
6 I agree **up to a point**.
7 You **have a point**.
8 I think we've reached **the point of no return**.

4 Think of one word only which can be used in each set of three sentences.

1 I felt a .... of rain on my face.
Is this the .... where you saw him fall?
What's that .... on your face?
2 Let's leave a .... The service was good.
He gave me a useful .... for how to warm up.
They live on the northern .... of the island.
3 When buying a car, you need to take into .... how much petrol it uses.
The police asked me to give them a full .... of the accident.
She put all the money into her bank ....
4 The bench was very .... and uncomfortable.
This year we're having a .... winter with lots of snow and low temperatures.
Is this exercise .... or can you do it?
5 The water is beautiful and .... here.
You need to give .... instructions.
It's .... that you can't win without a lot of training.
6 It's going to .... my heart if we lose.
We need to get away and have a proper ....
The actor got his first big .... when he appeared in an ad for a famous brand of trainers.
7 I think it's boring when a match ends as a ....
I'd like to .... your attention to the next point.
Some people claim that they can't even .... a straight line with a ruler.
8 We need to run faster to .... the others up.
I'm sorry, I didn't .... your name.
I sincerely hope they .... the person who did this.

5 Write down the meanings of any new words or phrases in 4.

6 Work with a partner. Use your dictionary to find a word that has three different meanings. Write three sentences, leaving a gap for the word as in 4. Swap sentences with another pair and guess the missing word.

Appreciating *literature*

LIFE SKILLS OBJECTIVES

- To evaluate books you've read
- To consider the benefits of reading
- To appreciate how books can inspire and influence

KEY CONCEPTS

insight [n]: *Reading gives you insights into why people think, feel and behave the way they do. It helps you to understand them.*

1 SPEAKING **Read the list of the top ten books for young adults, voted for by people in the UK for World Book Day. Work with a partner. Answer these questions.**

1. Have you read any of the books on the list? If so, did you enjoy them?
2. Which book or books would you add to the list?

THE TOP 10 BOOKS

1. THE HUNGER GAMES by Suzanne Collins
2. THE FAULT IN OUR STARS by John Green
3. To Kill a Mockingbird by Harper Lee
4. Harry Potter series by J. K. Rowling
5. Nineteen Eighty-Four by George Orwell
6. The Diary of a Young Girl by Anne Frank
7. A Street Cat Named Bob by James Bowen
8. THE LORD OF THE RINGS by J. R. R. Tolkien
9. THE PERKS OF BEING A WALLFLOWER by Stephen Chbosky
10. JANE EYRE by Charlotte Brontë

2 **Read the line from a book called *Paperboy* by Christopher Fowler. What do you understand by it?**

'If life is a series of locked doors you must find ways to open, books provided me the first of many keys.'

3 READING **Read the article. What is the connection with the line above?**

THE SECRETS OF FICTION

For many people, there's nothing like curling up with a good book for an afternoon. But are novels simply a pleasant way to pass the time, or could it be true that reading fiction is actually beneficial for our lives?

One of the joys of fiction is that it can take us to places that our lives won't. It can transport us to 17th-century France, to war-torn Germany, or to a small, southern-US town dominated by racial prejudice. It can take us to a future world in which television dominates and books are banned, or a fantasy world where people battle it out for food.

Fiction can also introduce us to a whole range of people that we don't know or haven't yet met. And this, according to Keith Oatley, a Canadian novelist and academic, is perhaps the real benefit of stories. For Oatley, fiction is a kind of simulation of the real world. Just as a person learning to fly an aeroplane would spend time in a flight simulator, reading fiction allows us to experience the lives of other people and so help us to understand them better.

> "Fiction is a kind of simulation of the real world."

Oatley has carried out a number of experiments which show that

4 Read the article again and complete the sentences.

1 In stories, we learn about places and people that …
2 For Oatley, fiction is like a flight simulator because …
3 The experiment with the Chekhov story shows that …
4 People who read fiction are better able to …
5 Oatley says that reading helps us to …
6 The abilities may be useful for …

5 SPEAKING Work with a partner. Discuss these questions.

1 Do you enjoy reading literature? Why?
2 How often and when do you read?
3 What's the best book you've read?
4 What book has influenced or inspired you most?
5 What fictional character do you most identify with and why?

6 LISTENING 24 Some students are answering questions from 5. Watch or listen. Which question does each person answer?

7 LISTENING 24 Watch or listen again and make notes about their answers to each question.

LIFE TASK

You're going to make a video or presentation about one of the following:

- *a book that you love*
- *a fictional character that you identify with*

Follow this plan:

1 *Choose from one of the options above.*
2 *Prepare what you are going to say. Make notes, but don't write complete sentences.*
3 *Practise your presentation. Use your notes to help you, but try not to read.*
4 *If making a video, record your video.*
5 *Show your video or make your presentation to the class.*

> "Fiction can help to increase empathy and social understanding."

fiction can help to increase empathy and social understanding. In one study, participants were asked to read either a short story by Chekhov, or a version of the story in documentary form. Those who were given the fictionalised version were found to have gone through greater changes in personality – empathising with the characters and becoming a little more like them.

In another study, participants were shown photos of the eyes of people who were feeling and thinking different things. The people who read fiction were better able to interpret those thoughts and feelings than those who didn't read.

Oatley explains that when we read fiction, we enter into the minds of the characters. We think about why they behave in a certain way, and what they are likely to do next, rather than just looking at the exterior as we usually do. Just as we might become more knowledgeable about genetics or astronomy if we read about genetics or astronomy, we get better at this kind of social thinking if we read fiction. This helps us see the difference between the interior and more limited exterior of people and improves our understanding of the thoughts and feelings of those around us in real life.

This ability for empathy and social understanding is important, not just in the general way by making the world a better place by improving interpersonal relations, but also in specific areas such as politics, business and education where interaction and understanding of others' actions are key. Reading fiction should perhaps therefore be more highly valued than it is at present because it can have a positive influence on society and behaviour.

Listening

1 SPEAKING **Work with a partner. Read A–H in 2, Task 1, below. Have any of these things happened to you? Tell your partner about them.**

✓ EXAM SUCCESS

You are going to do a listening activity where you match speakers with pieces of information or ideas. Remember that speakers may express the same ideas as in the questions, but using different words or expressions. Remember also that other speakers may use the actual words that come in the questions, but that does not necessarily mean that this is the correct speaker.

➤ EXAM SUCCESS page 149

2 LISTENING 25 **You are going to listen to five people talking about special moments in their lives. Look at the two listening tasks. Listen and complete both tasks at the same time.**

Task 1

For questions 1–5, choose from the list (A–H) what the special moment in each speaker's life was. There are three extra letters which you do not need to use.

A I won a prize.
B I did something brave.
C My work was recognised and appreciated.
D I made an incredible physical effort.
E I learnt I had a special ability.
F I made a big mistake.
G I met someone who changed my life.
H I gained in self-confidence.

Speaker 1 **1** ....
Speaker 2 **2** ....
Speaker 3 **3** ....
Speaker 4 **4** ....
Speaker 5 **5** ....

Task 2

For questions 6–10, choose from the list (A–H) what each speaker felt after the special moment. There are three extra letters which you do not need to use.

A regret
B optimism
C indifference
D excitement
E anxiety
F relief
G embarrassment
H annoyance

Speaker 1 **6** ....
Speaker 2 **7** ....
Speaker 3 **8** ....
Speaker 4 **9** ....
Speaker 5 **10** ....

3 LISTENING 25 **Listen again and check your answers.**

4 SPEAKING **What about *you*?**

1 Each of the speakers did something new. What was it?
2 Which would you find easiest and most difficult to do?
3 How important is it to try new activities? What are some possible benefits?

Developing speaking

Discussions based on visual stimuli

1 SPEAKING **Work with a partner. Discuss these questions.**

1 Do you enjoy doing outdoor activities? Why/Why not?
2 Which of the activities in the photos have you done? When?
3 What do you think are the pros and cons of doing outdoor activities?

2 **Read the task. Is it asking you to describe the photos?**

Look at the three photos. A British friend is coming to stay with you this weekend. You know that he/she likes outdoor activities, so you want to take him/her out somewhere. You have three activities to choose from.

- Choose the activity that in your opinion is the most suitable and explain your choice.
- Explain why you have rejected the other two.

✓ EXAM SUCCESS

When there are photos or other visual material in a speaking exam, you are not always required to give a description of what you can see. It may be that the visuals are there to prompt you to perform another task or set of tasks. Make sure you read or listen to the instructions carefully so that everything you say is relevant to the task.

➤ EXAM SUCCESS page 152

3 LISTENING 26 **Listen to a student doing the task. Which activity does she choose and why? What are the other two questions that she answers?**

Flipped classroom: watch the grammar presentation video.

4 Look at the expressions in the Speaking bank. What do these expressions allow the speaker to do? How could you complete the title of the Speaking bank in a suitable way?

SPEAKING BANK

Useful expressions to ……………………

- Let me see, …
- Well, I guess …
- Let me think about that for a second …
- How can I put it?
- I suppose that what I'm saying is …
- What I mean/meant is/was …
- In other words …
- The thing is …
- Actually, …
- That's a good question.
- The truth is …

Making and modifying comparisons

5 Look at the sentences below and answer the questions.

a It's a great deal easier to chat if you're all walking together.

b It's considerably better for you to be breathing fresh air than to be stuck inside all day.

c It's not the same doing sport indoors as being outside.

d Young people spend significantly less time outdoors.

e Young people aren't nearly so active as they used to be.

f Far fewer young people walk nowadays.

g By far the most popular pastimes are things that you usually do indoors.

h More and more young people are starting to do outdoor activities again.

1 Look at sentences d and f. When do we use *less* and when do we use *fewer*?

2 In sentence e, can we replace *so* with *as*? Could we use *so* if the sentence was affirmative?

3 In sentence c, do we continue the expression *(not) the same …* with *as*, *so* or *than*?

4 What effect do the words and expressions *a great deal*, *considerably*, *significantly*, *nearly*, *far*, *easily* and *by far* have in comparisons?

5 Which of the words or expressions above do we use with normal comparatives? Which do we use with superlatives? Which do we use with *(not) as/so … as*?

GRAMMAR REFERENCE ➤ PAGE 106

6 Choose the correct alternative.

1 In my opinion, canoeing is *by far/far more* exciting than hiking.

2 Walking in the mountains can be *as/so* tiring as running.

3 I think I have the same opinion *as/than* the student who did the task.

4 I would say that cycling is slightly *better/the best* for your health.

5 The more exercise you do, the *more fit/fitter* you get.

6 I guess there are *fewer/less* opportunities to get outdoors when you live in a big city.

7 We should get back soon because it's getting *dark/darker* and darker.

8 She's *easily/considerably* the fittest person I know.

7 SPEAKING Work with a partner. Compare different sports or outdoor activities. Use each of these words or structures at least once.

1 significantly
2 by far
3 (not) the same … as
4 fewer
5 more and more
6 less
7 (not) as … as
8 a great deal

PRACTICE MAKES PERFECT

8 SPEAKING Take it in turns to do this task. Use expressions from the Speaking bank and language of comparison.

Look at the three photos on page 164.
A British friend who is mad about sports is coming to stay with you this weekend. You want to take him/her to see a sports event in or near where you live. You have these three events to choose from.

- Choose the event that in your opinion is the most suitable and explain your choice.
- Explain why you have rejected the other two.

Student A: When you finish the first part of the task, answer these two questions.

1 Is it important for sport to be part of our lives? Why/Why not?

2 Do you think some sports like football have become too popular? Why/Why not?

Student B: When you finish the first part of the task, answer these two questions.

3 What do you think makes some sports more popular than others?

4 What disadvantages could there be with being a professional sportsperson?

Opinion and for-and-against essays

VOCABULARY Metaphors – happiness and sadness

1a Complete the metaphors with these words. What idea do they all give about happiness?

air • cloud • lift • moon • seventh • up • world

1 Things are *looking* ....
2 This will .... *your spirits.*
3 I've been *walking/floating on* .... since I got the news.
4 She's *over the* ....
5 They're *on top of the* ..../*on* .... *nine/in* .... *heaven.*

1b Do the same with these words. What idea do the expressions give?

bright • brightened • lit • tunnel

1 His face .... *up* when he saw her.
2 Things are *looking* .... for the future.
3 There's *light at the end of the* ....
4 They .... *up* when they heard what had happened.

1c These expressions all describe sadness. Which give an idea of being low or falling? Which give an idea of darkness or dark colours?

1 She's *feeling blue*.
2 Things are *looking gloomy/bleak*.
3 I've been *feeling* a bit *down/low* recently.
4 *My heart sank* when I found out.
5 It *cast a shadow over* the meal.
6 She's *in low spirits*.
7 I'm feeling *down in the dumps* today.

1d SPEAKING Work with a partner. Ask and answer these questions.

1 Would you say that you are generally in high or low spirits?
2 When's the last time you felt over the moon?
3 What types of things can make you feel down?
4 If your friend was feeling blue, what would you do to lift his/her spirits?

2 SPEAKING Work with a partner. You are going to read a short text about happiness. Before you read, discuss what you think the key to being happy is.

3 Read the text. Do you agree with what it says about happiness?

WHAT IS HAPPINESS, ANYWAY?

Everyone wants to be happy, but what does this really mean?

People have been asking this question for centuries, but only recently have scientists and psychologists joined the debate. Apparently, our genes play a big part in how happy we feel. And while money and material possessions can lift our spirits for a short time, it seems the real key to happiness is life experiences.

Buying new clothes or the latest electronic device may make us feel on top of the world for a short time, but after a while, the feeling starts to fade. We get used to seeing our possessions and our happiness loses its shine. What's more, we tend to compare ourselves to others and if we see someone with a better or newer version of what we've bought, it can leave us down in the dumps.

Life experiences, on the other hand, are more satisfying and bring more lasting happiness. Apart from the enjoyment of the actual experience, they give us memories that we keep our whole lifetime. Life experiences bring us closer to people, too. So the next time you're tempted to spend money on material possessions, try saving the cash for a life experience instead. As you look back on your life, you'll be grateful.

Happy people actually live up to nine years longer than unhappy people. That alone should be enough to brighten us up!

4 Look at this task. What similarities and differences are there between the two essays?

You have had a class discussion on happiness. Your teacher has now asked you to write **one** of these essays.

1 'Money can't buy you happiness.' Do you agree?
2 Some people claim that our modern lifestyle, with more money, material comforts and scientific progress does not make us any happier than in the past, perhaps even the opposite. Others say we have never been happier thanks to today's lifestyle. Discuss both these views and give your own opinion.

Write your essay.

✓ EXAM SUCCESS

In some essays we must give both sides of an argument, but in others we need only give our own opinion. This will make a big difference to the way we organise our essay and to our paragraph plan. However, in both cases it is important to justify and explain the arguments that we present, and the style in both types of essay will be formal.

➤ EXAM SUCCESS page 152

5 Read this student's essay, ignoring the gaps. Answer the questions.

1 Is the student writing essay 1 or 2 in the task in 4?

2 What is the purpose of each paragraph?

3 How would you organise the paragraphs differently if you were writing the other type of essay?

In today's materialistic society, it is not uncommon for people to say that money cannot buy happiness. We often hear that possessions are not essential to enjoy life, and that the path to happiness lies in simple pleasures. (a) ...., I (b) .... believe that money can make us happy, if it is spent wisely.

First and (c) ...., I believe that money allows us the freedom to travel, and pursue our hobbies and interests. It also makes it possible to spend more time with our family and friends. Too often people are so concerned about work and earning a living that they are unable to do the things that matter most. Money enables us to have the life experiences that enrich our lives.

(d) ...., I am (e) .... that one of the greatest sources of satisfaction is being able to give to others. Having money makes it possible to help people who are less well-off, both at home and abroad. To return to the example of working to earn a living, many of us are restricted by financial concerns and not able to think about wider issues. Many wealthy people donate to charities and invest in worthwhile causes. As a (f) ...., they often feel happier themselves.

Some people argue that we are too obsessed with money, since we only need a certain amount to survive. Whilst it is true that only the basics, such as food and a comfortable home, are necessary, I would maintain that money gives us the option to invest in experiences that will make us happy.

(g) .... in all, as far as I'm concerned, money in itself cannot buy happiness (though having little or no money can cause distress). Happiness comes from spending time and effort in a worthwhile way, and money allows us to do this.

6 Work with a partner. Try to complete the gaps in the essay in 5. Then look at the words and expressions in the Writing bank to check. Can you add any words or expressions to the different sections in the Writing bank?

WRITING BANK

Revision of useful expressions and linkers in essays

Introducing and sequencing arguments

- First and foremost,
- Secondly,
- Last but not least,

Adding arguments

- Furthermore,/Moreover,
- not only … but also
- a further advantage/disadvantage/criticism of
- What is more,

Making contrasts and giving counterarguments

- On the one hand,/On the other hand,
- despite/in spite of (+ noun/gerund/the fact that …)
- However,/Nevertheless,
- Whilst it is true that …

Expressing consequences

- Therefore,
- and so
- as a result

Expressing strong personal opinions

- To my mind, there is no question that …
- I certainly believe that …
- I am convinced that …
- As far as I'm concerned,

Expressing general or other people's opinions

- It is widely accepted that …
- Some people claim/argue/maintain that …
- It is often said that …

Concluding

- All in all
- To sum up

PRACTICE MAKES PERFECT

7 Choose one of the essays below. Then follow these steps.

1 Check that you know whether the essay is an opinion essay or a for-and-against essay.

2 Brainstorm ideas to include in your essay.

3 Decide on a paragraph plan and decide which of the ideas you have brainstormed will go into each paragraph.

4 Write your essay. Use words and expressions from the Writing bank.

1 Dangerous sporting activities should be banned. Do you agree with this statement?

2 Some people say that we should live for today. Others disagree and say that we should plan for the future. Discuss both these views and give your own opinion.

Write your essay.

WRITING BANK ➤ PAGES 155 AND 157

Grammar reference

Participle clauses

FORM

Using the present participle

__Walking__ to the shops, I bumped into an old friend.

__Having walked__ to the shops, I started to buy the items on my list.

Using the past participle

__Caught__ by the police, the gang confessed.

The subject of the participle clause must be the same as in the other half of the sentence.

Seeing him there, I waved.

~~*Seeing him there, he waved to me.*~~

USE

We use present participles (*doing, watching, walking*, etc.) to talk about actions happening at the same time.

__Running__ to catch the bus, I twisted my ankle. = When I was running to catch the bus, I twisted my ankle.

We use the perfect form of present participles (*having done, having watched, having walked*, etc.) to say that this activity happened before the next activity in the sentence.

__Having seen__ the weather forecast, we cancelled the excursion. = After we had seen the weather forecast, we cancelled the excursion.

We can also use participles to explain the reason for something.

__Needing__ a rest, I sat down. = Because I needed a rest, I sat down.

We use past participles as an alternative to the passive.

__Watched__ by millions, the programme was an immediate hit. = The programme was watched by millions and was an immediate hit.

Making comparisons

We use *less* with uncountable nouns and *fewer* with countable nouns.

We have __less__ money than before. We have __fewer__ chances of success.

We use *as … as* to say two things are the same. We use *not as … as* or *not so … as* to say that the second person or thing is *more … than* the first one.

Playing tennis __isn't so__ expensive __as__ paragliding.

We use *(not) the same … as* to compare nouns.

This sport does__n't__ offer __the same__ excitement __as__ motor racing.

We use double comparatives (*more and more, bigger and bigger, more and more important*) to talk about continuing changes.

She's getting __more__ and __more tired__.

She's getting __taller__ and __taller.__

We use *The + comparative, the + comparative* to talk about two things that happen together.

__The faster__ I run, __the more tired__ I feel.

__The harder__ you study, __the better__ your results.

Modifying comparisons

We can use these words and expressions to modify basic comparatives:

slightly, a bit, a lot, a great deal, much, far, twice/three times …

He's __far__ better at tennis than me.

We can use these words and expressions to modify superlatives:

by far, easily, by a long way

She's __by far__ the best athlete in the world right now.

We can use these words and expressions to modify *(not) as … as:*

quite, nearly, almost, just, twice/three times, nowhere near, nothing like

She's not __nearly__ as careful as me.

Vocabulary

For words with more than one meaning, compound adjectives, and metaphors, see wordlist page 142.

Grammar revision

Participle clauses
/ 8 points

1 Complete the sentences with the correct form of these verbs.

eat • give • hurt • not know • practise • use • wash • write

1 .... the email, she sent it.
2 The man .... in the accident is making good progress in hospital.
3 When .... a mobile phone in public, you should try not to disturb others.
4 .... the money by my parents, I went to do the shopping.
5 .... breakfast, I brushed my teeth.
6 .... every day, you should become a guitarist one day.
7 .... the way, I think I may get lost.
8 .... by hand, this jumper should stay in perfect condition.

Making comparisons
/ 6 points

2 Decide if the sentences are correct. Tick (✓) the correct sentences and rewrite the incorrect sentences.

1 I'm convinced that snowboarding is so easy as skateboarding.
2 Fewer and fewer people walk for 30 minutes a day.
3 It seems that life is getting more and more fast.
4 Young people today don't have the same problems than young people in the 1950s.
5 I think people enjoy extreme sports because they take less risks in their day-to-day routines.
6 The earlier you leave, sooner you'll get there.

Modifying comparisons
/ 6 points

3 Put these words and expressions in the correct place. Use each once.

a great deal • by far • far • nearly • slightly • twice

1 This is the most exciting holiday I've ever had.
2 He was faster than me because he finished in 22 seconds and I finished in 23 seconds.
3 Russia is bigger than Ireland.
4 Running isn't as dangerous as paragliding.
5 The economy has grown as fast as predicted, expanding by 0.8% instead of 0.4%.
6 Gold is more valuable than steel.

Vocabulary revision

WORDS WITH MORE THAN ONE MEANING
/ 7 points

1 Write an explanation for the words in bold. Then write a different explanation.

1 I can't see what the **point** is of going to her house when we know she isn't in.
2 We need to **cover** a lot of ground before we can stop and rest.
3 The purpose of the exercise is **clear**.
4 Please write an **account** of what happened.
5 X marks the **spot**.
6 This could be the **break** the band needs.
7 Sorry, I didn't **catch** your name.

COMPOUND ADJECTIVES – PARTS OF THE BODY
/ 7 points

2 Complete the compound noun in each sentence.

ear • eye • hair • heart • nail • neck • soul

1 It's .... to see hungry children in the world.
2 The police drove at .... speed to catch the thief.
3 Come on our new, ... roller coaster ride!
4 What a .... finish! We scored in the last minute.
5 It's .... to see people do voluntary work.
6 That dress is ...., with so many bright colours.
7 There was an .... scream that made me jump.

METAPHORS – HAPPINESS AND SADNESS
/ 6 points

3 Match 1–6 with a–f to make sentences. Then complete the sentences with the correct preposition.

1 I'm so happy I feel like I'm walking
2 Watching my favourite group play live, I'm
3 I had an argument with my friend and now I'm down
4 Things will get better, there's always light
5 The tragic news cast a shadow
6 I won the competition! I feel on top

a .... air.
b .... the world.
c .... the rest of the evening.
d .... the end of the tunnel.
e .... seventh heaven.
f .... the dumps.

Total: / 40 points

Reading

➤ TIP FOR READING EXAMS

In multiple-choice activities, remember …
You may find the same words in the text and in one of the options, but this does not mean it is the correct answer. The correct option will probably express the information in the text using different words.

➤ EXAM SUCCESS page 149

1 Read the text and choose the best answer (A, B, C or D).

1 The writer suggests that Red Bull's success is surprising because
- **A** the company didn't use to be particularly big.
- **B** the firm is not a multinational.
- **C** they need to spend a lot of money on events.
- **D** you wouldn't expect it, based on the product they sell.

2 Red Bull events are
- **A** for professionals only.
- **B** more spectacular than other events.
- **C** connected with famous sports stars.
- **D** frequent and common.

3 When Baumgartner jumped from the edge of space,
- **A** it cost Red Bull much more than they expected.
- **B** it made him a star.
- **C** it was widely publicised by Red Bull.
- **D** it promoted Red Bull around the world.

4 The Red Bull events
- **A** are devised by the company executives.
- **B** have often proved fatal.
- **C** have caused some negative publicity.
- **D** are always suggested by the athletes themselves.

5 When Pepsi launched its orange drink,
- **A** it was the first time it had promoted a drink in India.
- **B** it was the first time that Pepsi had used extreme sports to promote a drink.
- **C** it was unusual because people shared videos of the event online.
- **D** the Xtreme Tour increased online activity related to the product.

EXTREME MARKETING

Brands attract customers with hair-raising experiences

Tired of the routine commercials and sponsorships deals, some brands are turning to ever-more spectacular feats in order to promote their products.

Recently, the freerunner Ryan Doyle travelled the world, jumping off stones at Machu Picchu in Peru and from the Great Wall of China, and somersaulting against a backdrop of the Taj Mahal. Doyle is part of an elite group of extreme sports enthusiasts who have become brand ambassadors for the energy drink Red Bull. These stars don't sit in front of a camera, but film themselves doing extraordinary stunts and post their videos on the company website, where they are shared by millions of fans.

Over two decades, Red Bull has rewritten the rule book on how to sell a product, focusing on the drink's energy-giving properties while projecting a high-adrenalin image. The small Austrian firm has become a huge marketing success story, growing from a relatively small Austrian company in 1987 to a global juggernaut, earning its founders multi-million pound fortunes.

The company has built its success on sports sponsorships – it owns two teams in Formula One and several football teams – and the staging of global extreme sports events. The most notable of these are the Red Bull Air Race, which involves pilots navigating challenging obstacle courses in the sky, the Red Bull Flugtag, in which competitors are invited to create their own human-powered flying machines that are propelled off a pier into the sea or a lake, and the famous cliff diving competitions.

While the idea isn't new – it has long been forgotten, for example, that the Tour de France started life as a publicity stunt for a struggling French newspaper – Red Bull has taken its events to a whole new level. Perhaps the most memorable of these was when it partnered with Felix Baumgartner for his record-breaking skydive. Baumgartner's jump from the edge of space was shown live around the world with more than eight million people watching him online. Meanwhile, three million tweets were sent about the jump, including those from people encouraged by Red Bull to send their questions for Baumgartner's post-jump press conference. Though the star was Baumgartner, the real winner was its sponsor. The approximate cost, reportedly around $70,000, was easily paid off in terms of the amount of publicity it generated.

Many of the ideas for events and stunts come from the athletes themselves. In the case of the Air Race series, for example, the concept evolved from a chat between a Hungarian aerobatic pilot, Peter Besenyei, and some Red Bull executives. Recently, however, there has been some criticism against the brand for encouraging such risk-taking. One pilot crashed his jet during the Flying Bulls event, and three others, a skier, a parachuter and a base jumper, were all filmed during the action that killed them.

In spite of this, the trend for spectacular displays seems to be catching on with other companies. For instance, when Pepsi launched a new orange drink, it brought in international skateboarders and well-known athletes from the world of BMX and FMX for its Xtreme Tour of five Indian cities. The event, the first of its kind in the country, prompted a spurt of content online when people posted their personal videos of stunts on wheels. And it's not only sports. When Intel launched the Ultrabook, it got the world-famous magician David Blaine to go without sleep or food for 72 hours surrounded by one million volts of electricity which was controlled by the Ultrabook.

As one commentator said, there is pressure to perform ever-more dangerous acts, and while there is a demand to see them, these athletes are likely to continue to push themselves to even greater limits.

Use of English

➤ TIP FOR USE OF ENGLISH

In word-formation cloze tests, remember …
Read the text once quickly to know the general meaning. Then, when you look closer at each gap, read to the end of the sentence, not just to the end of the line.

➤ EXAM SUCCESS page 148

2 Read the text below. Use the word given in capitals at the end of some of the lines to form a word that fits in the gap in the same line.

Felix Baumgartner is **(a)** .... about extreme sports, and loves pushing himself to the limits.	PASSION
In 2012, he became famous for making the **(b)** .... jump from a helium balloon at a height of 120,000 feet, in the upper stratosphere.	SPECTACLE
He was the first man to travel faster than sound without vehicular power.	
Even though the details of the jump were calculated and **(c)** .... nothing would go wrong, it was still taking a huge risk. When American Joe Kittinger jumped from a balloon at 76,000 feet in 1959, he lost	THEORY
(d) .... and started to spin round and round at a speed of 120 mph. It was only his automatic parachute opener that saved his life. According to him, the higher you go, the more hostile the environment is, and the	CONSCIOUS
(e) .... you fall, the friendlier it is.	FAR
(f) .... for such an experienced adventurer, Baumgartner claimed that he was not afraid. He is certainly no	SURPRISE
stranger to **(g)** .... exploits. In the 1990s he began BASE jumping, which is basically parachuting from buildings	DANGER
or bridges, often **(h)** ...., as with	LEGAL
his **(i)** .... jump from the hand of the statue of Christ the Redeemer in Rio de Janeiro. Nevertheless, Baumgartner insists that he didn't just do the jump for the thrills. He wanted to prove that astronauts can get safely back to Earth if they are forced to jump out of their craft	MEMORY
at these amazing **(j)**	HIGH

Speaking

➤ TIP FOR SPEAKING EXAMS

In collaborative tasks, remember …
Make sure you know whether you must come to an agreement or decision or not.

➤ EXAM SUCCESS page 152

3 Work with a partner. Do the task.

Talk to each other about why these experiences would be memorable. Then decide which two experiences would be most memorable.

- winning a sports trophy
- getting married
- participating in an extreme sports event
- graduating from university
- having a baby
- travelling to a new country

Writing

➤ TIP FOR WRITING EXAMS

For guidance on writing reports, see page 152.
For guidance on opinion essays, see page 152.

➤ EXAM SUCCESS page 152

4 Choose one of these two tasks.

1 A local sports club wants to know about attitudes of teenagers towards sports and outdoor activities. As a member of the club, you have been asked to write a report.

Read the memo from the sports club on which you have made some notes, and the results of a survey you carried out at school. Then write your report.

We are keen to encourage more teenagers to participate in sports. In order to offer suitable activities, we would like to know what sports and outdoor activities are popular, and what sports and activities teenagers would be interested in trying in the future. We would also like to hear your suggestions for courses we could offer.

reduced rates for students

free Saturday activities?

team sports preferred

We appreciate your cooperation!

Lee Samson

RESULTS OF STUDENT SURVEY

- **Currently member of a sports club:** yes 45% no 55%
- **Currently popular:** football, basketball, volleyball, handboard, skateboarding, swimming, aerobics
- **Possible interest:** dance, martial arts, snowboarding

2 'Advertising has a profoundly negative impact on our lifestyle.' Do you agree with this statement?

9 Career openings

Reading

VOCABULARY Life and career developments

1a Read the text and match some of the words and expressions in bold with the definitions 1–8.

When Andy left school, he decided to (a) **follow in** his older sister's **footsteps** and (b) **enrol on** a course to become a chef. The course he chose involved (c) **serving an apprenticeship** in a well-known restaurant. Working in the restaurant (d) **gave him valuable insight into** how a professional kitchen works. It took a while for him to (e) **settle in** and (f) **find his feet**. He also had to (g) **overcome** some important **setbacks** in his personal life during the course, but he didn't (h) **put** his career **on hold** for them. Andy has (i) **lots of aspirations and drive**. He wants to (j) **get on in life** and isn't afraid to (k) **try his hand at** anything. He has already (l) **accomplished** so much in a short time. Since he started the course, he's (m) **never looked back** and now he's at (n) **the top of his game**. One day he could even (o) **end up** running his own restaurant.

1 succeeded in doing something
2 learn about a job by actually doing it
3 do an activity for the first time, to see if you like it
4 put your name on an official list of students
5 get a chance to understand something or learn more about it
6 become familiar with something new
7 succeed in dealing with problems
8 stop something from happening now, but it may happen later

1b Check that you understand the other words and expressions in bold in 1a. Use your dictionary if necessary.

1c Complete the sentences with one word from 1a.

1 I have lots of .... and ambition.
2 In a new situation, I need time to find my ....
3 I would try my .... at anything to be famous.
4 I would like to .... an apprenticeship when I leave school.
5 I'm going to .... at university when I finish school.
6 I'm not interested in following in anyone's ....
7 I have overcome one or two .... in my life.
8 I would never put my career on .... to raise a family.

2 Read the article quickly. What did the four people train to become?

A .... B .... C .... D ....

✔ EXAM SUCCESS

When you have to match questions or statements with different texts, answer the questions that you are sure about first and then go back to the ones where you have doubts.

➤ EXAM SUCCESS page 148

3 Read the article again. For questions 1–12, choose from the people (A–D). The people may be chosen more than once.

Which person

- jumped at an unexpected opportunity? 1 ....
- has clear plans for the future? 2 .... 3 ....
- didn't end up doing what he/she set out to do? 4 ....
- turned down academic opportunities to do an apprenticeship? 5 ....
- read about the apprenticeship by chance? 6 .... 7 ....
- feels the apprenticeship has helped him/her to be mature? 8 ....
- has already earned a lot of money for his/her company? 9 ....
- had to do something that he/she wasn't prepared for? 10 ....
- feels the apprenticeship has relaunched his/her career? 11 ....
- works in different locations? 12 ....

4 CRITICAL THINKING

Think! Then compare ideas with your class.

- How important is chance in finding a job?

5 Guess the meaning of the underlined words from the context. Then use your dictionary to check.

6 SPEAKING What about *you*?

1 Which is preferable, working for a company or starting your own business? What are the advantages and disadvantages of each?
2 Do you expect to do the same job all your life? Why /Why not?

Career Paths

Apprenticeship case studies

Home | News | Careers | Advice | Message Board | Login

A Despite graduating with a first-class degree, Louisa Troughton, 30, drifted between temping jobs before landing a costume apprenticeship at the Royal Opera House in London.

Louisa had studied publishing, but she found it hard to find work in her chosen field. She'd always loved dressmaking, so she saved up and did a part-time one-year course in tailoring while continuing to work in a shop. At college one day, she saw a poster advertising the two-year apprenticeship; she applied and beat 70 applicants to win the place.

On her first day, she expected to be pressing clothes, but instead was asked to make a waistcoat for a production of *Nabucco* by Verdi. It took a week and when she saw it being worn in the final rehearsal, she was terrified in case it fell apart. Now, a year on, her confidence has grown.

> *The best bit is bringing friends to watch ballets.*

'Everyone here is at the top of their game and so inspiring,' she says. 'The best bit is bringing friends to watch ballets and operas that I have contributed to.'

Although Louisa isn't guaranteed a job at the end of her apprenticeship, she believes it will show future employers she has experienced real situations in a work environment.

B After completing his final year at college, Andrew Pidgeon, 18, was interested in finding full-time employment which allowed him to continue to learn. One day he stumbled upon information about apprenticeships and decided that he would apply for a position in marketing.

> *I now feel that my career is really moving forward.*

Soon he was organising events, updating the website and creating case studies as a member of the Truro and Penwith College Business Centre team. But it was his report on a new smartphone application that gained him recognition. The college was asked to trial an app which allows the user to find apprenticeship vacancies across the country on their mobile. Andrew's report gave important feedback and offered advice on how the user experience could be improved. The National Apprentice Service was so impressed that the report was used in their national marketing activities. He has since created a special Twitter account specifically for young people interested in apprenticeships.

Andrew intends to continue his career in marketing and would like to work for a multinational company in the future. 'When I finished college, it felt like my progression had ground to a halt, but I now feel that my career is really moving forward,' he says.

C Jessica Kirby, 19, didn't know what an apprenticeship was until a chance meeting in a restaurant. She'd turned down a place at university because of the high cost of tuition fees, and was working as a waitress while deciding what to do. When a customer suggested that the restaurant should have a mailing list, Jessica immediately made one and asked the woman to fill in her details. 'If you didn't work here, I'd offer you a job,' she said.

> *My proactive approach swung it.*

The next day Jessica emailed the woman to see if she was serious, and was offered an interview for an apprenticeship. It turned out that the customer was the chairwoman of a PR company. 'She told me that my proactive approach had swung it, and I got the position,' Jessica says.

Although Jessica was worried she would be doing basic office work, within two weeks she was writing press releases and organising launches. And with two months to go until the end of her apprenticeship, she has been offered a permanent job with the company.

Jessica has no regrets about not going to university. 'I can't just lie in bed and skip a lecture. I have to be responsible, but that's a good thing,' she says.

D When Ged left school at 17, he decided to do an apprenticeship rather than go to university. It may seem a surprising choice to some but Ged, now 20, is confident he made the right decision. 'I left school when I was 17 with 4 university offers, but chose to do an apprenticeship with IBM. I chose an apprenticeship because I think that having real job experience is much more valuable these days than having a degree,' he explains.

Ged works at IBM across the UK, leading a team of software developers to help clients in the insurance industry, working closely with them to ensure technical problems are resolved and customers are happy.

And he is finding the experience invaluable. According to Ged, the best thing about being an apprentice is working with some of the brightest people in the industry, giving him the opportunity to learn from the best and push himself out of his comfort zone every day. He also loves helping to create technology that is used by billions of people every day.

> *In the future I would love to start my own company.*

Ged has already achieved a lot in his short career so far, including delivering a software demonstration that resulted in a six-figure deal for IBM. And it seems the sky's the limit for this ambitious young apprentice. 'I'd like to gain more skills and experiences and eventually work for IBM in a foreign country. I would love to start my own company.'

Serving an IT apprenticeship can give you valuable insight into the industry.

Flipped classroom: watch the grammar presentation video.

Articles – 1

1 Match each sentence a–i with a rule 1–8. Rule 8 has two sentences.

a Louisa drifted between temping jobs before landing **a** costume apprenticeship.

b At college one day, she saw a poster advertising **the** two-year apprenticeship.

c She believes it will show (-) future employers she has experienced real situations.

d (-) Initiative is something that employers look for.

e The woman turned out to be **the** chairwoman.

f **The** best bit is bringing friends to watch ballets and operas that I have contributed to.

g She did a part-time one-year course in tailoring while continuing to work in **a** shop.

h It was an apprenticeship aimed at **the** unemployed.

i She was working as **a** waitress while deciding what she wanted to do.

We use *the*:

1 to refer to a thing or person that has been previously mentioned or that we already know about.

2 when there is only one thing or person.

3 with superlative adjectives and *first, last, only, same.*

4 with an adjective to talk about a group.

We use *a/an*:

5 to refer to a thing or person for the first time.

6 to say what somebody's job is in general.

7 to talk about one of a number of things without being specific.

We use no article:

8 with uncountable nouns and plural countable nouns to make general statements.

GRAMMAR REFERENCE ➤ PAGE 120

2 Choose the correct alternative.

1 My ambition is to become *a/the/–* professional singer one day.

2 I'm not sure if he has *a/the/–* drive to get to the top.

3 *A/The/–* young need opportunities to get on in life.

4 There must be *a/the/–* way to get promoted in this company.

5 She has *a/the/–* high aspirations.

6 Today *a/the/–* prime minister is going to announce new job creation schemes.

7 *A/The/–* money isn't the main reason to choose a job.

8 Yesterday I had *an/the/–* accident at work.

9 It's *an/the/–* only job I've ever really wanted to do.

10 Life as *an/the/–* electrician is harder than you think.

3 Complete the text with *a/an, the* or – .

Sarah Maycott served (a) .... apprenticeship in Smithco, (b) .... company that makes (c) .... musical instruments. Her boss says: 'Sarah has done more for (d) .... company in her two years here than many people do in (e) .... lifetime.' Sarah works as (f) .... personal assistant in (g) .... marketing department, but she is also mad about (h) .... music. Sarah says: '(i) .... guitar is my favourite instrument, which is lucky because it's also (j) .... most important instrument in our catalogue.' Sarah really enjoyed (k) .... practical aspect of her apprenticeship. 'In general, I think it's great when (l) .... students can do something they enjoy, get (m) .... useful qualification and earn (n) .... money all at the same time!'

Articles – 2

4 Look at the sentences and complete the rules.

a I want to go to university one day.

b We went to the university to attend an open day where they explained what life is like there.

c We went to the hospital yesterday to see my cousin, who's ill.

d When she had her accident, she was in hospital for a week.

1 We *use/don't use the* with places like *university, school, hospital, prison* when we talk about the general idea of what these places are for.

2 We *use/don't use the* with places like *university, school, hospital, prison* when we talk about the physical buildings.

GRAMMAR REFERENCE ➤ PAGE 120

5 Add *the* to these sentences where necessary.

1 They put him in .... prison for stealing funds.

2 Do you know the way to .... university?

3 I've never been in .... hospital for anything.

4 I've heard builders are doing work at .... college.

5 When I leave .... school, I want to go to .... college to do a course in tourism.

6 We bought some flowers on our way to .... hospital to visit our cousin.

6 Correct the mistakes with articles in these questions.

1 What are your chances of becoming millionaire?

2 Do you have the aspirations? What are they?

3 What are biggest problems facing the young today?

4 Do you think the unemployment is rising or falling?

5 What is university nearest your home like?

6 What are challenges young people face in the world of work?

7 SPEAKING Work with a partner. Ask and answer the questions in 6.

Verb-noun collocations

1 Work with a partner. Match the verbs (1–6) with the list of nouns that they commonly go with (a–f).

1 embark on
2 gain
3 overcome
4 experience
5 take up
6 undertake

a adversity, fear, obstacle, resistance, problem, setback
b career, hobby, post, position
c career, course, project, venture
d confidence, insight, knowledge, experience, qualification, understanding
e problem, situation, pain, change
f investigation, study, survey, task, analysis

2 Use the collocations in 1 to rewrite the underlined section in each sentence. You may need to add other words.

1 I have too much free time. I should start a new pastime. *take up a new hobby*
2 He started working as a journalist.
3 We need to ask people their opinions of the product.
4 She's becoming more and more sure of herself each day.
5 I've dealt successfully with lots of negative issues since I started working here.
6 We began to understand how a company works.
7 He began to work as manager of the company in 2012.
8 I never want to live through a similar event again.

3 Match 1–8 with a–h to make common verb–noun collocations.

1 voice	a pressure
2 pay	b the consequences/the pros and cons
3 speak	c an opinion
4 cause	d attention
5 suffer	e confidence
6 inspire	f a setback
7 weigh up	g your mind
8 stand	h trouble

4 Complete the text with the correct form of these verbs.

cause • embark • experience • gain • overcome • pay
speak • stand • suffer • take up • voice • weigh

Helen (a) .... on a career in engineering in 2012. At university she studied maths and everyone thought that she would (b) .... teaching. While at university, she heard about an engineering apprenticeship scheme. She (c) .... up the pros and cons and decided to apply for it. At first, she (d) .... a few setbacks. She was one of only two female engineers in her company and she wondered if she would be able to (e) .... the pressure. She was too afraid to (f) .... her opinions and she never disagreed with anyone because she didn't want to (g) .... trouble. However, she realised though that no-one took her seriously or (h) .... any attention to her as a result. With time, Helen managed to (i) .... these problems. She decided to stand up for herself and (j) .... her mind, and discovered that people began to respect her more. She (k) .... confidence and didn't (l) .... any difficulties after that. She is now one of the most respected engineers in her company.

5 Complete the sentences with these nouns. Ignore the spaces at the start of the sentences.

attention • confidence • mind • opinions • pressure
pros and cons • setbacks • trouble

1 … inspires .... in other people.
2 … always speaks his/her ....
3 … is sometimes afraid of voicing his/her ....
4 … pays no .... to what other people say.
5 … has suffered .... in his/her career.
6 … never causes ....
7 … can stand a lot of ....
8 … usually weighs up the .... before he/she acts.

6 SPEAKING Work with a partner. Think of the best people, famous or otherwise, to go in the spaces at the start of the sentences in 5. Justify your choices.

Succeeding in INTERVIEWS

LIFE SKILLS OBJECTIVES

- To learn how to prepare for an interview
- To understand successful interview techniques
- To prepare and practise answering interview questions

KEY CONCEPTS

strengths and weaknesses [n]: *What are your strengths and weaknesses? My strength is my creativity. My weakness is that I'm a perfectionist.* **person specification [n]:** *The person specifications will tell you what type of person they're looking for.* **long-term goals [n]:** *My long-term goal is to take on a senior role in a marketing campaign.*

1 SPEAKING **Work with a partner. Discuss these questions.**

1 Have you ever had an interview? If so, when and what for?
2 When and why do you expect to be interviewed in the future?
3 How well-prepared for an interview do you think you are right now? Why?

2 Read these Dos and Don'ts from a website. Decide whether each one is a Do or a Don't for a job interview. Compare your ideas with a partner.

1 *Don't* lie.
2 *Do* turn off your mobile.
3 .... find out where the venue is beforehand, how to get there and how long it takes.
4 .... read from notes or your CV.
5 .... find out what kind of interview it will be beforehand so you can prepare.
6 .... prepare answers for the main questions – for example, 'Why do you want the job?'
7 .... quote real examples of when you've used certain skills.
8 .... ask about money.
9 .... ask for feedback on your performance at the interview.
10 .... be late.
11 .... dress smartly, look bright and attentive and speak clearly and coherently.
12 .... use slang words.
13 .... criticise former colleagues.
14 .... prepare some questions to ask at the end.

3 READING **Read the advice opposite about how to succeed during an interview. Compare the advice to your ideas in 2.**

4 Read the tips again. Answer these questions.

1 What are the different styles of interview referred to?
2 How can you predict the kind of questions you're going to be asked?
3 Why can talking about your weaknesses be an opportunity?
4 Why is it important to dress smartly and speak confidently?
5 What is the real purpose of an interview?
6 What do you think are the reasons behind the 'things to avoid'?

5 LISTENING 27 **Two students, Hector and Jennifer, are practising for an interview. Watch the video or listen. Make notes about how successful Hector is in the following areas:**

- his clothes
- his body language
- the language he uses
- how prepared he is to answer questions

6 LISTENING 27 **Watch or listen again to the interview. Make a note of the questions the interviewer asks.**

INTERVIEW TIPS

Good preparation is essential to a successful interview. Here are some tips to make the best first impression.

BEFORE THE INTERVIEW

1 Do find out what type of interview you can expect to have. It may be an interview with a panel, or just one person interviewing several candidates at the same time. If you have a group interview, it's often because the interviewer wants to see how you interact with people, to find out if you are a leader or a team player. The style of interview should be indicated on the letter you receive, but if you have doubts, do contact the company in advance to find out.

2 Find out as much as possible about the company you are applying to, and the particular job they are offering. The job description and the person specification will tell you the type of person that the company is looking for. This will enable you to predict the questions that you are likely to be asked.

3 Prepare your answers to probable questions in advance of the interview. An interviewer will usually ask about your strengths and weaknesses. Do give concrete examples to illustrate your strengths, and be constructive about your weaknesses by saying what positive steps you have taken to overcome them.

4 Prepare two or three questions that you can ask at the end of the interview. These should be about the company or the role and demonstrate that you are really interested in the company.

5 Study your CV and application form carefully before the interview so that the information you give about yourself and your experience is consistent with what you have written.

6 Find out the location of the venue for your interview, how to get there and how long it will take so that you arrive in plenty of time on the day.

THE DAY OF THE INTERVIEW

7 Aim to create a positive first impression by dressing smartly. Showing up in jeans and trainers won't make a great first impression. Knowing the type of organisation you have applied to will help you decide what is best to wear.

8 Speak confidently and clearly. Only seven per cent of the interviewer's opinion of you will be formed by what you say – the rest will be judged on how you look and sound. If you feel nervous, breathe slowly and deeply to help you stay calm. Remember that an interview is for the company to find out if you are the right person for them, and if it is right for you.

9 Be as enthusiastic as possible about the role and the company. Smile and let your personality shine through.

THINGS TO AVOID

- *Arriving late or in a hurry*
- *Criticising former employers or colleagues*
- *Lying about your skills and experience*
- *Asking about the salary*
- *Asking for feedback on your performance at the end of the interview*

LIFE TASK

You are going to practise your interview technique.

Follow this plan:

1 *Make notes about your answers to the questions that the interviewer used in 5.*

2 *Choose one person to interview and one person to be the interviewee. Practise your interview.*

3 *Discuss how successful the interview was and any suggestions for improvement.*

4 *Swap roles and repeat stages 2 and 3.*

1 SPEAKING **Work with a partner. Discuss these questions.**

1 What do you think is the best way to get started in your chosen career?
2 Do you know anyone who has done an internship?
3 How common are internships in your country?

internship (n): A temporary job that a student or recent graduate takes in order to get experience in the area they want to work in.
intern (n): A person who does an internship.

2 SPEAKING **Work with a partner. Look at the photos and answer the questions.**

1 Who can you see in the photos? What are they doing?
2 What are the similarities and differences between what they are doing? Compare and contrast.
3 How useful do you think what they are doing is? Why?

VOCABULARY **Talking about internships**

3a Look at the sentences. What do you think the words and expressions in bold mean?

1 Your parents have to **support** you financially.
2 Regular workers think you're just **passing through**.
3 You **reach the point** where you want a decent salary.
4 You have to learn to **stand up for yourself**.
5 You **get a foot in the business**.
6 You're **under the nose** of the people who are recruiting.
7 Companies **take you for granted** and don't give proper training.
8 It's sometimes difficult to **make ends meet** without a proper salary.

3b Match these definitions, explanations and synonyms with the words and phrases in bold in 3a.

a expect you to always be there and don't value you enough
b arrive at a time or situation
c have just enough money to survive
d be assertive about your needs
e get the opportunity to start working in a particular field
f provide money, food or accommodation to enable you to live
g clearly visible because you are near
h be at a place for a short time before moving on to another place

4 SPEAKING **Work with a partner. Decide if these are possible advantages or disadvantages of an internship.**

a heavy workload • career advancement
insight into how a company works
long/antisocial hours • mundane tasks
networking opportunities
on the job training • perks

✓ EXAM SUCCESS

In the next listening activity, you have to answer comprehension questions, but there is a limit to the number of words you can write. The words that you write will actually appear in the recording. It is not necessary to change them at all. But make sure that you do not write more than the number of words given in the instructions or you will lose marks.

➤ EXAM SUCCESS page 153

5 LISTENING 28 **Listen to a podcast about internships. Write no more than three words for each answer.**

1 What type of company did Amy do her internship in?

....

2 What did she expect from her internship?

....

3 What does Jane think that most companies offer interns?

....

4 Apart from experience, what other benefit does Peter say internships offer?

....

5 What do you have to do as an intern, according to Jane?

....

6 How do many companies recruit these days?

....

7 What does Amy believe you must be to do an internship?

....

8 What money does Peter have to pay his expenses?

....

6 SPEAKING **What about *you*?**

1 What ideas that you heard justify internships?
2 What drawbacks are there, both for the intern and other workers?
3 Would you consider doing an internship in the future? Why/Why not?
4 What would you suggest to stop companies from taking advantage of interns?

Collaborative tasks - 2

1 **Look at the jobs. How would you rate them in terms of job satisfaction? Put them in order from the most satisfying (1) to the least satisfying (6).**

- artist
- doctor
- sportsman/woman
- humanitarian aid worker
- business owner
- journalist

2 SPEAKING **Work with a partner and compare your ideas in 1. Give reasons for your choices.**

3 **Read the task. Is it necessary to come to a decision?**

> Talk together about whether you think these jobs would provide job satisfaction. Give reasons for your answers.

4 LISTENING 29 **Listen to two students doing the task. Did they mention the same things you talked about in 2?**

5 **PRACTICE MAKES PERFECT** SPEAKING **Work with a partner and do this task. Use expressions from the Speaking bank.**

> Look at the task on page 165. You will see different reasons why people choose jobs. Talk together about how important you think these factors are in choosing a job.

✓ EXAM SUCCESS

Don't panic if the person you are talking to disagrees with you or asks you to explain something in more detail. This is to see if you can come up with new ideas and arguments spontaneously.

➤ EXAM SUCCESS page 152

SPEAKING BANK

Useful words and expressions to make generalisations

- Usually,/Normally,
- Most people
- Mostly …
- The majority of
- In most cases,
- On the whole
- In general,
- To a great extent
- By and large
- Broadly speaking

A covering letter

1 SPEAKING **Work with a partner. Read this job advertisement, ignoring the notes. Would you be interested in applying for any of the different posts? Why/Why not?**

2 **Read this task based on the advertisement and notes in 1, then read the letter. Does the letter contain all the information required?**

> You are looking for a job and have seen an advertisement for posts on a cruise ship, which you are very interested in. Write a covering letter including all the information in the notes.

12 Coltrane Drive
Newcastle
NE01 33E

20th June 2016

Recruitment Officer
K+P Cruises
20 Atlantic Parade
Plymouth

Dear Sir/Madam,

1 I am writing in response to your advertisement which appeared in the Newcastle Times on 19th June. I am particularly interested in the position of waitress.

2 I am 18 years old and have just finished secondary school. I am planning to study modern languages at university in 12 months' time but feel that it would be beneficial to me to experience the world of work before resuming my full-time studies. I would welcome the opportunity to work and travel on a cruise ship.

3 I believe that I am well-suited for this job. Last summer I had experience of working as a waitress in La Casa Italia, a busy Italian restaurant in which I worked part-time for two months. In addition to this, I can speak French and Spanish fluently and believe that knowledge of three languages would be highly useful on a cruise ship with international passengers, some of whom will speak no English.

4 As for my personal qualities, I consider myself to be very dynamic, being keen on all types of sports. I also believe I am highly sociable as I love meeting new people. I feel sure that these two qualities will help me to give prompt, friendly service.

5 I would be delighted to attend an interview at your earliest convenience. As requested, I enclose my curriculum vitae and the contact details of my referee, Mr Colin Hughes, for whom I worked at La Casa Italia.

Yours faithfully,

Grace Day

GREAT SALARY, NO EXPENSES, FREE TRAVEL!

We are looking for keen young people for different positions on board our latest cruise ship.

We need:

- Waiters/waitresses
- Child monitors
- Gift shop assistants
- Physical fitness coaches
- Entertainment staff

Yes! worked for a month in a pizza restaurant

love sports and social activities

Are you young, dynamic and trustworthy?

Have you got any special skills?

speak French and Spanish

Send your CV and a covering letter clearly stating the post you wish to apply for and the name of a referee to:
Recruitment Officer, K+P Cruises,
20 Atlantic Parade, Plymouth

referee = former boss at restaurant

3 **Read the letter again. Which paragraph:**

1 gives basic information about the applicant and why they are applying for the job? ....
2 says why the person is writing and which job the person is applying for? ....
3 gives information so that the company can continue further with the application? ....
4 gives information about the applicant's character? ....
5 states the applicant's relevant experience and/or relevant skills? ....

✓ EXAM SUCCESS

In this type of task, it is essential to identify the person you are writing to, the style you need to use and the pieces of information to be included. You lose marks if any information is missing. But remember that if you are given notes, you should expand them and give details to add realistic context.

➤ EXAM SUCCESS page 151

4 **Find the incomplete expressions in the letter in 2. Then complete the Writing bank.**

WRITING BANK

Useful words and expressions in covering letters

- I am writing in .... to/in connection with …
- I am .... interested in the job/post/position of …
- I would welcome the .... to work for your company.
- I believe that I am well-.................... for this job since …
- I have experience .... working …
- I have a working knowledge of …
- I .... myself to be …
- I was in charge of …
- I would be .... to attend an interview at your earliest ....
- I .... my curriculum vitae.

Prepositions in relative clauses

5a Look at these pairs of sentences. Which alternative in bold in each pair is more formal?

1a La Casa Italia is a busy restaurant **in which** I worked for two months.

1b La Casa Italia is a busy restaurant **which** I worked **in** for two months.

2a My referee is Mr Colin Hughes, **for whom** I worked at La Casa Italia.

2b My referee is Mr Colin Hughes, **who** I worked **for** at La Casa Italia.

5b Look at the sentences again. Do we use *that* when the preposition goes just before the relative pronoun? When do we use *whom* rather than *who*?

5c Look at these two sentences then read the information below.

3a This is useful for international passengers, **some of whom** will speak no English.

3b I hope that you find my curriculum vitae of interest, **in which case** I would be delighted to attend an interview.

1 In 3a, *some of whom* is a noun phrase containing a relative pronoun. Other similar phrases are *many of whom/which, most of whom/which, the first/last of which/whom.*

2 In 3b, *in which case* is an adverbial phrase containing a relative pronoun. Other similar phrases are *at which point, for which reason.*

GRAMMAR REFERENCE ➤ PAGE 120

6 **Rewrite these sentences to make them more formal.**

1 Your company is the first which I have made a formal application to.

Your company is the first to which I have made a formal application.

2 The recruitment officer is the person who I spoke to.

3 She is the teacher whose class I studied in.

4 They are the colleagues that I worked with.

5 The director was a person I had great respect for.

6 There are some things that we have no control over.

7 **Join the sentences using a noun or adverbial phrase containing a relative pronoun.**

1 In this job I met many new people. A large number of them are now good friends of mine.

In this job I met many new people, a large number of whom are now good friends of mine.

2 I will be available until June. At that point I will resume my studies.

3 I have had several jobs. The last was working in a department store.

4 I have worked with a number of chefs. The first one was a famous French chef.

5 You may decide you need another referee. In that case, I will send you the details upon request.

6 I have two sisters. One of them runs her own company.

8 **Read the advert. How appealing is the job to you? Why?**

Summer on the farm!

Working with acres of organic gardens, teaching children about the environment, enjoying beautiful swimming in the river. Sound appealing?

Edalan Farm is looking for seasonal staff from June to September. Duties include light work on the farm, meal preparation, organising and leading activities for children.

Reasonable pay and accommodation provided. Good level of English essential. Driving licence preferred.

A great opportunity to spend the summer in England.

Please send CV and covering letter to:
Recruitments, Edalan Farm
PO Box 18736 Kent NX3 794

9 **PRACTICE MAKES PERFECT Do the task below. Make a paragraph plan with the main information to include in each section, and use expressions from the Writing bank.**

Write a covering letter for the job in 8. Include that:

- You are learning to drive at the moment.
- You are quick to learn new skills.
- You have been studying English for many years.
- You have experience of working at a supermarket.

WRITING BANK ➤ PAGE 161

Grammar reference

Articles

A/An

We use *a/an* with singular, countable nouns. We use it:

when we mention something for the first time, or to say that the person or thing is one of a number of things or people.

*She's got **a** car.*

to say what somebody's profession is.

*He's **a** researcher.*

The

We use *the* with countable (singular and plural) and uncountable nouns. We use it:

to refer to something or somebody previously mentioned or that we already know about.

*She's got a car. **The** car's brand new.*

to talk about specific things or people.

***The** car she bought was expensive.*

***The** people who work there are really helpful.*

to talk about something unique, something that there is only one of.

***the** Sun, **the** government (in a particular country), **the** floor, **the** sky, **the** world*

with superlative adjectives and adverbs, and *first/last/only/same*.

*It's always **the** same story.*

with singular nouns to refer in general to all members of a group.

***The** piano is a difficult instrument to play.*

with an adjective to talk about a group. In this case, the verb is always plural.

***The** unemployed are suffering more than most.*

No article

We do not use an article:

with plural countable nouns or uncountable nouns when we are talking about people or things in general.

Economists say there will be more jobs next year.

Society needs to change.

with a person's job title or their unique position in a company.

My brother is Head of Finance at the university.

Articles with school, university, etc.

USE

We do not use an article with *school, university, hospital, college, prison, church* when we talk about what these places are for.

My sister is at university. = She's a student, not there right now.

We use *the* with *school, university, hospital, college, prison, church* when we talk about the physical buildings.

*Builders are doing work at **the** university.*

Prepositions in relative clauses

When we need a preposition with the relative pronouns *which, whom* or *whose*, the preposition can come before the relative pronoun. This is generally more formal.

*I studied with an American professor **from whom** I learnt many fascinating things. = more formal*

*I studied with an American professor **who** I learnt many fascinating things **from**. = less formal*

*This is the office **in which** I worked. = more formal*

*This is the office **which** I worked **in**. = less formal*

We cannot use *that* after prepositions.

After a preposition, *who* becomes *whom*.

Prepositions appear in several noun phrases which contain relative pronouns, e.g.

some of which/whom, many of which/whom, most of which/whom, the first/last of which/whom.

They also appear in several adverbial phrases which contain relative pronouns, e.g.

in which case, at which point, for which reason.

Vocabulary

For verb-noun collocations, life and career developments and internships, see wordlist page 143.

Grammar revision

Articles / 13 points

1 Decide if the sentences are correct. Tick (✓) the correct sentences and rewrite the incorrect sentences.

1 When I finish university I want to be a doctor.
2 The snow leopard is in danger of extinction.
3 I think it's a best idea to go by car.
4 She's just become head of the marketing.
5 His job is to protect the innocent.
6 It's an only chance we have.
7 I don't believe that the books will disappear because of new technologies.

2 Choose the correct alternative.

1 My parents met while studying at *–/the* university.
2 The teachers wanted to know why I hadn't gone to *–/the* school yesterday.
3 We went to *–/the* church to take photos of it.
4 The journalist went to *–/the* prison to interview a notorious criminal.
5 He stayed in *–/the* hospital while they did tests.
6 He went to *–/the* university to hear a talk.

Prepositions in relative clauses / 7 points

3 Complete the sentences with these words.

all of whom • at which • at which point • for which • for whom • in which case • on whom

1 I have lots of things ………… to be grateful.
2 You might need some help, ………… just call me.
3 I have many colleagues ………… I know I can rely.
4 I admire the works of Tolstoy, Dostoyevsky and Chekhov, ………… were Russian.
5 He'll speak from 5 pm to 6 pm, ………… there will be a short break.
6 There are students ………… this type of approach is rather tricky.
7 This is the moment ………… we should stop.

Vocabulary revision

VERB–NOUN COLLOCATIONS / 7 points

1 Match 1–7 with a–g to make sentences.

1 He has suffered
2 He isn't afraid to speak
3 The actor is about to embark on
4 He usually voices
5 I think he should gain
6 He always inspires
7 He has overcome

a a deeper understanding of how the job really works.
b his mind because he believes in being sincere.
c his fear of flying.
d confidence because he really knows what he's doing.
e a new project with his wife.
f a major setback as he's just been fired.
g opinions that few people agree with.

LIFE AND CAREER DEVELOPMENTS / 7 points

2 Read the definitions and complete the expressions.

1 start to feel confident and able to deal with something = ………… *your feet*
2 stop something from happening now, but it may happen later = *put something on* …………
3 be successful in life = *get* ………… *in life*
4 do an activity for the first time, to see if you like it or are good at it = *try your* ………… *at something*
5 do the same work or achieve the same success as someone before you = *follow in somebody's* …………
6 learn about a job by actually doing it = *serve an* …………
7 be in a particular situation after doing something = *end* ………… *doing something*

INTERNSHIPS / 6 points

3 Complete the sentences with an appropriate verb.

1 After three internships, she ………… the point when she wanted to be paid.
2 He learnt to ………… up for himself.
3 It was hard to ………… ends meet so he got a loan.
4 I didn't know other workers. I was just ………… through.
5 The company was ………… him for granted so he left.
6 The internship helped him ………… a foot in the business.

Total: / 40 points

10 Found in translation

Reading

VOCABULARY Communication/communication breakdown

1 Match these expressions with six definitions. What do the other expressions mean?

find something puzzling • get the wrong end of the stick • imply something • make a gaffe • make a (witty) remark • misinterpret something/someone offend someone unintentionally • take something literally • talk at cross purposes • understand nuances

1 misunderstand something (colloquial)
2 when two people think they're talking about the same thing but in fact they aren't
3 make someone upset and angry without meaning to
4 make an embarrassing mistake in public, especially one that upsets someone
5 say something (clever and funny)
6 understand slight differences that may be difficult to notice but are important

2 Read the three texts about translation. Then write a one or two-sentence summary of each one.

✓ EXAM SUCCESS

In reading activities where you complete tables, summaries or sentences, read the instructions carefully to know whether you can write any words, or any number of words, in the spaces. Sometimes you are given a list of words or phrases to choose from.

➤ EXAM SUCCESS page 153

3 Read text A again and complete this summary. Use words from the text. Use no more than three words for each answer.

When companies launch brands, they try to keep the words in slogans to (a) .... Even so, slogans sometimes have to be adapted. For example, 'small talk', which means a conversation about (b) .... in English, was changed for other countries, even where the language is (c) .... Mistranslations can be expensive. When (d) .... made a mistake in their slogan, it cost the company millions. In Japan, a mistranslation by (e) .... led to a change a national custom. Now women buy chocolate for their (f) .... on Valentine's Day.

4 Read text B again and complete the table. Use no more than two words.

Language	English words	Comments
Spanish	'reddish brown' or 'dark red'	Actual meaning is 'sour cherry'. There is (a) .... in English.
Vietnamese	blue and green	Same word used for (b) .... and ....
Hanuno'o	black, white, red, green	There are only (c) .... for colours.
Pirahã	(d)	Speakers use a comparison – 'like blood'
Navajo	black	Two words to describe (e) .... and ....
Spanish	brown	There is a (f) .... words, depending on what it describes.

5 Read text C again and decide if the statements are True (T), False (F) or if the information is Not Given (NG).

1 There are over 500 interpreters in the European Parliament. T/F/NG
2 Interpreters make sure that the language in treaties can't be misinterpreted. T/F/NG
3 They are able to agree the language used in treaties quickly. T/F/NG
4 There wasn't a Dzongkha speaker in the US State Department when the letter was received. T/F/NG
5 The first Dzongkha expert was unable to translate the letter from the King of Bhutan. T/F/NG
6 The US State Department was relieved when they discovered what the letter said. T/F/NG

6 CRITICAL THINKING

Think! Then compare ideas with your class.

- How does language shape the way we think?

7 Guess the meaning of the underlined words from the context. Then use your dictionary to check.

8 SPEAKING What about *you*?

Do you think technology is as effective as humans when it comes to translation? Why/Why not?

TRANSLATION

HOW LANGUAGE SHAPES OUR LIVES

A In the global economy, language is crucial. Companies often work hard to create brands that are recognisable throughout the world, and at the same time try to keep words to a minimum in their logos and advertising campaigns.

When the iPod shuffle came out, the campaign was based on two words: 'small talk'. In English, this refers to superficial conversation about trivial things like weather, but many languages don't use these words in the same way. So instead of translating the slogan, the company adapted it. In fact, it had to be adapted differently even for countries that speak the same language. In Spain, the phrase used was 'Ya sabe hablar', which is something that parents say when children start talking. In Latin American Spanish, the message read 'mira quien habla', or 'look who's talking'. France chose the slogan 'donnez lui de la voix', or 'let him speak' while in French Canada it was 'petit parleur, grand faiseur' meaning 'says little, does much'.

Mistranslating words can cost a company millions, as in the case of one banking giant. The slogan for their advertising campaign 'Assume Nothing' was mistranslated in several countries as 'Do Nothing'. The mistake cost $10,000 to correct.

In Japan, a mistranslation changed a national custom. In the mid 1950s, department stores began to introduce the idea of Valentine's Day. However, a statement from a company executive was incorrectly translated, leading people to believe that it was traditional for women to give chocolate to men. Japan now has a separate holiday on 14th March, when men buy white chocolate for their loved ones. On 14th February, it's still the women who buy chocolate for the men.

B Colours are one of the first things most children learn to say, both in a first and second language, so you'd think that they'd be easy to translate. Apparently not! Some words don't have a direct translation. The Spanish word *guindo,* for example, actually means 'sour cherry', but it's difficult to convey the same bright colour in English. The only way to describe it is by using approximates, like 'reddish brown' or 'dark red'.

Other colours present even greater challenges. A surprising number of languages have the same word for both 'blue' and 'green'. Vietnamese, which has millions of speakers, uses the same word *xanh* to refer to both the sky and leaves on trees. In Japanese and Korean, a green traffic light can also be called a blue light.

Meanwhile, a language which is spoken in the Philippines called Hanuno'o has only four words to talk about colours – black, white, red and green. Pirahã, an Amazonian tribal language, has no words for colours at all! The only way to describe a colour is by comparing it to something else, such as 'like blood' for the colour red.

Some languages, on the other hand, have a number of words for just one colour. The Native American speakers of Navajo have two words for black. There's the black that is associated with darkness and another for the colour of coal. And in Spanish, there is a whole range of words to say 'brown', depending on whether it describes animals, hair colour, coffee or sugar.

C Logically, language plays an important part when it comes to international relations. In the European Parliament alone, 23 different languages are spoken. The Parliament relies on the assistance of hundreds of interpreters to do their work. Twenty-three languages may not seem much, but when you consider the many combinations, for example Swedish into Greek or Latvian into Maltese, there are 506 language combinations. It's not surprising that the writer Umberto Eco once said: 'The language of Europe is translation.'

When it comes to negotiating international treaties, interpreters are hard at work behind the scenes. They make sure that the language selected is acceptable to both sides and that it means exactly what it is intended to mean. In fact, the nuances of a single word are often debated for many hours before an agreement can be reached.

Virtually every communication between countries must be translated, even the simplest document. When President Obama received a letter from the King of Bhutan, the US State Department had to find someone familiar with the Dzongkha language to translate. After seaching everywhere, they managed to locate a specialist in the language. Unfortunately, he refused to do the translation, explaining that the letter was written in Royal Dzongkha, a language he felt he was not worthy to read. Anxious about possible diplomatic repercussions, the department's translation team eventually found another Dzongkha specialist. He was happy to report that the letter contained greetings to the President and wished him a happy new year.

Grammar in context

Gerunds and infinitives – rules and revision

1a Look at the sentences below. With a partner, discuss why you think the gerund or infinitive is used in each one.

a Many people can't stand **seeing** mistranslations of their own language.

b In Spanish there is a whole range of words **to say** 'brown'.

c Instead of **translating** the slogan, the company adapted it.

d **Mistranslating words** can cost a company millions.

e Even the words for colours can be too difficult **to translate**.

f It's difficult **to convey** the same bright colour in English.

g The US State Department had to find someone **to translate**.

h It's no use **trying** to negotiate a treaty if you don't have interpreters.

1b Do you usually use a gerund or an infinitive in these situations? Which sentence in 1a is an example of each?

1 after prepositions *gerund c*
2 after *too*, *enough*, *the first*, *the last*
3 to talk about purpose or use
4 after verbs of liking or disliking
5 as the subject/object of a sentence
6 after these noun phrases: *It's no good/use, It's (not) worth, There's no point (in), have difficulty/problems/trouble (in/with)*
7 immediately after adjectives
8 immediately after indefinite pronouns (somewhere, something, etc.)

GRAMMAR REFERENCE ➤ PAGE 132

2 Choose the correct alternative.

1 Many people believe it's worth *to keep/keeping* languages alive.
2 The last person *to speak/speaking* Wampanoag died a hundred years ago.
3 These Native Americans are now on a mission *to reclaim/reclaiming* it.
4 *Reviving/To revive* a language isn't easy.
5 One woman has succeeded in *to learn/learning* it from texts.
6 She now has classes *to teach/teaching* others to speak it, too.
7 She believes the language is something *to be/being* proud of.
8 She thinks it's important *to know/knowing* about the tribe's cultural heritage.

3 Complete the text with the correct form of the verbs given.

What's in a name? Well, some people say our name may make the difference between **(a)** .... (be) happy or unhappy in life. **(b)** .... (call) your child something unusual like Brooklyn, Romeo or Cruz is a question of personal taste, but your surname is a different matter. A British newspaper conducted a survey **(c)** .... (find out) if their readers' surnames influenced their lives. They wanted to know whether **(d)** .... (have) a surname with a letter nearer the start of the alphabet made you more successful than those with names nearer the end. Of course, people whose surnames begin with A are the first **(e)** .... (appear) on any list, whether it's a school register, a list of job interviewees or in a phone book. Do people whose surnames beginning with Y, for example, have trouble **(f)** .... (adapt) to that? **(g)** .... (do) the experiment, people had to give their surname, age and sex and then say how successful they had been according to various categories. It was interesting **(h)** .... (see) that the results showed that, in terms of career, people with surnames at the start of the alphabet were indeed more successful. Men seem **(i)** .... (be) affected by this effect more than women. Despite this, the survey proved that it's not worth **(j)** .... (worry) about having a surname starting with a late letter in the alphabet since the effects were very slight.

4 Complete the sentences with a verb in the gerund or infinitive. Make the sentences true for you.

1 I don't think there's any point in …
2 In my opinion, it's worth …
3 I think it's difficult …
4 After …, I feel really good.
5 I reckon … is a complete waste of time.
6 I can't stand …
7 I never have any problems …
8 At weekends, I try to do something …

5 SPEAKING Work with a partner. Compare your sentences in 4. Do you agree or disagree?

Phrasal verbs – communication

1 Match the phrasal verbs in bold with the explanations 1–10.

In a university staff meeting, Jacqueline **(a) brought up** the subject of whether computers should replace pen and paper in exams. She **(b) pointed out** that nowadays most pupils don't write everything down by hand. Bill **(c) picked up on** her point, mentioning that some of his students could hardly write anymore because they used computers for all their schoolwork. However, quite a few people **(d) spoke out** in favour of paper and pen, especially Karen. But every time Karen started saying something, Bill would **(e) cut in** and add another point himself. Because the conversation was quite heated, it was difficult for most people to **(f) make out** what Karen and Bill were saying. Karen got really angry with Bill's tone. She felt that he was **(g) talking down to** her, but he claimed he was just trying to **(h) spell out** his thoughts. What became clear was that neither side could **(i) get through to** the other, and so they all decided to **(j) turn to** another important issue.

1 change from one subject to another
2 make someone understand what you are trying to say
3 tell someone something
4 talk to someone as if you think they are not as clever or as important as you
5 start discussing
6 state your opinion firmly and publicly to protest against or defend something
7 interrupt
8 understand someone or something with difficulty
9 explain something very clearly, often because someone has not understood
10 talk in more detail about something that someone has mentioned

2 Rewrite each sentence using a phrasal verb in 1.

1 I finally made them understand what I was saying.
I finally got through to them.
2 Would you please stop interrupting!
3 Don't speak to me as if I was a child!
4 I'm going to explain my opinion as clearly as possible.
5 I'd like to introduce the issue of how the Internet influences language.
6 Then I'd like to change the topic and talk about teenage slang.
7 She isn't afraid of stating openly that she's against all forms of censorship.
8 Speak up, please, because I can't hear what you're saying.
9 Can I just say that this wasn't my idea?
10 I'd like to make a more detailed comment about what my colleague has just said.

3 Read the article and think of the word which best fits each gap. Use one word only in each gap.

IS WRITING BECOMING JUST AN ART FORM?

How often do people write nowadays? For many of us, the answer is 'not very often'. There are not many jobs in (a) .... people have to write by hand, so maybe all you write is the occasional shopping list or a quick message to someone that you leave on your desk or (b) .... home. By far (c) .... most common situation is where people type everything they write, either on a computer keyboard or on their mobile phone. If you've ever looked at handwriting from a hundred years ago or more, it can be almost impossible to make (d) .... what the words are. But some people predict that in the future handwriting will only (e) .... understood by a few experts in the subject (although it has been pointed (f) .... that even today it takes an expert to read a doctor's handwriting!). Some companies do insist on job applicants handing in handwritten covering letters, in (g) .... case the handwriting is usually analysed to build up a character portrait of the candidate. Not everybody would agree that good handwriting is the best evidence (h) .... which to base the decision to employ someone or not, but it is true that really good handwriting can create a great impression. If we turn (i) .... China and Japan, handwriting there really is an art form, but it's not such (j) .... easy one for kids to learn as there are over 3,000 different characters to memorise. The problem is not to recognise them, it's to remember the strokes of the pen you need to actually make them. A great number of children spend all their time texting (k) .... other and working at the computer keyboard. They certainly almost never pick up a pen or a paintbrush in order to write anything. (l) .... a result, there is now a new Chinese word, *tibiwangzi*, which means 'take pen, forget character'.

✔ EXAM SUCCESS

When you finish, read the complete text with your answers in place and see if your answers (a) make sense and (b) fit grammatically with the words around them. Check that you have used one word, and only one word, for each space.

➤ EXAM SUCCESS page 151

4 SPEAKING What about *you*?

1 Do you think handwriting will disappear in the future? Why/Why not?
2 Do you think it matters if handwriting disappears? Why/Why not?

Taking NOTES

ACADEMIC SKILLS OBJECTIVES

- To evaluate your current note-taking skills
- To learn some strategies for taking good notes
- To learn common abbreviations and symbols for taking notes

KEY CONCEPTS

abbreviations [n]: *Use abbreviations instead of writing complete words.* **highlight [v]:** *Highlight key points in colour so that they are easily recognisable.* **bullet points [n]:** *Organise the information on the page using bullet points or a mind map.*

1 SPEAKING **Work with a partner. Answer these questions.**

1. How do you usually make notes during lessons?
2. Do you review your notes after the lesson? If so, how do you do it? If not, why not?
3. Look at the notebooks. Which of these ways of taking notes would you find most useful? Why?

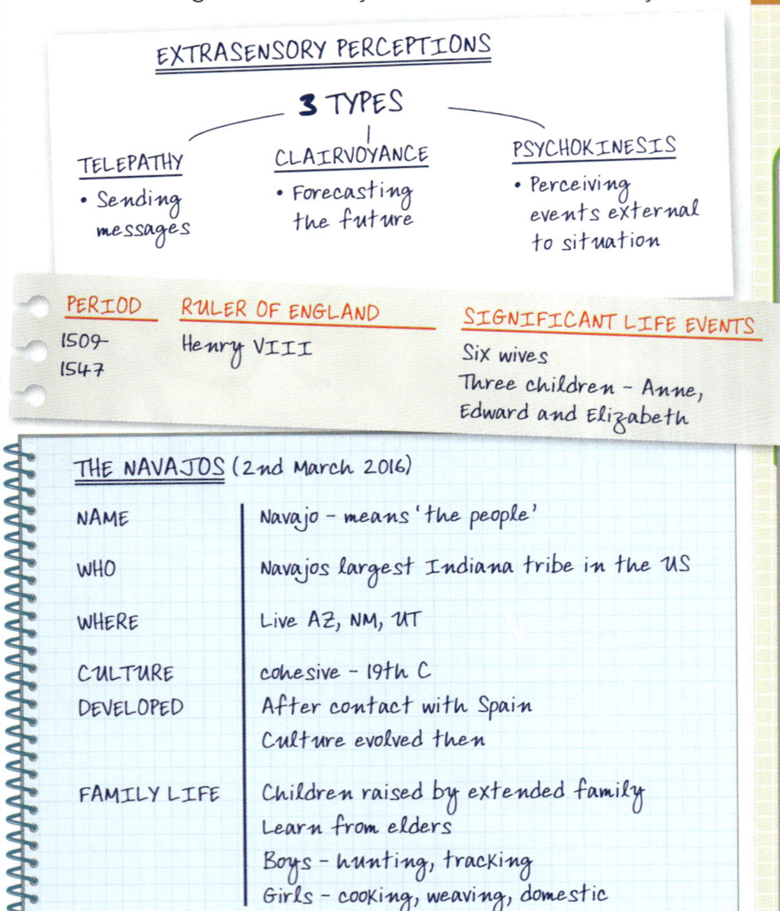

2 **Read the suggestions about note-taking. Which do you think are good ideas? Why? Why aren't the other ideas helpful?**

1. Write the date at the top of a new page.
2. Try to write down everything that the teacher says.
3. Write full sentences.
4. Use abbreviations or mathematical symbols.
5. Highlight key points in colour.
6. Write up your notes at home later.

3 READING **Read the advice about note-taking and check your answers in 2.**

NOTE-TAKING

Note-taking skills are essential, but not everyone knows how to do it. It's not simply a case of writing down everything the teacher says. Good note-taking requires students to evaluate, organise and summarise information and is a key life skill for students to learn. Students who take notes are seven times more likely to remember information one week after a lesson than those who simply listen. There are different ways to record information, and it's best to find the system that suits your learning style, but here are some suggestions to help.

Before the lesson

- Start by reviewing the notes from the previous lesson and look at the major ideas or specific facts that you were taught. Think of questions you would like to ask the teacher. This will help refresh your memory and get you ready for the lesson to come.
- Start a new page, and write the date.
- Organise your page in a way that suits you best. One way to do this is to draw a line down the centre of the page, leaving about two thirds of the width to the right, and a third to the left. The right-hand section is where you will write your notes during the lesson, and the left-hand side is for reviewing and organising later.

During the lesson

- Don't try to write down everything the teacher says. The average student writes only 1/3 of a word per second, while the average teacher says 2–3 words. Keep your notes brief. Write an outline of the key concepts, with supporting facts and examples using short phrases or sentences only.

4 Read the advice again. Answer the questions.

1. Why is it a good idea to read your notes before the lesson starts?
2. If you divide the page, what goes on the left of the line? And what goes on the right?
3. What aspects of a lecture should you try to write down?
4. What should you listen for to help you organise your notes?
5. When should you review your notes? Why?
6. Why isn't it necessary to write up your notes at home?

HOME | ABOUT US | FAQS | BLOGS | CONTACT US

SKILLS

- Develop your own system of abbreviations, such as w/ for 'with' or use mathematical symbols, e.g. <, =. Aim to be consistent with these so that you recognise them easily when you re-read your notes.
- Listen for clues from the teacher about how to organise your notes. Often a lesson will begin with a summary of the points that will be covered. Then the teacher will use phrases to signal what's important, e.g. 'There are two points of view …', "The third reason is … .' The lesson may then also end with a summary of what has been said.
- Organise the main points on the page in a way that suits you best, for example using bullet points, or a mind map.

After the lesson

- As soon as the lesson finishes, take a moment to look over your notes. Use this time to highlight in colour, circle or underline key concepts, or to write questions if anything isn't clear.
- Within 24 hours, look at your notes again to help transfer information from your short- to long-term memory. If you've left a margin on the left of the page, write here key words that summarise the main ideas of the lesson. If the notes are clear, you won't need to waste time writing everything up again.
- Regularly reviewing, reciting and practising your notes is the best way to learn and remember them.

5 SPEAKING Work with a partner. Discuss the advice for taking notes.

1. What things do you already do when taking notes?
2. What aspects of your note-taking do you think you should change?
3. What one idea in particular would you like to try?

6 Look at the common abbreviations. Work with a partner. What do you think the abbreviations mean?

1 +	**5** x	**9** info
2 =	**6** ?	**10** w/, w/o
3 ↑	**7** c	**11** →
4 ∴	**8** cf.	**12** v.

7 Match the abbreviations in 6 with the meanings a–l.

a compared to	**h** very
b increase	**i** with, without
c information	**j** possibly/uncertain/unproven
d about	**k** is the same as/results in
e so, therefore	**l** leads to, produces, causes
f and	
g no, not correct	

8 LISTENING 30 You're going to hear a lecture about language. First, re-read the advice and prepare your page. Then watch the video or listen to the lecture and take notes.

ACADEMIC TASK

You're going to write a short summary of the lecture. Work with a partner.

Follow this plan:

1. *Discuss and evaluate your note-taking. Are your notes clear? How could you improve them?*
2. *Compare the information in your notes. Do you have the same information?*
3. *Select the most important information in the lecture.*
4. *Write a short summary of the lecture.*
5. *Compare your summary with that of others in the class.*

Flipped classroom: watch the grammar presentation video.

1 SPEAKING **Work with a partner. Answer these questions.**

1. How common is it to dub foreign language films and TV shows in your country?
2. Do you prefer to watch films and TV shows that are dubbed or in the original version? Why?
3. What are some advantages and disadvantages of watching with subtitles?

✔ EXAM SUCCESS

In the next listening activity, you have to complete sentences. Remember that usually you need to write between one and three words in each space. Check whether you have to write the words you actually hear or whether they can be different. Correct spelling is also important.

➤ EXAM SUCCESS pages 151–2

2 LISTENING ▶ 31 **You are going to hear a podcast about creating subtitles. Complete the summary. Use a maximum of three words or numbers. You must use the words you hear. You can listen twice.**

Perhaps the first subtitles were 'intertitles', or pieces of **(a)** ………………………… that appeared in silent films. Subtitles in a foreign language were first used in *The Jazz Singer*, when it opened in **(b)** …………………………. Now, there is a whole industry dedicated to translating subtitles. In France, a subtitler is called 'an adapter' because they have to **(c)** …………………………. This is because the average person reads only **(d)** ………………………… a second, and it's impossible to keep up with the words that appear on the screen. More recently, **(e)** ………………………… has meant that people have access to more films and TV shows and online platforms such as Viki have appeared. These allow people to **(f)** ………………………… subtitles collaboratively. TV shows and films are posted online and then **(g)** ………………………… translate them. Viki has translators in **(h)** ………………………… languages and they've translated **(i)** ………………………… words. Some do it because they feel that the subtitles they read aren't **(j)** ………………………… and they want to improve them. Surprisingly, one of the most popular shows on the site is a **(k)** …………………………. Platforms like Viki are **(l)** …………………………, which is a positive thing for language learners.

3 SPEAKING **What about *you*?**

1. What impact does dubbing have on foreign language learning?
2. Do you think all TV shows should be shown in the original version with subtitles? Why/Why not?
3. To what extent does the government subsidise local films and TV shows? In your opinion, should it do more to support them?

Whatever, wherever, whoever, etc.

4 Look at the sentences and choose the correct alternative in the rules below.

a **Whenever** you watch a foreign language film, you have two choices.

b People can translate subtitles **wherever** they are in the world.

c **Whatever** the reason translators do it, it must be a good thing.

d **However hard** it may be to work for nothing, at least she feels satisfied.

1. We use *whoever*, *whenever*, *whichever*, etc. when it *makes a/doesn't make any* difference who, when, which, etc.
2. We use *however* + adjective/adverb to say it *matters/doesn't matter* how much you do something or how big/small/difficult something is.

GRAMMAR REFERENCE ➤ PAGE 132

5 Complete the sentences with these words.

however • whatever • whenever • wherever
whichever • whoever

1. He gets nervous ……………… he has to speak in English on the phone.
2. People tend to speak English ……………… you go.
3. You can never learn all the words in a language, ……………… long you study it.
4. We can meet ……………… day you like.
5. In my opinion, ……………… says that they can speak 20 languages fluently is lying.
6. ……………… happens, I'll always love you.

6 Complete these sentences with *whatever, whoever*, etc.

1. I eat popcorn …
2. At the weekend, I wear …
3. I like to go … on holiday.
4. When I watch TV, I usually watch …
5. I couldn't …, … I tried.
6. I'll marry …

Presentations – 2

1 SPEAKING **Work with a partner. Look at the photos on p165. Student A: compare two of the pictures. Student B: say how important you think language is in these situations and how you think the people feel.**

2 **Look at this exam task and, individually, spend one minute making notes.**

> You will have to talk about this topic for one to two minutes. You have one minute to think about what you are going to say. You can make some notes to help you.
> *Describe a time you had a problem with language, either your own language or another language.*
> *You should say:*
> - *where and when it was.*
> - *what the problem was.*
> - *if/how the problem was resolved.*
>
> *Also, explain what you learnt from the experience.*

3 LISTENING 32 **Listen to a student doing the task and identify the main points he would have made in his notes.**

Ellipsis

4a **Look at these sentences. What words are 'missing' after the words in bold?**

1 I'd never been to the UK before, but I'd wanted **to**.
2 I stopped asking him because I was too embarrassed **to**.
3 I don't usually listen to other accents, but I **should**.
4 I've been to England, but my friend **hasn't**.

4b **Why do we sometimes miss out words as in the examples in 4a?**

GRAMMAR REFERENCE ➤ PAGE 132

5 **Complete the sentences with these words. What words are being missed out in each sentence?**

don't • forgot to • have to • like to • might • ready to • used to • won't

1 My friend speaks with a strong accent, but I ....
2 I don't have problems understanding accents now, but I ....
3 I was going to point out some useful expressions, but I ....
4 My older sister stopped learning English when she left school. When I finish school next year, I .... because I enjoy it.
5 He's never studied German, but one day he'd ....
6 I never dared to do this exam. Now I'm ....
7 I don't really know if I'll go to the US one day. I think I ....
8 We don't want to translate this text, but the teacher says we ....

6 SPEAKING **Work with a partner. Do the task in 2 using the notes you made. Use expressions from the Speaking bank.**

SPEAKING BANK

Useful words to talk about past personal experiences

- I seem to remember that …
- I recall …
- I have a vague memory/recollection of/that …
- What sticks in my mind is that …
- The most vivid memory I have is …
- What struck me was …
- As far as I (can) remember …
- To the best of my recollection,
- If my memory serves me,

7 SPEAKING **After a presentation you will often be asked follow-up discussion questions. With a partner, ask and answer these questions.**

Student A:
1 How important is it to be able to speak more than one language? Why?
2 Which language do you think is the most useful to learn? Why?

Student B:
1 How well do people in your country speak English? Why?
2 How difficult do you think it is to learn another language? Why?

PRACTICE MAKES PERFECT

8a SPEAKING **Work with a partner. Look at the task on p165. Take it in turns to do the task.**

8b **Take it in turns to discuss the follow-up questions on page 165.**

A proposal

1 SPEAKING **Work with a partner. Discuss these questions.**

1 What would be some reasons for joining an English club?

2 What would you expect to do at the club?

3 Would you be interested in joining a club? Why/Why not?

2 Read the memo from a school principal to student representatives. Think of three suggestions you would make in response to the memo. Then compare your ideas with a partner.

From: The Principal

To: Student Representatives

We are considering setting up an English Club as an after-school activity to encourage students to develop their proficiency in English. We wondered if you could send a proposal with ideas to help to attract members and make the club a success.

Thanks,

J. Barnes

3 Read the proposal. Does it contain the same ideas you discussed in 2?

4 SPEAKING **Read the proposal again and discuss these questions with a partner.**

1 Who is the proposal written for?

2 Is the style formal or informal?

3 What aspects of the language make it formal?

4 How is the proposal organised?

5 What similarities or differences can you find between a proposal and a report?

✓ EXAM SUCCESS

The style of a proposal is usually formal, unless it is written for a group of peers, in which case the language can be less formal. A proposal contains factual information about the current situation, and suggestions under headings. Sometimes the proposal is written on behalf of others, so remember to refer to their opinions.

➤ EXAM SUCCESS page 153

Proposal to attract members to the English Club

Introduction

The aim of this proposal is to outline ways to attract students to attend a school English Club, and to give reasons for these suggestions. The school currently has 600 students, and we estimate that around 50 would be interested in attending. We believe that the club would be a valuable addition to the school's extracurricular activities.

1 Variety of activities

We have conducted a survey and in the light of students' comments, we propose that the club's organisers provide a variety of activities for those who attend. There are a number of activities that would be popular, including films in English, and group quizzes. We suggest that the club also includes debates, storytelling, an essay competition and a games night. We could also increase participation further by inviting speakers from different backgrounds to come to the club to give presentations.

2 Information

With regard to promoting the club, we suggest that organisers provide information about the activities on offer. An effective way to do this would be to put a notice on a weekly basis in each of the classrooms, as well as in the main entrance. Additionally, the club could be given prominence on the school website, with regular updates about forthcoming activities, and photos of previous events.

3 Excursions

Excursions have proven to be very popular and we recommend that the club should organise regular excursions, at least one every six weeks. These excursions could include going to a concert, an art gallery or a museum, or having a picnic. Also worthy of mentioning is the fact that there are similar clubs at other schools in the area. We propose that these are contacted with a view to planning activities together.

4 Conclusions

To sum up, the English Club is considered to be of interest to a number of students in the school. To attract participation in the club, we propose that organisers provide a varied and appealing range of activities. This would include regular excursions. We also recommend that everything possible is done to inform students about the club within the school.

5 Complete the Writing bank with expressions from the proposal in 3.

WRITING BANK

Useful words and expressions in proposals

Introduction

- ....
- This proposal relates to …
- This proposal describes/outlines …
- This proposal looks at …

Outlining the current situation

- It is clear from (students' comments) … that …
- With regard to …, the general view seems to be …
- ....
- It is beyond dispute that …

Suggestions

- I/We recommend/propose/suggest that we (should) …
- We could also … If we …, we could …
- ....

Adding information

- ....
- ....

Conclusions

- ....
- In conclusion, I would say that …
- On balance, we are of the opinion that …

6 SPEAKING Work with a partner. Read the memo and discuss ideas for your proposal.

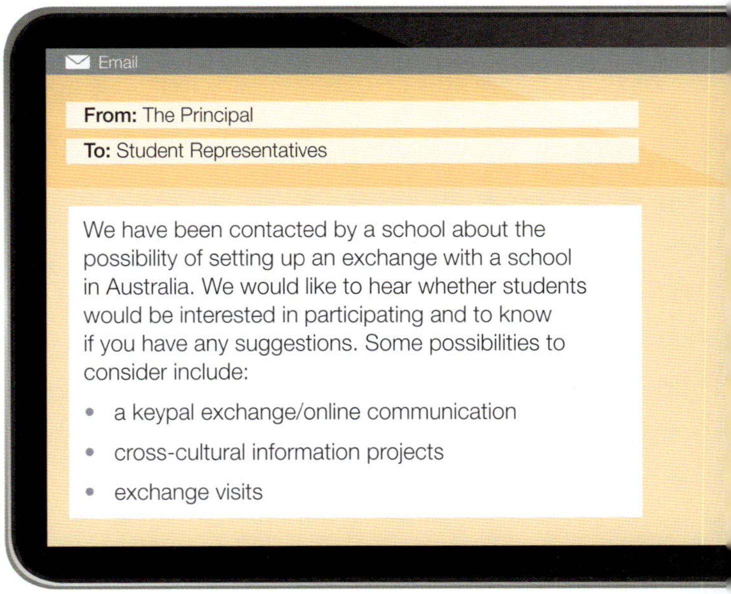

Email

From: The Principal

To: Student Representatives

We have been contacted by a school about the possibility of setting up an exchange with a school in Australia. We would like to hear whether students would be interested in participating and to know if you have any suggestions. Some possibilities to consider include:

- a keypal exchange/online communication
- cross-cultural information projects
- exchange visits

7 PRACTICE MAKES PERFECT Write your proposal to the school principal. Use the information in the Writing bank and in Exam success to help you.

WRITING BANK ➤ PAGE 160

Grammar reference

Gerunds and infinitives – rules

We use the gerund:	We use the infinitive:
as the **subject** or **object** of a sentence. *__Listening__ to podcasts helps you to understand more.* *He described __listening__ to the band as torture.*	to explain **why** somebody does something. *__To buy__ a good computer, you need to think carefully what you want.*
after **prepositions**. *I'm tired __of making__ mistakes.*	immediately after **adjectives**. *It's __essential to think__ before you answer.*
after **verbs of liking or disliking**, e.g. *like, love, enjoy, can't stand, don't mind, hate*. *I __adore__ eating in that restaurant.*	after **too**, **enough**, **the first**, **the last**. *I'm __the first to admit__ it.*
after these noun phrases: *It's no good/use, It's (not) worth, There's no point (in), have difficulty/problems/trouble (in/with)* *It's __not worth__ crying over.*	after indefinite pronouns (*somewhere, something*, etc.). *I haven't got __anything to wear__.*
with **go** to talk about physical activities. *go runn__ing__, swimm__ing__, cycl__ing__, shopp__ing__, swimm__ing__, fish__ing__*	after certain verbs: afford • agree • appear • arrange • decide • expect fail • happen • help • hope • manage • pretend promise • refuse • seem • volunteer • wait
after certain verbs: admit • avoid • carry on • consider • deny • face • feel like • finish • give up • include • keep (on) • practise recommend • risk • suggest • take up	

Whatever, wherever, whoever, etc.

We use *whoever, whenever, whichever, whatever, however* when it doesn't make any difference who, when, which, etc. The clause which contains *whatever, whoever*, etc. can come at the start of the sentence or in the middle.

__Whatever__ I do, you're always angry with me.

You're always angry with me, __whatever__ I do.

We use *however* + adjective/adverb to say it doesn't matter how much you do something, or how big/small/difficult something is. The clause which contains *however* can come at the start of the sentence or in the middle.

__However__ fast you run, you'll never beat me.

You'll never beat me, __however__ fast you run.

Ellipsis

Ellipsis is when we leave out words because they are not necessary and to avoid repetition.

One of the most common examples is when we omit an infinitive to avoid repeating the verb again.

Lisa wanted to swim, but I couldn't [__swim__] because I didn't have my swimsuit.

She ate early, but I didn't want to [__eat early__].

Rob went up the stairs in the dark, but I was frightened to [__go up the stairs in the dark__].

It is also common to leave out the main verb after a modal or auxiliary verb.

Mark won't help you, but I will [__help you__].

She hasn't seen the film, but I have [__seen the film__].

Vocabulary

For phrasal verbs about communication and communication breakdown, see wordlist page 144.

Grammar revision

Gerunds and infinitives – rules and revision / 8 points

1 Choose the correct alternative.

1 I certainly don't mind *to wait/waiting* for you.
2 It's no good *to cry/crying* every time you have a problem to face.
3 In my family I'm usually the first person *to wake/waking* up.
4 Can you manage *to see/seeing* what's happening?
5 I used the knife *to open/opening* the letter.
6 There's just no point *to argue/arguing* with them.
7 Does *to think/thinking* about food make you hungry?
8 They managed to resolve the problem without *to lose/losing* face.

Whatever, wherever, whoever, etc. / 7 points

2 Decide if the words in bold are used incorrectly. Tick (✓) the correct sentences and rewrite the incorrect sentences.

1 **Whatever** busy I am, I always have time for you.
2 **Wherever** I go to your house, you're always wearing your pyjamas!
3 I want to pass the test **however** I can.
4 **Whichever** you wear, you always look great.
5 I can't help smiling **whenever** I think about what happened.
6 She always believed **however** he told her.
7 **Whatever** hard I try, I never seem to please them.

Ellipsis / 7 points

3 Rewrite each sentence to avoid repetition.

1 I didn't read the whole of the book, even though I should have read it.
2 I'd already finished eating my lunch, but my friends hadn't finished it.
3 She didn't cook because she was too tired to cook.
4 Jo could speak French when she was little, but she can't speak French now.
5 We never used to worry about them, but we've started to worry about them.
6 They moved all the chairs, but they shouldn't have moved them.
7 I'd love to go, but I don't think I'll be able to go.

Vocabulary revision

PHRASAL VERBS – COMMUNICATION / 8 points

1 Choose the correct particles.

1 interrupt = cut *in/up*
2 state your opinion firmly = speak *out/on*
3 start discussing = bring *on/up*
4 change from one subject to another = turn *to/in*
5 make someone understand what you are trying to say = get *to/through*
6 understand something with difficulty = make *out/up*
7 talk to someone as if you think they are not as clever as you = talk *across to/down to*
8 talk in detail about something that someone has mentioned = pick *up on/out on*

COMMUNICATION/COMMUNICATION BREAKDOWN / 10 points

2 Complete the sentences with these words.

gaffe • implied • literally • misinterpreted • nuances
offended • purposes • puzzling • remark • stick

1 He made a terrible .... when he called her Mr.
2 I found his remarks .... What exactly did he mean by what he said?
3 I got the wrong end of the .... and misunderstood you.
4 You made me laugh with your witty ....
5 I think we're talking at cross .... because I was talking about your French teacher, not your English teacher.
6 I think I .... him when I said he looks older.
7 She didn't actually say it, but she .... that I'm stupid.
8 It's quite easy to learn new vocabulary, but it's hard to understand the .... of specific words.
9 When I said I never wanted to see him again, I didn't expect him to take it ....
10 They .... her silence for agreement with their plan.

Total: / 40 points

Reading

> ➤ **TIP FOR READING EXAMS**
>
> In activities where you complete summaries, notes or tables, remember …
> When you read the table, summary or sentences that you need to complete, be aware that they will probably not use exactly the same words as in the text.
>
> ➤ EXAM SUCCESS page 153

1 Read the article and complete the summary with words from the text. Use no more than two words in each answer.

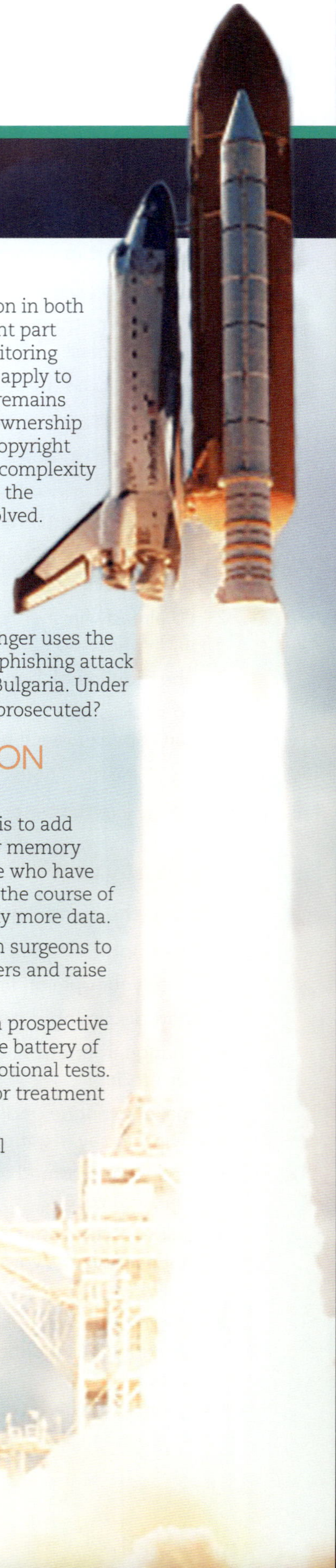

JOBS OF THE FUTURE

What will you be doing in 20 years' time? Chances are you'll be working in a job that doesn't yet exist. A report published by the research company Fast Future predicts that advances in science and technology, together with the onset of climate change, could make for career paths that are virtually unrecognisable today. The most popular jobs of the future could include: body part maker, vertical farmer, virtual lawyer, memory augmentation surgeon and space pilot.

THE BODY PART MAKER

A day would typically start with scanning the most critical or urgent new requests for repairs and complete body parts, and checking on component deliveries to help schedule the day's work plan. Requests would be reviewed to determine whether entire limbs or organs were required or just component subsystems (e.g. a new kneecap) and where multiple copies were required, e.g. for athletes. A visit to the incubator would follow to check on the progress of body parts currently being grown and to perform staged quality control tests.

Much of the day would be spent working at the laboratory bench designing and assembling body parts and testing their performance under various conditions as specified by the owner. Throughout the day the body part maker would be engaged in video conferences with surgeons around the world to discuss their requirements, provide advice on appropriate body part design and review the results of past body part replacement surgeries.

THE VERTICAL FARMER

Many models can be envisaged for how such farms could be run. One would involve a professional farm manager supported by a mix of human and robotic farmhands and specialist scientists. Another model envisages such farms being part of new community developments with the local residents donating time as farm labour in return for a regular supply of fresh produce and a share of the commercial returns from the farm.

A typical day would start with monitoring plant health, atmospheric conditions and crop growth. A number of routine daily tasks would be performed including tending the plants, planting, harvesting, irrigating the various plants, waste recycling and maintaining the ventilation equipment and other machinery. Each day, time would be dedicated to working on new developments in special areas of the farm given over to experimentation on new crops and growing techniques.

THE VIRTUAL LAWYER

The Internet is a major facilitator of innovation in both the legal and illegal realms. Hence a significant part of the virtual lawyer's time will be spent monitoring new legal developments and precedents that apply to the virtual world. Much of the legal territory remains the same, e.g. disputes, contractual failures, ownership issues, intellectual property theft, sabotage, copyright infringements and trademarks. However, the complexity comes from the global nature of the Web and the different legal jurisdictions that could be involved.

Some of the most interesting challenges will arise from dealing with international web-based criminal acts. For example, consider a British passenger on a flight from Paris to Singapore on an Australian airline. The passenger uses the on-board web access to commit a hacking or phishing attack on victims in Luxembourg whilst flying over Bulgaria. Under whose legal jurisdiction should the crime be prosecuted?

THE MEMORY AUGMENTATION SURGEON

This is a new category of surgeon whose role is to add memory to people who want to increase their memory capacity. A key service would be helping those who have literally been overloaded with information in the course of their life and simply can no longer take on any more data.

Leading companies will increasingly hire such surgeons to enhance the capabilities of their top performers and raise the standards of the entire workforce.

A typical day would involve consultation with prospective patients – including the review of an extensive battery of cognitive, psychological, neurological and emotional tests. These will determine if a patient is suitable for treatment and the appropriate interventions to make.

Surgeons will have to be part of a professional association. The association will play a key role in trying to address the ethical outcry and influencing the debate around memory enhancement.

SUMMARY

Advances in science and technology mean that in 20 years' time, people will be doing jobs that don't **(a)** .... today. For example, people will be employed to work as body part makers. These will grow body parts for people such as **(b)** .... They will also be responsible for dealing with **(c)** .... of existing body parts. They will work closely with **(d)** .... from all over the world, who will order the body parts and perform surgeries.

Another job will be that of the vertical farmer. Some experts believe that in the future, these farmers will manage teams of people and **(e)** .... workers who will do manual labour on the farms. Others think that **(f)** .... will work on the farm and receive food from the farms and profits in return for their labour. They will also carry out experiments to develop **(g)** .... and ways of farming.

Virtual lawyers will deal with similar legal matters as now, but they will specialise in problems relating to the **(h)** .... One of the main areas of their work will be to work out how to prosecute criminals who commit **(i)** .... in more than one country.

Finally, surgeons will be employed by **(j)** .... to increase the memory capabilities of their top workers. Memory augmentation surgeons will need to decide which patients should receive **(k)** .... and what type of procedures to perform. They will also have to belong to associations in order to deal with the **(l)** .... questions that will arise as a result of memory enhancement.

Speaking

➤ TIP FOR SPEAKING EXAMS

In activities where you have to work with other speakers, remember …

There aren't usually any right or wrong answers. The important thing is to have an opinion, to explain it clearly, to justify it and to give examples to support it.

➤ EXAM SUCCESS page 152

2 SPEAKING **Work with a partner. Do the task.**

Talk to each other about the most important requirements for learning a language.

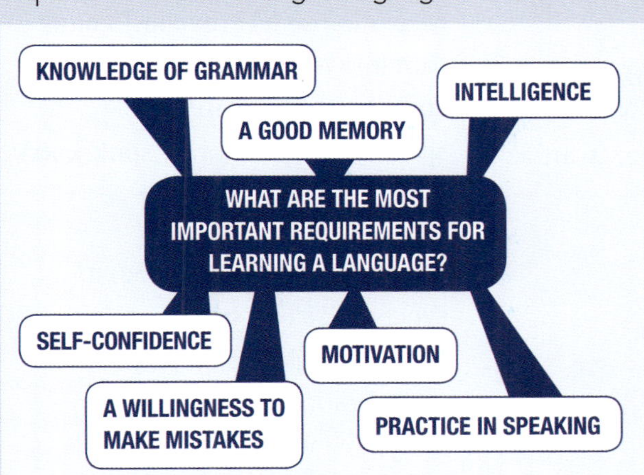

Writing

➤ TIP FOR WRITING EXAMS

For guidance on writing proposals, see page 153.
For guidance on writing formal letters, see page 151.

➤ EXAM SUCCESS pages 151 and 153

3 Choose one of these two tasks.

1 Your school is planning to hold a careers day for students to give them information and advice about careers and training courses. The principal has asked you to write a proposal to include what should happen on the day and how it should be organised.

Read the information from the school website forum which students wrote after a previous careers day and some notes that you have made. Then write your proposal to the principal.

1 … really wanted to meet ex-students who had just started jobs or courses
2 … not enough about future job market
3 … long queues, so didn't get to speak to everyone I wanted
4 … didn't seem very practical
5 … same old careers advice – was hoping for something different

1 invite ex-students to share insights?
2 invite external speakers – specialists in science, engineering, etc?
invite expert on future job market?
3 over two days?
4 practice interviews? workshops?
5 question and answer session?

2 You have seen the following advertisement and decide to apply. Write your letter of application.

SUMMER CAMP MONITORS

We have several vacancies for summer camp helpers to work at various camps across the UK.

Duties include supervising children aged 8–15, and leading various activities, including swimming, football, nature discovery walks, etc.

Good pay and accommodation provided. Good level of English essential. Driving licence preferred.

A great opportunity to travel, make great friends from all over the world, and experience a summer speaking English.

Please send CV and covering letter to: Recruitments, PJL Summer Camps, PO Box 18736, London E1 1B

(adj) = adjective
(adv) = adverb
(conj) = conjunction
(det) = determiner
(n/n pl) = noun/noun plural
(phr) = phrase
(prep) = preposition
(pron) = pronoun
(v) = verb

The most common and useful words in English are marked according to the Macmillan Dictionary 'star rating'. This is so you can easily recognise the vocabulary you need to know especially well.

★★★ = very common words ★★ = common words ★ = fairly common words

If there is no star next to the word, this means that it is not very common.

In the Macmillan Dictionary, (r) is used to indicate where the sound /r/ is pronounced in American English and some other regional varieties of English. In a standard British accent, (r) is only pronounced if it occurs at the end of a word which is followed by another word starting with a vowel sound, for example *far away* /fɑːr əˈweɪ/.

Unit 1

Word formation – noun suffixes

Abstract nouns and things

accuracy (n) ★★ /ˈækjʊrəsi/
activity (n) ★★★ /ækˈtɪvəti/
argument (n) ★★★ /ˈɑː(r)gjʊmənt/
coincidence (n) ★ /kəʊˈɪnsɪd(ə)ns/
conclusion (n) ★★★ /kənˈkluːʒ(ə)n/
decency (n) /ˈdiːs(ə)nsi/
description (n) ★★★ /dɪˈskrɪpʃ(ə)n/
difference (n) ★★★ /ˈdɪfrəns/
explanation (n) ★★★ /ˌekspləˈneɪʃ(ə)n/
failure (n) ★★★ /ˈfeɪljə(r)/
freedom (n) ★★★ /ˈfriːdəm/
frequency (n) ★★★ /ˈfriːkwənsi/
friendship (n) ★★ /ˈfren(d)ʃɪp/
happiness (n) ★★ /ˈhæpinəs/
honesty (n) ★ /ˈɒnɪsti/
importance (n) ★★★ /ɪmˈpɔː(r)t(ə)ns/
intelligence (n) ★★ /ɪnˈtelɪdʒ(ə)ns/
interaction (n) ★★ /ˌɪntərˈækʃ(ə)n/
invention (n) ★★ /ɪnˈvenʃ(ə)n/
loneliness (n) /ˈləʊnlinəs/
movement (n) ★★★ /ˈmuːvmənt/
personality (n) ★★★ /ˌpɜː(r)səˈnæləti/
popularity (n) ★★ /ˌpɒpjʊˈlærəti/
protection (n) ★★★ /prəˈtekʃ(ə)n/
safety (n) ★★★ /ˈseɪfti/
similarity (n) ★★ /ˌsɪməˈlærəti/
sincerity (n) /sɪnˈserəti/

People

actor (n) ★★★ /ˈæktə(r)/
participant (n) ★★ /pɑː(r)ˈtɪsɪpənt/
psychologist (n) ★★ /saɪˈkɒlədʒɪst/
researcher (n) /rɪˈsɜː(r)tʃə(r)/
scientist (n) ★★★ /ˈsaɪəntɪst/
speaker (n) ★★★ /ˈspiːkə(r)/

Body idioms and human interaction

be under someone's thumb (phr) /biː ˌʌndə(r) sʌmwʌnz ˈθʌm/
do something behind someone's back (phr) /ˌduː sʌmθɪŋ bɪˌhaɪnd sʌmwʌnz ˈbæk/
get something off your chest (phr) /ˌget sʌmθɪŋ ˌɒf jɔː(r) ˈtʃest/
give someone the cold shoulder (phr) /ˌgɪv sʌmwʌn ðə ˌkəʊld ˈʃəʊldə(r)/
lend someone a hand (phr) /ˌlend sʌmwʌn ə ˈhænd/
pull someone's leg (phr) /ˌpʊl sʌmwʌnz ˈleg/
see eye-to-eye with someone (phr) /siː ˌaɪ tu ˈaɪ wɪð ˌsʌmwʌn/
stick your neck out for someone (phr) /ˌstɪk jɔː(r) ˈnek aʊt fə(r) ˌsʌmwʌn/

Similes

as clear as mud (phr) /əz ˌklɪər əz ˈmʌd/
as cold as ice (phr) /əz ˌkəʊld əz ˈaɪs/
as cool as a cucumber (phr) /əz ˌkuːl əz ə ˈkjuːˌkʌmbə(r)/
as easy as ABC (phr) /əz ˌiːzi əz eɪbiˈsiː/
as fresh as a daisy (phr) /əz ˌfreʃ əz ə ˈdeɪzi/
as light as a feather (phr) /əz ˌlaɪt əz ə ˈfeðə(r)/
as quick as a flash (phr) /əz ˌkwɪk əz ə ˈflæʃ/
as quiet as a mouse (phr) /əz ˌkwaɪət əz ə ˈmaʊs/
as solid as a rock (phr) /əz ˌsɒlɪd əz ə ˈrɒk/
as strong as an ox (phr) /əz ˌstrɒŋ əz ən ˈɒks/
as white as a sheet (phr) /əz ˌwaɪt əz ə ˈʃiːt/

Ways of talking

gasp (v) ★ /gɑːsp/
groan (v) ★ /grəʊn/
mutter (v) ★★ /ˈmʌtə(r)/
shriek (v) /ʃriːk/
sigh (v) ★★ /saɪ/
whine (v) /waɪn/
whisper (v) ★★ /ˈwɪspə(r)/
yell (v) ★ /jel/

Other words and phrases

accommodate (v) ★ /əˈkɒmədeɪt/
amass (v) /əˈmæs/
anticipate (v) ★★ /ænˈtɪsɪpeɪt/
applause (n) /əˈplɔːz/
beneficial (adj) ★★ /ˌbenɪˈfɪʃ(ə)l/
bond (n & v) ★★ /bɒnd/
claim (v) ★★★ /kleɪm/
close (adj) ★★★ /kləʊs/
commuter (n) ★ /kəˈmjuːtə(r)/
devise (v) ★★ /dɪˈvaɪz/
fraternity (n) /frəˈtɜː(r)nəti/
fundraising (n) /ˈfʌndreɪzɪŋ/
get across (v phr) /ˌget əˈkrɒs/
household (n) ★★★ /ˈhaʊsˌhəʊld/
hunter-gatherer (adj & n) /ˌhʌntə(r) ˈgæθərə(r)/
initiation (n) /ɪˌnɪʃiˈeɪʃ(ə)n/
keep to yourself (phr) /ˌkiːp tə jə(r)ˈself/
like-minded (adj) /ˈlaɪkˌmaɪndɪd/
look out for yourself (phr) /lʊk ˌaʊt fə(r) jə(r)ˈself/
precise (adj) ★★ /prɪˈsaɪs/
rehearse (v) ★ /rɪˈhɜː(r)s/
relate (v) ★★★ /rɪˈleɪt/
respectively (adv) ★ /rɪˈspektɪvli/
revolutionise (v) /ˌrevəˈluːʃəˌnaɪz/
root (n) ★★★ /ruːt/
sorority (n) /səˈrɒrəti/
speak your mind (phr) /ˌspiːk jɔː(r) ˈmaɪnd/
struggle (v) ★★ /ˈstrʌg(ə)l/
support (n & v) ★★★ /səˈpɔː(r)t/
synchronise (v) /ˈsɪŋkrənaɪz/
think through (v phr) /ˌθɪŋk ˈθruː/
undergraduate (n) /ˌʌndə(r)ˈgrædʒʊət/
upset (adj & v) ★★ /ʌpˈset/

Unit 2

Collocations with *take, make* and *do*

take (phr)

a call /ˌteɪk ə 'kɔːl/
a course /ˌteɪk ə 'kɔː(r)s/
a decision /ˌteɪk ə dɪ'sɪʒ(ə)n/
an interest /ˌteɪk ən 'ɪntrəst/
a risk /ˌteɪk ə 'rɪsk/
a test /ˌteɪk ə 'test/
control /ˌteɪk kən'trəʊl/
cover /ˌteɪk 'kʌvə(r)/
effect /ˌteɪk ɪ'fekt/
offence /ˌteɪk ə'fens/
place /ˌteɪk 'pleɪs/
power /ˌteɪk 'paʊə(r)/

make (phr)

an apology /ˌmeɪk ən ə'pɒlədʒi/
an attempt /ˌmeɪk ən ə'tempt/
a call /ˌmeɪk ə 'kɔːl/
a choice /ˌmeɪk ə 'tʃɔɪs/
a comment /ˌmeɪk ə 'kɒment/
a complaint /ˌmeɪk ə kəm'pleɪnt/
a decision /ˌmeɪk ə dɪ'sɪʒ(ə)n/
a difference /ˌmeɪk ə 'dɪfrəns/
an improvement /ˌmeɪk ən ɪm'pruːvmənt/
a mistake /ˌmeɪk ə mɪ'steɪk/
a suggestion /ˌmeɪk ə sə'dʒestʃ(ə)n/
changes /ˌmeɪk 'tʃeɪndʒɪz/
use of something /ˌmeɪk 'juːs əv ˌsʌmθɪŋ/

do (phr)

a course /ˌduː ə 'kɔː(r)s/
a test /ˌduː ə 'test/
business /ˌduː 'bɪznəs/
harm /ˌduː 'hɑː(r)m/
household chores /ˌduː haʊshəʊld 'tʃɔː(r)z/
research /ˌduː rɪ'sɜː(r)tʃ/, /ˌduː 'riːsɜː(r)tʃ/
your best /ˌduː jɔː(r) 'best/

Compound nouns – cars and the road

driving licence (n) /'draɪvɪŋ ˌlaɪs(ə)ns/
motorway (n) ★★ /'məʊtə(r)ˌweɪ/
petrol station (n) /'petrəl ˌsteɪʃ(ə)n/
road sign (n) /'rəʊd ˌsaɪn/
roundabout (n) ★ /'raʊndəˌbaʊt/
seat belt (n) /'siːt ˌbelt/
speed limit (n) /'spiːd ˌlɪmɪt/
steering wheel (n) /'stɪərɪŋ ˌwiːl/
traffic jam (n) /'træfɪk ˌdʒæm/
traffic light (n) /'træfɪk ˌlaɪt/

Other words and phrases

bother (v) ★★★ /'bɒðə(r)/
chauffeur (v) /'ʃəʊfə(r)/
cliff (n) ★★ /klɪf/
enforce (v) ★★ /ɪn'fɔː(r)s/
ensure (v) ★★★ /ɪn'ʃɔː(r)/
explain (v) /ɪk'spleɪn/
gain (v) ★★★ /geɪn/
goddess (n) /'gɒdes/
go down well (phr) /ˌgəʊ daʊn 'wel/
imminent (adj) /'ɪmɪnənt/
impetuous (adj) /ɪm'petʃuəs/
implement (v) ★★ /'ɪmplɪˌment/
impulsive (adj) /ɪm'pʌlsɪv/
leap (v) ★★ /liːp/
lower (v) /'ləʊə(r)/
provisional (adj) ★ /prə'vɪʒ(ə)nəl/
rash (adj) /ræʃ/
requirements (n pl) /rɪ'kwaɪə(r)mənts/
rolling (adj) /'rəʊlɪŋ/
rope (n) ★★ /rəʊp/
rush of adrenalin (phr) /ˌrʌʃ əv ə'drenəlɪn/
scenery (n) ★ /'siːnəri/
show off (v phr) /ˌʃəʊ 'ɒf/
slippery (adj) /'slɪpəri/
snap decision (n) /ˌsnæp dɪ'sɪʒ(ə)n/
support vehicle (n) /sə'pɔː(r)t ˌviːɪk(ə)l/
synapse (n) /'saɪnæps/
think ahead (v phr) /ˌθɪŋk ə'hed/
toss (a coin) (v) /tɒs/
toughen up (v phr) /ˌtʌf(ə)n 'ʌp/
widely (adv) ★★★ /'waɪdli/
wind (v) ★★ /waɪnd/

Gateway to exams: Units 1–2

adapt (v) ★★ /ə'dæpt/
age limit (n) /'eɪdʒ ˌlɪmɪt/
broaden (v) ★ /'brɔːd(ə)n/
challenge (v) ★★★ /'tʃælɪndʒ/
content (adj) ★★ /kən'tent/
custom (n) ★★ /'kʌstəm/
demanding (adj) ★★ /dɪ'mɑːndɪŋ/
dependent (adj) ★★★ /dɪ'pendənt/
drop-out (adj) /'drɒpaʊt/
enrol (v) /ɪn'rəʊl/
fair share (n) /ˌfeə(r) 'ʃeə(r)/
fashion (n) ★★★ /'fæʃ(ə)n/
for that matter (phr) /fə(r) ˌðæt 'mætə(r)/
found (v) ★★★ /faʊnd/
from scratch (phr) /ˌfrəm 'skrætʃ/
idol (n) /'aɪd(ə)l/
impressive (adj) ★★ /ɪm'presɪv/
logic (n) ★★ /'lɒdʒɪk/
long-distance (adj) ★ /ˌlɒŋ 'dɪstəns/
master (v) ★ /'mɑːstə(r)/
practical (adj) ★★★ /'præktɪk(ə)l/
rally (n) ★★ /'ræli/
relieved (adj) /rɪ'liːvd/
sink in (v phr) /ˌsɪŋk 'ɪn/
solidarity (n) /ˌsɒlɪ'dærəti/
stereotype (n) ★ /'steriəˌtaɪp/
take advantage (phr) /ˌteɪk əd'vɑːntɪdʒ/
unconditional (adj) /ˌʌnkən'dɪʃ(ə)nəl/
within (adv) ★★★ /wɪð'ɪn/

Unit 3

Phrasal verbs – the mind

catch on (v phr) /ˌkætʃ 'ɒn/
come up with (v phr) /ˌkʌm 'ʌp wɪð/
hit on (v phr) /'hɪt ɒn/
keep up with (v phr) /ˌkiːp 'ʌp wɪð/
leap out at (v phr) /ˌliːp 'aʊt æt/
pick up (v phr) /ˌpɪk 'ʌp/
piece together (v phr) /ˌpiːs tə'geðə(r)/
talk through (v phr) /ˌtɔːk 'θruː/

Other phrasal verbs

fit in (v phr) /ˌfɪt 'ɪn/
get on with (v phr) /ˌget 'ɒn wɪð/
look down on (v phr) /ˌlʊk 'daʊn ɒn/
look for (v phr) /'lʊk fɔː(r)/
stand out (v phr) /ˌstænd 'aʊt/
take up (v phr) /ˌteɪk 'ʌp/
work out (v phr) /ˌwɜː(r)k 'aʊt/
write down (v phr) /ˌraɪt 'daʊn/

The human mind

articulate (adj) /ɑː(r)'tɪkjʊlət/
bewildered (adj) /bɪ'wɪldə(r)d/
grasp (v) ★★ /grɑːsp/
have a gift for (phr) /ˌhæv ə 'gɪft fɔː(r)/
memorise (v) ★ /'meməraɪz/
perceive (v) ★★ /pə(r)'siːv/
recall (v) ★★★ /rɪ'kɔːl/
wander (v) ★★ /'wɒndə(r)/

Wordlist: Units 3–4

Prefixes

anti
co-
dis-/un-/im-/ir-/in-/il-
ex-
inter-
mis-
over-
post-
pre-
re-
sub-
super-
under-

Examples

disappointing (adj) ★ /ˌdɪsə'pɔɪntɪŋ/
disjointed (adj) /dɪs'dʒɔɪntɪd/
impenetrable (adj) /ɪm'penɪtrəb(ə)l/
miscast (v) /ˌmɪs'kɑːst/
overblown (adj) /ˌəʊvə(r)'bləʊn/
subconscious (adj) /ˌsʌb'kɒnʃəs/
underrated (adj) /ˌʌndə'reɪtɪd/
uninspiring (adj) /ˌʌnɪn'spaɪərɪŋ/
unpredictable (adj) ★ /ˌʌnprɪ'dɪktəb(ə)l/

Other words and phrases

a smash/flop (phr) /ə 'smæʃ/'flɒp/
adaptation (n) ★ /ˌædæp'teɪʃ(ə)n/
alter (v) ★★ /'ɔːltə(r)/
assign (v) ★★ /ə'saɪn/
appeal (n) ★★★ /ə'piːl/
big/low-budget (adj) /ˌbɪg/ˌləʊ 'bʌdʒɪt/
(the film) bombed (v) /bɒmd/
box office (n) /'bɒks ˌɒfɪs/
chunk (n) /tʃʌŋk/
clap of thunder (phr) /ˌklæp əv 'θʌndə(r)/
cliché (n) /'kliːʃeɪ/
cliffhanger (n) /'klɪfˌhæŋə(r)/
cope (with) (v) ★★★ /kəʊp/
critic (n) ★★★ /'krɪtɪk/
cursory (adj) /'kɜː(r)səri/
deliver a great performance (phr) /dɪˌlɪvə(r) ə ˌgreɪt pə(r)'fɔː(r)məns/
devise (v) ★★ /dɪ'vaɪz/
disjointed (adj) /dɪs'dʒɔɪntɪd/
display (v) ★★★ /dɪ'spleɪ/
emerge (v) ★★★ /ɪ'mɜː(r)dʒ/
empowerment (n) /ɪm'paʊə(r)mənt/
endearing (adj) /ɪn'dɪərɪŋ/
enhance (v) ★★ /ɪn'hɑːns/
epic (adj) /'epɪk/
expertise (n) ★★ /ˌekspə(r)'tiːz/
far-fetched (adj) /ˌfɑː(r) 'fetʃt/
fast-moving (adj) /ˌfɑːst 'muːvɪŋ/
flawed (adj) /flɔːd/
flawlessly (adv) /'flɔːləsli/
gatherer (n) /'gæθərə(r)/
get a lukewarm reception (phr) /ˌget ə ˌluːkwɔː(r)m rɪ'sepʃ(ə)n/
gripping (adj) /'grɪpɪŋ/
(the film) grossed ($10,000) (v) /grəʊst/
groundbreaking (adj) /'graʊn(d)ˌbreɪkɪŋ/
(the film) hit the big screen (phr) /ˌhɪt ðə ˌbɪg 'skriːn/
hug (v) ★ /hʌg/
hunter (n) ★ /'hʌntə(r)/
insight (n) ★★ /'ɪnsaɪt/
(un)inspiring (adj) /(ˌʌn)ɪn'spaɪərɪŋ/
intriguing (adj) /ɪn'triːgɪŋ/
lack (n) ★★★ /læk/
layer (n) ★★★ /'leɪə(r)/
light-hearted (adj) /ˌlaɪt 'hɑː(r)tɪd/
lightning speed (phr) /ˌlaɪtnɪŋ 'spiːd/
lock up (v phr) /ˌlɒk 'ʌp/
masterpiece (n) ★ /'mɑːstə(r)ˌpiːs/
memorable (adj) /'mem(ə)rəb(ə)l/
mesmerising (adj) /'mezməˌraɪzɪŋ/
mind-blowing (adj) /'maɪnd ˌbləʊɪŋ/
mnemonic device (n) /nɪˌmɒnɪk dɪ'vaɪs/
moving (adj) ★★ /'muːvɪŋ/
overhear (v) /ˌəʊvə(r)'hɪə(r)/
(critics) panned (the film) (v) /pænd/
pattern (n) ★★★ /'pætə(r)n/
portrayal (n) /pɔː(r)'treɪəl/
receive rave reviews (phr) /rɪˌsiːv ˌreɪv rɪ'vjuːz/
recite (v) /rɪ'saɪt/
risqué (adj) /'rɪskeɪ/
script (n) ★★ /skrɪpt/
scriptwriter (n) /'skrɪptˌraɪtə(r)/
sequel (n) /'siːkwəl/
setting (n) ★★★ /'setɪŋ/
shallow (adj) ★★ /'ʃæləʊ/
sharp (adj) ★★★ /ʃɑː(r)p/
soundtrack (n) /'saʊn(d)ˌtræk/
span (v) /spæn/
supporting actor (n) /səˌpɔː(r)tɪŋ 'æktə(r)/
sweep away (v phr) /ˌswiːp ə'weɪ/
thought-provoking (adj) /'θɔːt prəˌvəʊkɪŋ/
tinker (v) /'tɪŋkə(r)/
tool (n) ★★★ /tuːl/
twists and turns (of a plot) (n) /ˌtwɪsts ən(d) 'tɜː(r)nz/
(the story) unfolds (v) /ʌn'fəʊldz/
up-and-coming (adj) /ˌʌp ən(d) 'kʌmɪŋ/

Unit 4

Compound nouns and adjectives

Nouns

breakthrough (n) ★ /'breɪkˌθruː/
crackdown (n) /'krækˌdaʊn/
cutback (n) /'kʌtˌbæk/
drawback (n) /'drɔːˌbæk/
feedback (n) ★★ /'fiːdˌbæk/
lifetime (n) ★★ /'laɪfˌtaɪm/
offspring (n) ★ /'ɒfˌsprɪŋ/
outbreak (n) ★ /'aʊtˌbreɪk/
outcome (n) ★★★ /'aʊtˌkʌm/
outlook (n) ★ /'aʊtˌlʊk/
outset (n) ★ /'aʊtˌset/
setback (n) /'setˌbæk/

Adjectives

genetically modified (adj) /dʒəˌnetɪkli 'mɒdɪfaɪd/
worldwide (adj) ★ /ˌwɜː(r)ld'waɪd/
worthwhile (adj) ★★ /ˌwɜː(r)θ'waɪl/

Biology and scientific research

chromosome (n) /'krəʊməsəʊm/
contract (a disease) (v) ★★ /kən'trækt/
enzyme (n) ★ /'enzaɪm/
genetic engineering (n) /dʒəˌnetɪk ˌendʒɪ'nɪərɪŋ/
genetically modified (adj) /dʒəˌnetɪkli 'mɒdɪfaɪd/
parasite (n) /'pærəsaɪt/
prevalent (adj) /'prevələnt/
resistant (adj) /rɪ'zɪst(ə)nt/
species (n) ★★★ /'spiːʃiːz/
transmit (a disease) (v) ★★ /trænz'mɪt/

Causes, reasons and results

as (adv) ★★★ /æz/, /əz/
bring about (v phr) /ˌbrɪŋ ə'baʊt/
disastrous/catastrophic results (phr) /dɪˌzɑːstrəs/kætəˌstrɒfɪk rɪ'zʌlts/
due to (prep) ★★★ /'djuː tuː/
give rise to (phr) /ˌgɪv 'raɪz tuː/
in turn (phr) /ɪn 'tɜː(r)n/
lead to (v phr) /'liːd tuː/
owing to (prep) /'əʊɪŋ tuː/
prompt (someone to do something) (v) ★★ /prɒmpt/
repercussion (n) /ˌriːpə(r)'kʌʃ(ə)n/

side effect (n) ★ /ˈsaɪd ɪˌfekt/
spark off (v phr) /ˌspɑː(r)k ˈɒf/
stem from (v phr) /ˈstem frɒm/

Other words and phrases

acquire (v) ★★ /əˈkwaɪə(r)/
anomaly (n) /əˈnɒməli/
bar chart (n) /ˈbɑː(r) ˌtʃɑː(r)t/
causation (n) /kɔːˈzeɪʃ(ə)n/
conclusive (adj) ★ /kənˈkluːsɪv/
consumption (n) ★★ /kənˈsʌmpʃ(ə)n/
conversely (adv) ★ /ˈkɒnvɜː(r)sli/
corroborate (v) /kəˈrɒbəreɪt/
debilitate (v) /dɪˈbɪlɪteɪt/
decline (v) ★★★ /dɪˈklaɪn/
(non-)diagrammatic comparison (phr) /(ˌnɒn)ˌdaɪəgrəˌmætɪk kəmˈpærɪs(ə)n/
die out (v phr) /ˌdaɪ ˈaʊt/
double (v) ★★ /ˈdʌb(ə)l/
dramatic(ally) (adj, adv) ★★★/~ /drəˈmætɪk, drəˈmætɪkli/
drop (v) ★★★ /drɒp/
eradicate (v) /ɪˈrædɪkeɪt/
fluctuate (v) /ˈflʌktʃueɪt/
foremost (adj) /ˈfɔː(r)məʊst/
funding (n) ★★ /ˈfʌndɪŋ/
graze (v) /greɪz/
halt (v) ★ /hɔːlt/
keystone (n) /ˈkiːˌstəʊn/
level off (v phr) /ˌlev(ə)l ˈɒf/
life-threatening (adj) /ˈlaɪf ˌθret(ə)nɪŋ/
line graph (n) /ˈlaɪn ˌgrɑːf/
manipulate (v) ★★ /məˈnɪpjʊleɪt/
manipulation (n) ★ /məˌnɪpjʊˈleɪʃ(ə)n/
niche (n) /niːʃ/
pave the way (for) (phr) /ˌpeɪv ðə ˈweɪ/
pie chart (n) /ˈpaɪ ˌtʃɑː(r)t/
pioneer, pioneering (n, adj) ★/~ /ˌpaɪəˈnɪə(r), ˌpaɪəˈnɪə(r)ɪŋ/
plummet (v) /ˈplʌmɪt/
plunge (v) ★★ /plʌndʒ/
pose (v) ★★ /pəʊz/
proportion (n) ★★★ /prəˈpɔː(r)ʃ(ə)n/
reach a high/low (phr) /ˌriːtʃ ə ˈhaɪ/ˈləʊ/
rebound (v) /rɪˈbaʊnd/
rocket (v) /ˈrɒkɪt/
roughly (approximately) (adv) ★★ /ˈrʌfli/
self-sustaining (adj) /ˌself səˈsteɪnɪŋ/
sharp (adj) ★★★ /ʃɑː(r)p/
sharply (adv) ★★ /ˈʃɑː(r)pli/
stabilise (v) /ˈsteɪbəlaɪz/
steady, steadily (adj, adv) ★★/~ /ˈstedi/, /ˈstedəli/
striking (adj) ★ /ˈstraɪkɪŋ/
table (grid) (n) /ˈteɪb(ə)l/
tackle (v) ★★ /ˈtæk(ə)l/
the majority (n) ★★★ /ðə məˈdʒɒrəti/
the minority (n) ★★★ /ðə maɪˈnɒrəti/
the wild (n) /ðə ˈwaɪld/
treble (v) /ˈtreb(ə)l/
ultimately (adv) ★★ /ˈʌltɪmətli/
vulnerable (adj) ★★ /ˈvʌln(ə)rəb(ə)l/
wipe out (v phr) /ˌwaɪp ˈaʊt/
woolly mammoth (n) /ˌwʊli ˈmæməθ/

Gateway to exams: Units 3–4

anatomical (adj) /ˌænəˈtɒmɪk(ə)l/
archetypal (adj) /ˌɑː(r)kɪˈtaɪp(ə)l/
eligible (adj) ★★ /ˈelɪdʒəb(ə)l/
feat (n) /fiːt/
outsider (n) ★★ /aʊtˈsaɪdə(r)/
penmanship (n) /ˈpenmənʃɪp/
restraint (n) ★ /rɪˈstreɪnt/
switch (v) ★★★ /swɪtʃ/
unparalleled (adj) /ʌnˈpærəleld/
visionary (adj) /ˈvɪʒən(ə)ri/

Unit 5

Prepositional phrases

by means of (phr) /baɪ ˈmiːnz ɒv/
in addition to (phr) /ɪn əˈdɪʃ(ə)n tuː/
in aid of (phr) /ɪn ˈeɪd ɒv/
in the process of (phr) /ɪn ðə ˈprəʊses ɒv/
in/out of touch with (phr) /ɪn/aʊt əv ˈtʌtʃ wɪð/
on account of (phr) /ɒn əˈkaʊnt ɒv/
on behalf of (phr) /ɒn bɪˈhɑːf ɒv/
on the strength of (phr) /ɒn ðə ˈstreŋθ ɒv/

Minor offences and punishment

be banned (from) (phr) ★★ /biː ˈbænd frɒm/
be issued with a fine (phr) ★★★ /biː ˌɪʃuːd wɪð ə ˈfaɪn/
community service (n) /kəˌmjuːnəti ˈsɜː(r)vɪs/
court (n) ★★★ /kɔː(r)t/
criminal record (n) /ˌkrɪmɪn(ə)l ˈrekɔː(r)d/
judge (n & v) ★★★ /dʒʌdʒ/
litter (n & v) ★ /ˈlɪtə(r)/
lodge a (formal) complaint (phr) /ˌlɒdʒ ə (ˌfɔː(r)m(ə)l) kəmˈpleɪnt/
pay a small/heavy fine (phr) /ˌpeɪ ə ˌsmɔːl/ˌhevi ˈfaɪn/
prosecute (v) ★ /ˈprɒsɪˌkjuːt/
suspended sentence (n) /səˌspendɪd ˈsentəns/

Formal register

a (growing) number of (phr) /ə ˌgrəʊɪŋ ˈnʌmbə(r) ɒv/
highly (adv) ★★★ /ˈhaɪli/
merely (adv) ★★★ /ˈmɪə(r)li/
numerous (adj) ★★ /ˈnjuːmərəs/
provide (v) ★★★ /prəˈvaɪd/
the vast majority of (phr) /ðə ˌvɑːst məˈdʒɒrəti ɒv/

Other words and phrases

adverse (adj) ★ /ˈædvɜː(r)s/
alienate (v) /ˈeɪliəneɪt/
career (v) /kəˈrɪə(r)/
charge (v) ★★★ /tʃɑː(r)dʒ/
closed-circuit television (CCTV) (n) /ˌkləʊzd ˌsɜː(r)kɪt ˈtelɪˌvɪʒ(ə)n/
come into force (phr) /ˌkʌm ɪntuː ˈfɔː(r)s/
convict, conviction (v, n) ★★ /kənˈvɪkt, kənˈvɪkʃ(ə)n/
correspondence (n) ★★ /ˌkɒrɪˈspɒndəns/
council (n) ★★★ /ˈkaʊns(ə)l/
court summons (n) /ˈkɔː(r)t ˌsʌmənz/
data (n) ★★★ /ˈdeɪtə/
device (n) ★★★ /dɪˈvaɪs/
disrupt, disruption (v, n) ★ /dɪsˈrʌpt, dɪsˈrʌpʃ(ə)n/
disturbance (n) ★★ dɪˈstɜː(r)bəns
enforce, enforcement (v, n) ★★ /ɪnˈfɔː(r)s, ɪnˈfɔː(r)smənt/
expectation (n) ★★★ /ˌekspekˈteɪʃ(ə)n/
flaming (adj) /ˈfleɪmɪŋ/
forthcoming (adj) ★★ /fɔː(r)θˈkʌmɪŋ/
get tough on (phr) /ˌget ˈtʌf ɒn/
hop on/off (v phr) /ˌhɒp ˈɒn/ˈɒf/
integral (adj) ★ /ɪnˈtegrəl/
invasion of privacy (phr) /ɪnˌveɪʒ(ə)n əv ˈprɪvəsi/
knock over (v phr) /ˌnɒk ˈəʊvə(r)/
land in court (phr) /ˌlænd ɪn ˈkɔː(r)t/
litter bug (n) /ˈlɪtə(r) ˌbʌg/
lobby (n) ★ /ˈlɒbi/
magistrate (n) ★ /ˈmædʒɪˌstreɪt/

manoeuvre (n) ★ /mə'nuːvə(r)/
measure (n) ★★★ /'meʒə(r)/
merely (adv) ★★★ /'mɪə(r)li/
monitor (v) ★★ /'mɒnɪtə(r)/
nuisance (n) ★ /'njuːs(ə)ns/
on-the-spot (adj) /ˌɒn ðə 'spɒt/
pedestrian, pedestrianised (n, adj) ★/~ /pə'destriən, pə'destriənaɪzd/
peer (n) ★★ /pɪə(r)/
pinpoint (v) /'pɪnˌpɔɪnt/
place (v) ★★★ /pleɪs/
praise (n & v) ★★ /preɪz/
premises (n pl) ★★ /'premɪsɪz/
privacy (n) ★ /'prɪvəsi/
raise (v) ★★★ /reɪz/
recipient (n) /rɪ'sɪpiənt/
repercussions (n pl) /ˌriːpə(r)'kʌʃ(ə)nz/
slam (v) ★★ /slæm/
slang (n) /slæŋ/
spark concern (phr) ★ /ˌspɑː(r)k kən'sɜː(r)n/
spokesperson (n) /'spəʊksˌpɜː(r)s(ə)n/
state-owned (adj) /ˌsteɪt 'əʊnd/
summon (v) ★★ /'sʌmən/
summons (n) /'sʌmənz/
thrive (v) ★ /θraɪv/
track (v) ★ /træk/
troll, trolling (n) /trəʊl, 'trəʊlɪŋ/
urge (v) ★★ /ɜː(r)dʒ/
verge (n) /vɜː(r)dʒ/
wreck (v) ★ /rek/

Unit 6

Idiomatic expressions with *home*

not be anything to write home about (phr) /ˌnɒt biː ˌeniθɪŋ tə ˌraɪt 'həʊm əˌbaʊt/
be at home with (phr) /biː ət 'həʊm wɪð/
be home and dry (phr) /biː ˌhəʊm ən(d) 'draɪ/
be home from home (phr) /biː ˌhəʊm frəm 'həʊm/
bring something home to somebody (phr) /ˌbrɪŋ sʌmθɪŋ 'həʊm tə ˌsʌmbədi/
do something until the cows come home (phr) /ˌduː sʌmθɪŋ ənˌtɪl ðə 'kaʊz kʌm ˌhəʊm/
home truths (n pl) /ˌhəʊm 'truːðz/
take home (phr) /ˌteɪk 'həʊm/

Finding a place to live

flat-/house-hunt (v) /'flæt/'haʊs ˌhʌnt/
flat/house share (v) /'flæt/'haʊs ˌʃeə(r)/
landlord/landlady (n) ★★/★ /'læn(d)ˌlɔː(r)d/'læn(d)ˌleɪdi/
lodger (n) /'lɒdʒə(r)/
move in (v phr) /ˌmuːv 'ɪn/
pay a deposit (phr) /ˌpeɪ ə dɪ'pɒzɪt/
pay the rent (phr) /ˌpeɪ ðə 'rent/
sign a contract (phr) /ˌsaɪn ə 'kɒntrækt/
squatter (n) /'skwɒtə(r)/
studio flat (n) /'stjuːdiəʊ ˌflæt/
tenant (n) ★★ /'tenənt/

Describing cities and towns

atmospheric (adj) ★ /ˌætməs'ferɪk/
bustling (adj) /'bʌs(ə)lɪŋ/
cosmopolitan (adj) /ˌkɒzmə'pɒlɪt(ə)n/
crowded (adj) ★ /'kraʊdɪd/
filthy (adj) ★ /'fɪlθi/
hilly (adj) /'hɪli/
historic (adj) ★★ /hɪ'stɒrɪk/
industrial (adj) ★★★ /ɪn'dʌstriəl/
isolated (adj) ★ /'aɪsəˌleɪtɪd/
magnificent (adj) ★★ /mæg'nɪfɪs(ə)nt/
picturesque (adj) ★ /ˌpɪktʃə'resk/
quaint (adj) /kweɪnt/
renowned (for) (adj) /rɪ'naʊnd/
run-down (adj) /ˌrʌn 'daʊn/
shabby (adj) /'ʃæbi/
spotless (adj) /'spɒtləs/
sprawling (adj) /'sprɔːlɪŋ/
steeped in (adj) /'stiːpt ɪn/
thriving (adj) /'θraɪvɪŋ/
touristy (adj) /'tʊərɪsti/
vibrant (adj) /'vaɪbrənt/
welcoming (adj) /'welkəmɪŋ/
well-connected (adj) /ˌwel kə'nektɪd/
well-off (adj) /ˌwel 'ɒf/

Other words and phrases

affordable (adj) /ə'fɔː(r)dəb(ə)l/
barge (n) /bɑː(r)dʒ/
be in the same boat (phr) /biː ɪn ðə ˌseɪm 'bəʊt/
be worth (adj) /biː 'wɜː(r)θ/
(un)biased (adj) /(ʌn)'baɪəst/
boiler (n) /'bɔɪlə(r)/
bound (adj) ★★ /baʊnd/
budget (v) /'bʌdʒɪt/
collide (v) ★ /kə'laɪd/
compromise (v & n) ★/★★ /'kɒmprəmaɪz/
cool off (v phr) /ˌkuːl 'ɒf/
derelict (adj) /'derəlɪkt/
diligent (adj) /'dɪlɪdʒ(ə)nt/
DIY (do-it-yourself) (n) /ˌdiː aɪ 'waɪ/
dodgy (adj) /'dɒdʒi/
draw a line (work out where the lines are drawn) (phr) /ˌdrɔː ə 'laɪn/
fly the nest (phr) /ˌflaɪ ðə 'nest/
fund (v) ★★★ /fʌnd/
give notice (phr) /ˌgɪv 'nəʊtɪs/
go up in the world (phr) /ˌgəʊ 'ʌp ɪn ðə ˌwɜː(r)ld/
ground rules (n pl) /'graʊnd ˌruːlz/
guardian (n) /'gɑː(r)diən/
hall of residence (n) /ˌhɔːl əv 'rezɪd(ə)ns/
handy (adj) ★ /'hændi/
hassle (n) ★ /'hæs(ə)l/
helicopter pad (n) /'helɪˌkɒptə(r) ˌpæd/
high-profile (adj) /ˌhaɪ 'prəʊfaɪl/
housewarming party (n) /'haʊsˌwɔː(r)mɪŋ ˌpɑː(r)ti/
in short supply (phr) /ɪn ˌʃɔː(r)t sə'plaɪ/
liaise (with) (v) /li'eɪz/
lose your temper (phr) /ˌluːz jɔː(r) 'tempə(r)/
maintenance (n) ★★ /'meɪntənəns/
mingle (v) /'mɪŋg(ə)l/
mod cons (n pl) /ˌmɒd 'kɒnz/
moor (v) /mʊə(r)/
nightmare (n) ★★ /'naɪtˌmeə(r)/
opulence (n) /'ɒpjʊləns/
outskirts (n) /'aʊtˌskɜː(r)ts/
pokey (adj) /'pəʊki/
power shower (n) /'paʊə(r) ˌʃaʊə(r)/
prioritise (v) /praɪ'ɒrɪtaɪz/
recreation (n) ★ /ˌrekri'eɪʃ(ə)n/
refurbish (v) /riː'fɜː(r)bɪʃ/
renovate, renovation (v, n) /'renəveɪt, ˌrenə'veɪʃ(ə)n/
rental (n) ★ /'rent(ə)l/
respectful (adj) /rɪ'spektf(ə)l/
retail (n) /'riːteɪl/
rocketing (adj) /'rɒkɪtɪŋ/
running costs (n) /'rʌnɪŋ ˌkɒsts/
rush into (v phr) /ˌrʌʃ 'ɪntuː/
scandalous (adj) /'skænd(ə)ləs/
scenario (n) ★ /sə'nɑːriəʊ/
semi-detached (adj) /ˌsemi dɪ'tætʃt/

skyline (n) /ˈskaɪˌlaɪn/
slum (n) /slʌm/
solely (adv) ★★ /ˈsəʊlli/
spoilt for choice (phr) /ˌspɔɪlt fə(r) ˈtʃɔɪs/
staff (n) ★★★ /stɑːf/
stuff (n) ★★★ /stʌf/
trawl (v) /trɔːl/
turn up (v phr) /ˌtɜː(r)n ˈʌp/
unannounced (adv) /ˌʌnəˈnaʊnst/
update (v) ★★ /ʌpˈdeɪt/

Gateway to exams: Units 5–6

case (n) ★★★ /keɪs/
criminologist (n) /ˌkrɪmɪˈnɒlədʒɪst/
end up (v phr) /ˌend ˈʌp/
fraud (n) ★★ /frɔːd/
issue (v) ★★★ /ˈɪʃuː/
obligatory (adj) /əˈblɪgət(ə)ri/
take something for granted (phr) /ˌteɪk sʌmθɪŋ fə(r) ˈgrɑːntɪd/
transaction (n) ★★ /trænˈzækʃ(ə)n/
valid (adj) ★★ /ˈvælɪd/
watermark (n) /ˈwɔːtə(r)ˌmɑː(r)k/

Unit 7

Word formation – suffixes

Adjectives

accessible (adj) /əkˈsesəb(ə)l/
authentic (adj) ★ /ɔːˈθentɪk/
childish (adj) ★ /ˈtʃaɪldɪʃ/
collectable (adj) /kəˈlektəb(ə)l/
creative (adj) ★★ /kriˈeɪtɪv/
credible (adj) ★ /ˈkredəb(ə)l/
cynical (adj) ★ /ˈsɪnɪk(ə)l/
effective (adj) ★★★ /ɪˈfektɪv/
famous (adj) ★★★ /ˈfeɪməs/
funny (adj) ★★★ /ˈfʌni/
helpful (adj) ★★ /ˈhelpf(ə)l/
important (adj) ★★★ /ɪmˈpɔː(r)t(ə)nt/
innovative (adj) ★ /ˈɪnəveɪtɪv/
instantaneous (adj) /ˌɪnstənˈteɪniəs/
lucky (adj) ★★★ /ˈlʌki/
memorable (adj) /ˈmem(ə)rəb(ə)l/
optimistic (adj) ★★ /ˌɒptɪˈmɪstɪk/
original (adj) ★★★ /əˈrɪdʒ(ə)nəl/
pointless (adj) /ˈpɔɪntləs/
powerful (adj) ★★★ /ˈpaʊə(r)f(ə)l/
predictable (adj) ★ /prɪˈdɪktəb(ə)l/
resistant (adj) /rɪˈzɪst(ə)nt/
sensible (adj) ★★ /ˈsensəb(ə)l/
successful (adj) ★★★ /səkˈsesf(ə)l/
thoughtful/less (adj) ★ /ˈθɔːtf(ə)l/ləs/

Adverb suffixes

creatively (adv) /kriˈeɪtɪvli/
fortunately (adv) ★★ /ˈfɔː(r)tʃənətli/
luckily (adv) ★ /ˈlʌkɪli/
officially (adv) ★★ /əˈfɪʃ(ə)li/
optimistically (adv) /ˌɒptɪˈmɪstɪkli/
sensibly (adv) /ˈsensəbli/
successfully (adv) /səkˈsesf(ə)li/

Verb suffixes

intensify (v) /ɪnˈtensɪfaɪ/
modernise (v) /ˈmɒdə(r)naɪz/
standardise (v) /ˈstændə(r)daɪz/

Noun suffixes

criticism (n) ★★★ /ˈkrɪtɪˌsɪz(ə)m/
discovery (n) ★★★ /dɪˈskʌv(ə)ri/
endorsement (n) /ɪnˈdɔː(r)smənt/
imagination (n) ★★ /ɪˌmædʒɪˈneɪʃ(ə)n/
likelihood (n) ★ /ˈlaɪklihʊd/
originality (n) /əˌrɪdʒəˈnæləti/
readiness (n) /ˈredinəs/
variety (n) ★★★ /vəˈraɪəti/

Prefixes

autograph (n) /ˈɔːtəˌgrɑːf/
multi-purpose (adj) /ˌmʌlti ˈpɜː(r)pəs/
post-concert (adj) /ˌpəʊst ˈkɒnsə(r)t/
pre-concert (adj) /ˌpriː ˈkɒnsə(r)t/

Advertising and selling

banner (n) /ˈbænə(r)/
billboard (n) /ˈbɪlˌbɔː(r)d/
brand name (n) ★ /ˈbrænd ˌneɪm/
endorse a product (phr) /ɪnˌdɔː(r)s ə ˈprɒdʌkt/
give away a freebie (phr) /ˌgɪv əˌweɪ ə ˈfriːbi/
launch a marketing campaign (phr) /ˌlɔːntʃ ə ˈmɑː(r)kɪtɪŋ kæmˌpeɪn/
make cold calls (phr) /ˌmeɪk kəʊld ˈkɔːlz/
word-of-mouth publicity (phr) /ˌwɜː(r)d əv ˌmaʊθ pʌbˈlɪsəti/

Describing clothes and fashions

adventurous (adj) /ədˈventʃ(ə)rəs/
baggy (adj) /ˈbægi/
(be) in style (phr) /biː ɪn ˈstaɪl/
be seen dead in (phr) /biː ˌsiːn ˈded ɪn/
by means of (phr) /baɪ ˈmiːnz ɒv/
casual (adj) ★★ /ˈkæʒuəl/
check (n) ★★ /tʃek/
chic (adj) /ʃiːk/
classic (n) ★★ /ˈklæsɪk/
fit (v) ★★★ /fɪt/
flowery (adj) /ˈflaʊəri/
glamorous (adj) /ˈglæmərəs/
loose (adj) ★★ /luːs/
match (n & v) ★★★ /mætʃ/
old-fashioned (adj) ★★ /ˌəʊld ˈfæʃ(ə)nd/
plain (adj) ★★ /pleɪn/
scruffy (adj) /ˈskrʌfi/
set a trend (phr) /ˌset ə ˈtrend/
smart (adj) ★★ /smɑː(r)t/
sophisticated (adj) ★★ /səˈfɪstɪˌkeɪtɪd/
stripy (adj) /ˈstraɪpi/
suit (v) ★★★ /suːt/
tight (adj) ★★/taɪt/
trendy (adj) /ˈtrendi/

Other words and phrases

(a) fraction (of) (n) ★★ / (ə) ˈfrækʃ(ə)n (əv)/
aisle (n) /aɪl/
appliance (n) ★ /əˈplaɪəns/
assemble (v) ★★ /əˈsemb(ə)l/
blogger (n) /ˈblɒgə(r)/
brainwash (v) /ˈbreɪnˌwɒʃ/
buzz (n) /bʌz/
certification (n) /ˌsə(r)tɪfɪˈkeɪʃ(ə)n/
CFC (n) /ˌsiː ef ˈsiː/
challenge (v) ★★★ /ˈtʃæləndʒ/
customer-friendly (adj) /ˌkʌstəmə(r) ˈfren(d)li/
detail (v) ★ /ˈdiːteɪl/
developing country (n) /dɪˌveləpɪŋ ˈkʌntri/
economic growth (n) /ˌiːkənɒmɪk ˈgrəʊθ/
far-reaching (adj) /ˌfɑː(r) ˈriːtʃɪŋ/
following (n) ★ /ˈfɒləʊɪŋ/
globalisation (n) /ˌgləʊbəlaɪˈzeɪʃ(ə)n/
grab (v) ★★ /græb/
greenwashing (n) /ˈgriːnˌwɒʃɪŋ/
hashtag (n) /ˈhæʃˌtæg/
hold sway (phr) /ˌhəʊld ˈsweɪ/
icon, iconic (n, adj) ~/★ /ˈaɪkɒn, aɪˈkɒnɪk/
incentive (n) ★★ /ɪnˈsentɪv/
influencer (n) /ˈɪnfluənsə(r)/
interdependent (adj) /ˌɪntə(r)dɪˈpendənt/
pay off (v phr) /ˌpeɪ ˈɒf/
purchase (n) ★★ /ˈpɜː(r)tʃəs/

relatable (adj) /rɪ'leɪtəb(ə)l/
retailer (n) ★ /'riːˌteɪlə(r)/
savvy (n) /'sævi/
scanner (n) ★ /'skænə(r)/
selfie (n) /'selfi/
sizeable (adj) /'saɪzəb(ə)l/
vlogger (n) /'vlɒgə(r)/
wise (adj) ★★ /waɪz/

Unit 8

Words with more than one meaning

clear (adj) ★★★ /klɪə(r)/
cover (v) ★★★ /'kʌvə(r)/
fair (adj) ★★★ /feə(r)/
hard (adj) ★★★ /hɑː(r)d/
point (v & n) ★★★ /pɔɪnt/
since (adv, prep) ★★★ /sɪns/

point (phr)

get to the point (phr) /ˌget tə ðə 'pɔɪnt/
have a point (phr) /ˌhæv ə 'pɔɪnt/
miss the point (phr) /ˌmɪs ðə 'pɔɪnt/
on the point of (phr) /ɒn ðə 'pɔɪnt ɒv/
prove a point (phr) /ˌpruːv ə 'pɔɪnt/
see a point (phr) /ˌsiː ə 'pɔɪnt/
the point of no return (phr) /ðə ˌpɔɪnt əv ˌnəʊ rɪ'tɜː(r)n/
up to a point (phr) /ˌʌp tuː ə 'pɔɪnt/

Compound adjectives – parts of the body

breakneck (adj) /'breɪkˌnek/
ear-splitting (adj) /'ɪə(r) ˌsplɪtɪŋ/
eye-catching (adj) /'aɪ ˌkætʃɪŋ/
eye-opening (adj) /'aɪ ˌəʊp(ə)nɪŋ/
hair-raising (adj) /'heə(r) ˌreɪzɪŋ/
heart-stopping (adj) /'hɑː(r)t ˌstɒpɪŋ/
heartwarming (adj) /'hɑː(r)tˌwɔː(r)mɪŋ/
nail-biting (adj) /'neɪl ˌbaɪtɪŋ/
soul-destroying (adj) /'səʊl dɪˌstrɔɪɪŋ/

Metaphors – happiness and sadness

be/feel down in the dumps (phr) /biː/fiːl ˌdaʊn ɪn ðə 'dʌmps/
be/feel on top of the world (phr) /biː/fiːl ɒn ˌtɒp əv ðə 'wɜː(r)ld/
be in low spirits (phr) /biː ɪn ˌləʊ 'spɪrɪts/
be in seventh heaven (n) /biː ɪn ˌsev(ə)nθ 'hev(ə)n/
be on cloud nine (phr) /biː ɒn ˌklaʊd 'naɪn/
be over the moon (phr) /biː ˌəʊvə(r) ðə 'muːn/
brighten up (v phr) /ˌbraɪt(ə)n 'ʌp/
cast a shadow over (phr) /ˌkɑːst ə 'ʃædəʊ ˌəʊvə(r)/
feel blue (phr) /ˌfiːl 'bluː/
feel down/low (phr) /ˌfiːl 'daʊn/'ləʊ/
lift somebody's spirits (phr) /ˌlɪft sʌmbədiz 'spɪrɪts/
light at the end of the tunnel (phr) /ˌlaɪt ət ði ˌend əv ðə 'tʌn(ə)l/
light up (v phr) /ˌlaɪt 'ʌp/
look bright (phr) /ˌlʊk 'braɪt/
look gloomy/bleak (phr) /ˌlʊk 'gluːmi/'bliːk/
look up (v phr) /ˌlʊk 'ʌp/
somebody's heart sinks (phr) /ˌsʌmbədiz 'hɑː(r)t ˌsɪŋks/
walk/float on air (phr) /ˌwɔːk/ˌfləʊt ɒn 'eə(r)/

Other words and phrases

adamant (adj) /'ædəmənt/
adrenalin (n) /ə'drenəlɪn/
astounded (adj) /ə'staʊndɪd/
battle it out (for) (phr) /ˌbæt(ə)l ɪt 'aʊt fɔː(r)/
belongings (n pl) /bɪ'lɒŋɪŋz/
black out (v phr) /ˌblæk 'aʊt/
blur (n) /blɜː(r)/
bruise (n) /bruːz/
burst (n) /bɜː(r)st/
cling (v) ★★ /klɪŋ/
cord (n) ★ /kɔː(r)d/
curl up (v phr) /ˌkɜː(r)l 'ʌp/
dive (v) ★★ /daɪv/
drag (v) ★★ /dræg/
enrich (v) /ɪn'rɪtʃ/
essentially (adv) ★★★ /ɪ'senʃ(ə)li/
fade (v) ★★ /feɪd/
fearless (adj) /'fɪə(r)ləs/
fictionalised (adj) /'fɪkʃ(ə)nəlaɪzd/
float (v) ★★ /fləʊt/
give something a go (phr) /ˌgɪv sʌmθɪŋ ə 'gəʊ/
gorge (n) /gɔː(r)dʒ/
harness (n) /'hɑː(r)nɪs/
head over heels (in love) (phr) /ˌhed əʊvə(r) ˌhiːlz (ɪn 'lʌv)/
hike (v) /haɪk/
impact (n) ★★★ /'ɪmpækt/
infested (adj) /ɪn'festɪd/
ingest (v) /ɪn'dʒest/
jolt (n) /dʒəʊlt/
lifeboat (n) /'laɪfˌbəʊt/
lose your bottle (phr) /ˌluːz jɔː(r) 'bɒt(ə)l/
miraculous (adj) /mə'rækjʊləs/
mountaineer (n) /ˌmaʊntɪ'nɪə(r)/
quest (n) ★ /kwest/
rapids (n pl) /'ræpɪdz/
recoil (v) /rɪ'kɔɪl/
reject (v) ★★★ /rɪ'dʒekt/
roar (v) ★ /rɔː(r)/
rope (n) ★★ /rəʊp/
rule out (v phr) /ˌruːl 'aʊt/
rush (n) ★★ /rʌʃ/
simulator, simulation (n, n) ~/★ /'sɪmjʊˌleɪtə(r), ˌsɪmjʊ'leɪʃ(ə)n/
single-handed (adj) /ˌsɪŋg(ə)l 'hændɪd/
slap (v) ★ /slæp/
slip (v) ★★★ /slɪp/
speed (v) ★★ /spiːd/
spot (n) ★★★ /spɒt/
spread (v) ★★★ /spred/
strap together (v phr) /ˌstræp tə'geðə(r)/
thrill seeker (n) /'θrɪl ˌsiːkə(r)/
turbulent (adj) /'tɜː(r)bjʊlənt/
war-torn (adj) /'wɔː(r) ˌtɔː(r)n/
waterfall (n) ★ /'wɔːtə(r)ˌfɔːl/
wedge (v) /wedʒ/
whirlpool (n) /'wɜː(r)lˌpuːl/
witness (v) ★★ /'wɪtnəs/
zoom (v) /zuːm/

Gateway to exams: Units 7–8

backdrop (n) ★ /'bækˌdrɒp/
base jumper (n) /'beɪs ˌdʒʌmpə(r)/
cliff (n) ★★ /klɪf/
juggernaut (n) /'dʒʌgə(r)ˌnɔːt/
multinational (adj) ★ (n) /ˌmʌlti'næʃ(ə)nəl/
parachute (n) /'pærəˌʃuːt/
pier (n) ★ /pɪə(r)/
propel (v) /prə'pel/
publicise (v) /'pʌblɪsaɪz/
somersault (v & n) /'sʌmə(r)ˌsɔːlt/
sponsor (n) ★ /'spɒnsə(r)/
spurt (n) /spɜː(r)t/
stage (v) /steɪdʒ/
stunt (n) /stʌnt/

Unit 9

Verb-noun collocations

embark on a +

career (n) ★★★ /ɪmˌbɑː(r)k ɒn ə kə'rɪə(r)/

course (n) ★★★ /ɪmˌbɑː(r)k ɒn ə 'kɔː(r)s/

project (n) ★★★ /ɪmˌbɑː(r)k ɒn ə 'prɒdʒekt/

venture (n) ★ /ɪmˌbɑː(r)k ɒn ə 'ventʃə(r)/

gain +

a qualification (n) ★★★ /ˌgeɪn ə ˌkwɒlɪfɪ'keɪʃ(ə)n/

confidence (n) ★★★ /ˌgeɪn 'kɒnfɪd(ə)ns/

experience (n) ★★★ /ˌgeɪn ɪk'spɪəriəns/

insight (n) ★★ /ˌgeɪn 'ɪnsaɪt/

knowledge (n) ★★★ /ˌgeɪn 'nɒlɪdʒ/

understanding (n) ★★★ /ˌgeɪn ˌʌndə(r) 'stændɪŋ/

overcome +

adversity (n) /ˌəʊvə(r)ˌkʌm əd'vɜː(r)səti/

an obstacle (n) ★★ /ˌəʊvə(r)ˌkʌm ən 'ɒbstək(ə)l/

a problem (n) ★★★ /ˌəʊvə(r)ˌkʌm ə 'prɒbləm/

a setback (n) /ˌəʊvə(r)ˌkʌm ə 'setˌbæk/

fear (n) ★★★ /ˌəʊvə(r)ˌkʌm 'fɪə(r)/

resistance (n) ★★★ /ˌəʊvə(r)ˌkʌm rɪ'zɪst(ə)ns/

experience +

a situation (n) ★★★ /ɪkˌspɪəriəns ə ˌsɪtʃu'eɪʃ(ə)n/

change (n) ★★★ /ɪkˌspɪəriəns 'tʃeɪndʒ/

pain (n) ★★★ /ɪkˌspɪəriəns 'peɪn/

problems (n) ★★★ /ɪkˌspɪəriəns 'prɒbləmz/

take up a +

career (n) ★★★ /ˌteɪk ʌp ə kə'rɪə(r)/

hobby (n) ★ /ˌteɪk ʌp ə 'hɒbi/

position (n) ★★★ /ˌteɪk ʌp ə pə'zɪʃ(ə)n/

post (n) ★★★ /ˌteɪk ʌp ə 'pəʊst/

undertake +

analysis (n) ★★★ /ˌʌndə(r)ˌteɪk ə'næləsɪs/

an investigation (n) ★★★ /ˌʌndə(r)ˌteɪk ən ɪnˌvestɪ'geɪʃ(ə)n/

a study (n) ★★★ /ˌʌndə(r)ˌteɪk ə 'stʌdi/

a survey (n) ★★★ /ˌʌndə(r)ˌteɪk ə 'sɜː(r)veɪ/

a task (n) ★★★ /ˌʌndə(r)ˌteɪk ə 'tɑːsk/

Other collocations

cause trouble (phr) /ˌkɔːz 'trʌb(ə)l/

inspire confidence (phr) /ɪnˌspaɪə(r) 'kɒnfɪd(ə)ns/

pay attention (phr) /ˌpeɪ ə'tenʃ(ə)n/

speak your mind (phr) /ˌspiːk jɔː(r) 'maɪnd/

stand pressure (phr) /ˌstænd 'preʃə(r)/

suffer a setback (phr) /ˌsʌfər ə 'setˌbæk/

take control of (phr) /ˌteɪk kən'trəʊl ɒv/

take responsibility for (phr) /ˌteɪk rɪˌspɒnsə'bɪləti fɔː(r)/

voice an opinion (phr) /ˌvɔɪs ən ə'pɪnjən/

weigh up the consequences/the pros and cons (phr) /ˌweɪ ʌp ðə 'kɒnsɪkwənsɪz/ðə ˌprəʊz ən(d) 'kɒnz/

Life and career developments

accomplish (v) ★ /ə'kʌmplɪʃ/

end up (v phr) /ˌend 'ʌp/

enrol (on a course) (v) /ɪn'rəʊl/

find your feet (phr) /ˌfaɪnd jɔː(r) 'fiːt/

follow in somebody's footsteps (phr) /ˌfɒləʊ ɪn sʌmbədiz 'fʊtˌsteps/

get on in life (phr) /ˌget 'ɒn ɪn ˌlaɪf/

give somebody insight into (phr) /ˌgɪv sʌmbədi 'ɪnsaɪt ɪntuː/

have lots of aspirations and drive (phr) /hæv ˌlɒts əv ˌæspɪ'reɪʃ(ə)nz ən(d) 'draɪv/

never look back (phr) /ˌnevə(r) lʊk 'bæk/

overcome setbacks (phr) /ˌəʊvə(r) ˌkʌm 'setˌbæks/

put something on hold (phr) /ˌpʊt sʌmθɪŋ ɒn 'həʊld/

serve an apprenticeship (phr) /ˌsɜː(r)v ən ə'prentɪsʃɪp/

settle in (v phr) /ˌset(ə)l 'ɪn/

try your hand at something (phr) /ˌtraɪ jɔː(r) 'hænd æt/

Words and expressions connected with internships

career advancement (phr) /kə'rɪər ədˌvɑːnsmənt/

get a foot in the business (phr) /ˌget ə 'fʊt ɪn ðə ˌbɪznəs/

heavy workload (phr) /ˌhevi 'wɜː(r)kˌləʊd/

insight into how a company works (phr) /ˌɪnsaɪt ɪntuː ˌhaʊ ə ˌkʌmp(ə)ni 'wɜː(r)ks/

long/antisocial hours (phr) /ˌlɒŋ/ ˌæntiˌsəʊʃ(ə)l 'aʊə(r)z/

make ends meet (phr) /ˌmeɪk endz 'miːt/

mundane tasks (phr) /mʌnˌdeɪn 'tɑːsks/

networking opportunities (phr) /'netˌwɜː(r)kɪŋ ˌɒpə(r)ˌtjuːnətiz/

on the job training (phr) /ˌɒn ðə ˌdʒɒb 'treɪnɪŋ/

pass through (v phr) /ˌpɑːs 'θruː/

perks (n pl) /pɜː(r)ks/

reach the point (phr) /ˌriːtʃ ðə 'pɔɪnt/

stand up for (yourself) (v phr) /ˌstænd 'ʌp fə(r) jə(r)ˌself/

support financially (phr) /səˌpɔː(r)t faɪ'nænʃ(ə)li/

take for granted (phr) /ˌteɪk fə(r) 'grɑːntɪd/

under the nose of (phr) /ˌʌndə(r) ðə 'nəʊz ɒv/

Other words and phrases

accomplished (adj) /ə'kʌmplɪʃt/

accomplishment (n) /ə'kʌmplɪʃmənt/

applicant (n) ★ /'æplɪkənt/

by and large (phr) /ˌbaɪ ən(d) 'lɑː(r)dʒ/

drift (v) ★★ /drɪft/

fall apart (v phr) /ˌfɔːl ə'pɑː(r)t/

get the ball rolling (phr) /ˌget ðə ˌbɔːl 'rəʊlɪŋ/

grind to a halt (phr) /ˌgraɪnd tuː ə 'hɔːlt/

hands-on (adj) /ˌhændz 'ɒn/

highly-regarded (adj) /ˌhaɪli rɪ'gɑː(r)dɪd/

intern (n) /'ɪntɜː(r)n/

jump at an opportunity (phr) /'dʒʌmp ət ən ˌɒpə(r)ˌtjuːnəti/

liaise (v) /li'eɪz/

long-/short-term (adj) ★★★/★★ /'lɒŋ/'ʃɔː(r)t ˌtɜː(r)m/

mentor (n & v) /'mentɔː(r)/

panel (n) ★★★ /'pæn(ə)l/

placement (n) /'pleɪsmənt/

proactive (adj) /prəʊ'æktɪv/

prompt (adj) /prɒmpt/

pursue (v) ★★ /pə(r)'sjuː/

recognition (n) ★★★ /ˌrekəg'nɪʃ(ə)n/

recruit (v) ★★ /rɪ'kruːt/

referee (n) ★★ /ˌrefə'riː/

run a company (phr) ★★★ /ˌrʌn ə 'kʌmp(ə)ni/
short-staffed (adj) /ˌʃɔː(r)t 'stɑːft/
skip (v) ★ /skɪp/
slang (n) /slæŋ/
specification (n) ★★ /ˌspesɪfɪ'keɪʃ(ə)n/
straightforward (adj) ★★ /ˌstreɪt'fɔː(r)wə(r)d/
strength (n) ★★★ /streŋθ/
stumble on/upon (v phr) /'stʌmb(ə)l ɒn/əpɒn/
swing it (phr) /'swɪŋ ɪt/
tailor (n) /'teɪlə(r)/
temp (n) /temp/
trail (v) ★★ /treɪl/
turn down (v phr) /ˌtɜː(r)n 'daʊn/
vacancy (n) ★ /'veɪkənsi/
venue (n) ★★ /'venjuː/
venture (n) ★ /'ventʃə(r)/
weakness (n) ★★ /'wiːknəs/

Unit 10

Phrasal verbs – communication

bring up (v phr) /ˌbrɪŋ 'ʌp/
cut in (v phr) /ˌkʌt 'ɪn/
get through to (v phr) /ˌget 'θruː tuː/
make out (v phr) /ˌmeɪk 'aʊt/
pick up on (v phr) /ˌpɪk 'ʌp ɒn/
point out (v phr) /ˌpɔɪnt 'aʊt/
speak out (v phr) /ˌspiːk 'aʊt/
spell out (v phr) /ˌspel 'aʊt/
talk down to (v phr) /ˌtɔːk 'daʊn tuː/
turn to (v phr) /'tɜː(r)n tuː/

Communication and communication breakdown

find something puzzling (phr) /ˌfaɪnd sʌmθɪŋ 'pʌz(ə)lɪŋ/
get the wrong end of the stick (phr) /ˌget ðə rɒŋ ˌend əv ðə 'stɪk/
imply (v) /ɪm'plaɪ/
make a gaffe (phr) /ˌmeɪk ə 'gæf/
make a (witty) remark (phr) /ˌmeɪk ə ˌwɪti rɪ'mɑː(r)k/
misinterpret (v) /ˌmɪsɪn'tɜː(r)prɪt/
offend somebody unintentionally (phr) /əˌfend sʌmbədi ˌʌnɪn'tenʃ(ə)nəli/
take something literally (phr) /ˌteɪk sʌmθɪŋ 'lɪt(ə)rəli/
talk at cross purposes (phr) /ˌtɔːk ət ˌkrɒs 'pɜː(r)pəsɪz/
understand nuances (phr) /ˌʌndə(r)ˌstænd 'njuːɒnsɪz/

Other words and phrases

abbreviation (n) ★ /əˌbriːvi'eɪʃ(ə)n/
acquire (v) ★★ /ə'kwaɪə(r)/
approximate (n) /ə'prɒksɪmət/
assume (v) ★★★ /ə'sjuːm/
behind the scenes (phr) /bɪˌhaɪnd ðə 'siːnz/
bullet point (n) /'bʊlɪt ˌpɔɪnt/
censorship (n) /'sensə(r)ʃɪp/
consistent (adj) ★★ /kən'sɪstənt/
convey (v) ★★ /kən'veɪ/
crowd-sourced (adj) /'kraʊd ˌsɔː(r)st/
cut off (from) (v phr) /ˌkʌt 'ɒf (frɒm)/
dedicated (adj) /'dedɪˌkeɪtɪd/
digitalisation (n) /ˌdɪdʒɪt(ə)laɪ'zeɪʃ(ə)n/
dubbed (adj) /dʌbd/
excursion (n) /ɪk'skɜː(r)ʃ(ə)n/
get in the way (phr) /ˌget ɪn ðə 'weɪ/
hard at work (phr) /ˌhɑː(r)d ət 'wɜː(r)k/
highlight (v) ★★ /'haɪˌlaɪt/
integrate (v) ★★ /'ɪntɪˌgreɪt/
in the light of (phr) /ɪn ðə 'laɪt ɒv/
isolated (adj) ★ /'aɪsəˌleɪtɪd/
lead people to believe something (phr) /ˌliːd ˌpiːp(ə)l tə bɪ'liːv sʌmθɪŋ/
mistranslate, mistranslation (v, n) /ˌmɪstræns'leɪt, ˌmɪstræns'leɪʃ(ə)n/
outline (v) ★★ /'aʊtlaɪn/
proficient (adj) /prə'fɪʃ(ə)nt/
prominence (n) /'prɒmɪnəns/
propose (v) ★★ /prə'pəʊz/
prove popular (phr) /ˌpruːv 'pɒpjʊlə(r)/
range (n) ★★★ /reɪndʒ/
small talk (n) /'smɔːl ˌtɔːk/
sour (adj) ★ /'saʊə(r)/
statement (n) ★★★ /'steɪtmənt/
strike (v) ★★★ /straɪk/
stroke of the pen (phr) /ˌstrəʊk əv ðə 'pen/
subtitler (n) /'sʌbˌtaɪt(ə)lə(r)/
subtitles (n pl) /'sʌbˌtaɪt(ə)lz/
superficial (adj) ★ /ˌsuːpə(r)'fɪʃ(ə)l/
synchronised (adj) /'sɪŋkrənaɪzd/
treaty (n) ★★ /'triːti/
turn something on its head (phr) /ˌtɜː(r)n sʌmθɪŋ ɒn ɪts 'hed/
undergo (v) ★★ /ˌʌndə(r)'gəʊ/
virtually (adv) ★★★ /'vɜː(r)tʃʊəli/
word play (n) /'wɜː(r)d ˌpleɪ/
worthy (adj) ★★★ /'wɜː(r)ði/

Gateway to exams: Units 9–10

arise (from) (v) ★★★ /ə'raɪz/
augment, augmentation (v, n) /ɔːg'ment, ˌɔːgmen'teɪʃ(ə)n/
bench (n) ★★ /bentʃ/
commercial returns (n pl) /kəˌmɜː(r)ʃ(ə)l rɪ'tɜː(r)nz/
component (n) ★★ /kəm'pəʊnənt/
critical (adj) ★★★ /'krɪtɪk(ə)l/
crop (n) ★★ /krɒp/
dispute (n) ★★★ /dɪ'spjuːt/, /'dɪspjuːt/
enhance (v) ★★ /ɪn'hɑːns/
envisage (v) ★★ /ɪn'vɪzɪdʒ/
facilitator (n) /fə'sɪləteɪtə(r)/
harvest (v) /'hɑː(r)vɪst/
incubator (n) /'ɪŋkjʊˌbeɪtə(r)/
infringement (n) /ɪn'frɪndʒmənt/
irrigate (v) /'ɪrɪgeɪt/
kneecap (n) /'niːˌkæp/
legal jurisdiction (n) /ˌliːg(ə)l ˌdʒʊərɪs'dɪkʃ(ə)n/
limb (n) ★★ /lɪm/
onset (n) ★ /'ɒnˌset/
outcry (n) /'aʊtˌkraɪ/
precedent (n) ★ /'presɪdənt/
quality control (n) /'kwɒləti kənˌtrəʊl/
realm (n) ★ /relm/
sabotage (n) /'sæbətɑːʒ/
staged (adj) /steɪdʒd/
surgeon (n) ★★ /'sɜː(r)dʒ(ə)n/
tend (plants) (v) ★★★ /tend/
trademark (n) /'treɪdˌmɑː(r)k/

Suffixes

Adjective suffixes:

-*ful* (usually added to nouns)
insightful, painful, helpful, thoughtful, successful, careful, colourful, hopeful, painful, peaceful, useful, wonderful

-*less* (usually added to nouns)
helpless, thoughtless, meaningless, painless, fearless, hopeless, sleepless, useless, pointless, powerless

-*al* (usually added to nouns)
personal, accidental, biographical, astrological, commercial, national, economical, environmental, global, industrial, logical, musical, original, political, professional, provisional, regional, sentimental

-*ic* (usually added to nouns)
optimistic, scientific, artistic, economic, pessimistic, poetic

-*y* (usually added to nouns)
lucky, cloudy, dirty, dusty, funny, hairy, hungry, rainy, sleepy, sunny, thirsty

-*able* (usually added to verbs)
considerable, likeable, enjoyable, believable, predictable, acceptable, available, comfortable, irritable, knowledgeable, memorable, profitable, questionable, reasonable, recognisable, understandable, washable, useable/usable

-*ible* (usually added to verbs)
terrible, accessible, comprehensible, convertible, edible, sensible, horrible

-*ant* (usually added to verbs)
important, expectant, resistant, observant

-*ive* (usually added to verbs)
productive, active, attractive, competitive, constructive, creative, deceptive, decisive, destructive, effective, impressive, impulsive, perceptive, receptive, supportive

-*ish* (meaning: more or less, usually added to another adjective)
tallish, straightish, youngish, brownish

Noun suffixes – abstract/things:

-*ity* (usually added to adjectives)
similarity, personality, ability, productivity, activity, availability, complexity, creativity, curiosity, density, equality, formality, fraternity, generosity, humidity, ingenuity, reality, security, stupidity, superiority

-*ence* (usually added to adjectives)
coincidence, intelligence, existence, adolescence, confidence, correspondence, difference, independence, obedience, patience, presence, residence, violence

-*ance* (usually added to adjectives)
abundance, (dis)appearance, appliance, assurance, elegance, extravagance, ignorance, importance, insurance, relevance, surveillance

-*ety* (usually added to adjectives)
anxiety, safety

-*ness* (usually added to adjectives)
happiness, awareness, blindness, darkness, eagerness, illness, loneliness, madness, sadness, selfishness, weakness

-*dom* (usually added to adjectives)
freedom, boredom, kingdom

-*cy* (usually added to adjectives)
frequency, accuracy, decency, diplomacy, efficiency, fluency, privacy, urgency, vacancy

-*ment* (usually added to verbs)
argument, enjoyment, improvement, (un)employment, amusement, appointment, arrangement, assessment, attachment, accomplishment, adjustment, development, embarrassment, empowerment, enhancement, excitement, government, instalment, recruitment, requirement, retirement

-*ion* (usually added to verbs)
description, creation, production, action, adaptation, affection, attention, prediction, destruction, discussion, education, explanation, expression, hesitation, implication, impression, invention, investigation, isolation, operation, organisation, probation

-*ure* (usually added to verbs)
failure, pleasure, pressure

-*ship* (usually added to another noun)
citizenship, censorship, relationship, friendship, membership, leadership, hardship, ownership

Noun suffixes – people:

-*or* (usually added to verbs)
actor, creator, inventor

-*er* (usually added to verbs)
astrologer, researcher, believer, producer, player, hunter, gatherer, publisher, bystander, plumber

-*ant* (usually added to verbs)
participant, assistant, attendant, applicant

-ist **(usually added to another noun)**
graphologist, psychologist, scientist, artist, optimist, guitarist, physicist

Adverb suffix:

-ly **(usually added to adjectives)**
deliberately, virtually, nationally, productively, actively, willingly

Prefixes

anti- **(meaning: *against*)**
anticlockwise, antisocial, anti-hero

co- **(meaning: *with, together*)**
co-star, coproduce, coexist, cooperate, coordination, co-pilot

dis- **(meaning: *the opposite, not*)**
disappointing, disjointed, disabled, disability, disappear, disadvantage, disapprove, discomfort, disconnect, dishonest, disloyal, disobey, disorder, disorganise, disqualify

ex- **(meaning: *a position or situation that existed before, but not now*)**
ex-husband, ex-president

il- **(meaning: *the opposite, not*)**
illegal, illegible, illegitimate, illiterate, illogical

im- **(meaning: *the opposite, not*)**
impenetrable, immature, impatient, imperfect, impolite, impossible, impractical, improbable

in- **(meaning: *the opposite, not*)**
inability, inactive, inadequate, incapable, inconsolable, incorrect, inefficient, inexperienced, informal, insecure, invisible

inter- **(meaning: *between*)**
international, interact, interactive, interchange, interconnect, interdependent, interface, intermediary

ir- **(meaning: *the opposite, not*)**
irrational, irregular, irrelevant, irresistible, irresponsible

mis- **(meaning: *wrong, incorrect*)**
miscast, mishap, misinterpret, misfortune, misbehave, miscalculate, misconception, misdemeanour, mishear, misinform, misjudge, mislead, mismanage, misprint, mispronounce, misread, mistimed, mistreat, mistrust, misunderstand

over- **(meaning: *too much*)**
overblown, overcritical, overcook, overbook, overbearing, overdo, overemphasise, overestimate, overflow, overhang, overload, overpaid, overpopulated, overpriced, overreact, oversleep, overweight, overwork

non- **(meaning: *the opposite, not*)**
non-profit, non-smoking, non-resident, non-stop, non-verbal

pre- **(meaning: *before*)**
preconception, precook, pre-school

post- **(meaning: *after*)**
postgraduate, postmodern, post-war

re- **(meaning: *again*)**
remake, reproduce, react, rediscover, readjust, reappear, reassess, rebuild, reclassify, reconsider, rediscover, redo, replay

sub- **(meaning: *below*)**
subconscious, sub-plot, subway, sub-zero, submarine

super- **(meaning: *more, bigger, better*)**
superhero, superhuman, superimpose, supernatural, superpower

un- **(meaning: *the opposite, not*)**
unpredictable, uninspiring, unnatural, unable, uncooked, unacceptable, unbelievable, uncertain, unconscious, unconventional, undo, unemployed, unfair, unfortunate, unkind, unlock, unpack, unreal, unreliable

under- **(meaning: *not enough*)**
underrated, undercook, underestimate, underprivileged, undervalued, underweight

Infinitive	Past simple	Past participle
be	was/were	been
beat	beat	beaten
become	became	become
begin	began	begun
break	broke	broken
bring	brought	brought
build	built	built
burn	burnt	burnt
buy	bought	bought
catch	caught	caught
choose	chose	chosen
come	came	come
cost	cost	cost
cut	cut	cut
do	did	done
draw	drew	drawn
drink	drank	drunk
drive	drove	driven
eat	ate	eaten
fall	fell	fallen
feel	felt	felt
find	found	found
fly	flew	flown
forget	forgot	forgotten
forgive	forgave	forgiven
get	got	got
give	gave	given
go	went	gone
grow	grew	grown
hang out	hung out	hung out
have	had	had
hear	heard	heard
hide	hid	hidden
hit	hit	hit
hurt	hurt	hurt
keep	kept	kept
know	knew	known
lay	laid	laid
leave	left	left
learn	learned/learnt	learned/learnt

Infinitive	Past simple	Past participle
let	let	let
lie	lay	lain
lose	lost	lost
make	made	made
mean	meant	meant
meet	met	met
pay	paid	paid
put	put	put
read	read	read
ride	rode	ridden
ring	rang	rung
run	ran	run
say	said	said
see	saw	seen
sell	sold	sold
send	sent	sent
set up	set up	set up
shine	shone	shone
shoot	shot	shot
show	showed	shown
sing	sang	sung
sit	sat	sat
sleep	slept	slept
speak	spoke	spoken
speed	sped	sped
spell	spelt	spelt
spend	spent	spent
split up	split up	split up
stand up	stood up	stood up
steal	stole	stolen
swim	swam	swum
take	took	taken
teach	taught	taught
tell	told	told
think	thought	thought
understand	understood	understood
wake up	woke up	woken up
wear	wore	worn
win	won	won
write	wrote	written

Unit 1

READING: MULTIPLE MATCHING (UNITS 1 AND 9)

In this type of activity, you have to say which text or part of a text contains a piece of information or answers a question.

Step 1: Read all the texts or parts of the text quickly to get a general understanding.

Step 2: Read the piece(s) of information that you need to find. Underline key words in the questions. Are there any special words that help you to find the text or part of the text which contains the information? Remember that in the text the same information will probably be expressed with different words.

Step 3: Read again in more detail the specific text or part of the text where you think the information comes. It can be useful to underline the section of the text where you think the answer comes.

Step 4: If you are not sure that you have found the correct answer, read other sections again in more detail.

Step 5: When you finish, check that you have an answer for each question. Never leave answers blank in an exam.

USE OF ENGLISH: WORD-FORMATION CLOZE (UNITS 1 AND 7)

In this type of activity you must use the word given to form a word that fits in the gap. The words can be any type – noun, adjective, adverb or verb.

Step 1: Read the text once quickly to know the general meaning.

Step 2: When you look closer at each gap, read to the end of the sentence, not just to the end of the line. This will help you to decide if you need to change the meaning of the word, e.g. making it negative. Usually to change the meaning of the word you will need a prefix (e.g. *im-*, *re-*).

Step 3: Then look carefully at the words just before and after the gap. They can help you to decide what type of word you need. Usually to change the type of word you will need a suffix (e.g. *-ion* to make a noun, *-ly* to make an adverb).

Step 4: Remember that you may need to change the spelling of the word they give you. For example, from the word STRONG you may need to make the noun STRENGTH. Also, look carefully to decide if your word needs to be in the singular or plural form. If the word is a verb, put it in the correct form according to the context.

Step 5: Read the completed sentence and check your answer. Check that you have an answer for each question. Never leave answers blank in an exam.

LISTENING: TRUE/FALSE/NOT GIVEN

In this type of activity you have to listen and decide if answers are true, false or if the information is not stated. Put *Not Given* if you cannot hear the information when you listen to the text. You usually hear the text twice. The questions are usually in the order that you hear them in the recording.

Step 1: Read the answers *before* you listen. They can give you ideas about the topic of the text and the vocabulary you are going to hear in it.

Step 2: You can usually hear the recording twice. Do not panic if you do not understand information the first time. If you don't hear the answer to one question, start listening immediately for the answer to the next question.

Step 3: Use the second listening to find the answers you didn't hear the first time and to check the answers you already have.

Step 4: When you finish, check that you have an answer for each question. Never leave answers blank in an exam.

WRITING: STORIES

- Before you write a story, make a plan. Make sure that your story has a beginning, a middle and an end. Sometimes you can change the order of these three sections in a story, but always make sure the sequence of events and the chronology are clear. We can use linkers of time and sequence to do this.
- Make the main events of the story clear. What happened? Why? What happened later? How did the story end? We usually use the past simple for this.
- Give background information so that we know about the characters and the situation. We usually use the past perfect simple and continuous for this.
- Make the story interesting by describing scenes in detail. We often use the past continuous for this.
- Short sections of direct speech can bring your story to life, as can the descriptive use of adjectives, adverbs and similes.
- For more information on writing stories, see page 154 of the Writing bank.

Unit 2

USE OF ENGLISH: MULTIPLE-CHOICE CLOZE

Step 1: Read the text or sentences to get a general idea of the overall meaning. This is to get a general understanding.
Do not worry about the gaps at first.

Step 2: Read the text in more detail and try to predict which word or phrase comes in each gap. Look especially at the words which come just before and after the gap. Do those words need a special preposition? Is an article or auxiliary verb missing? Think about the type of word you need (noun, verb, pronoun, article, etc.) and the general meaning.

Step 3: Look at the alternatives. Is one of them the same as the word you thought of in Step 2? Be careful because often the meaning of the different options can be very similar, but the difference may be that each word goes with a different preposition, for example. Also remember that some words typically go with other words. We call this collocation.

Step 4: If you aren't sure which answer is right, think about why other answers are definitely wrong and eliminate them.

Step 5: When you finish, check that you have an answer for each question. Never leave answers blank in an exam.

LISTENING: MULTIPLE CHOICE

In this type of activity you choose the best answer from three or four different answers.
You usually hear the text twice. The questions are usually (but not always!) in the order that you hear them in the recording.

Step 1: Read the different answers before you listen. They can give you ideas about the topic of the text and the vocabulary you are going to hear in it. Remember that sometimes the difference between two answers is just one word.

Step 2: When you listen, remember that you may hear the correct answer but expressed in different words. You may also hear a word or words that come in one of the possible answers, but this does not mean it is the answer. The word(s) may be there just to distract you.

Step 3: You usually hear the recording twice. Do not panic if you do not understand information the first time. If you don't hear the answer to one question, start listening immediately for the answer to the next question.

Step 4: Use the second listening to find the answers you didn't hear the first time and to check the answers you already have.

Step 5: When you finish, check that you have an answer for each question. Never leave answers blank in an exam.

SPEAKING: DISCUSSING PHOTOS (UNITS 2 AND 6)

In this type of activity you have one or more photos to discuss and answer a question or questions about the photo(s) or related to the same topic.

- Listen very carefully to the examiner's instructions. Your marks will depend on completing the whole task, so if you only complete one part, you will lose marks. If you aren't sure that you have understood what the examiner says, ask them to repeat.
- If you have two or more photos, you shouldn't describe each photo in great detail. The important thing is to compare and contrast the two photos.
- Don't just describe the photos, make speculations about them.
- Try to speak for exactly the right amount of time. The more you practise, the easier it will become.
- Give your own opinion if the examiner asks for it and give reasons to justify your opinions. There is not usually a right or wrong answer. The examiner wants to hear you speak English.
- Try to use a wide range of grammar and vocabulary to show the examiners what you know.
- Speak loudly and clearly so that the examiner can hear you.
- Don't let mistakes stop you from speaking. Correct your own mistakes if possible, or start the sentence again, but don't stop completely.
- Use *Well*, *Hmm* or *Let me think* to give you time to think of what you want to say next.

WRITING: OPINION ESSAYS

- In opinion essays you can just give your own side of the argument. You do not have to present both sides of an argument, although you can state arguments against your opinion and then give counterarguments to defend your opinion.
- Before you begin, decide your opinion and the points you want to make. Think about how to organise these points in a logical way.
- In the conclusion, we do not usually present new ideas or opinions. We restate the major point(s) already made.
- The style in opinion essays should be formal or neutral.
- Remember that there are no right or wrong answers. The examiner wants to see that you can write and express yourself clearly and effectively.
- For more information on writing opinion essays, see page 155 of the Writing bank.

Unit 3

READING: MULTIPLE CHOICE (UNITS 3 AND 7)

In this type of activity you read a text, or several short texts, and answer questions about it/them by choosing the best answer from three or four different options. You must choose the correct option according to the information in the text, not according to your own opinion or prior knowledge of the topic.

Step 1: Read the text quickly to get a general understanding.

Step 2: Read all the answers carefully. Sometimes the difference between two options is just one word.

Step 3: Find the section of the text where you think each answer comes and read it again slowly, in more detail. You may find the same words in the text and in one of the options, but this does not mean it is the correct answer. The correct option will probably express the information in the text using different words. Sometimes the question is not about facts but about opinions, attitudes or feelings, so be ready to 'read between the lines'. The answers usually come in order in the text.

Step 4: If you aren't 100% sure which answer is best, take away any answers which you know are not correct.

Step 5: When you finish, check that you have an answer for each question. Never leave answers blank in an exam.

LISTENING: MULTIPLE MATCHING (UNITS 3 AND 8)

In this type of activity you match different speakers with the information, ideas and/or attitudes that they express. If there are two tasks in the same activity, you may hear the answer to the second task before the answer to the first one.

Before you listen,

- think about the topic of what you are going to listen to. Think of words that could appear in the listening text.
- read the questions and underline important information. This can help you to know what the people may say and helps you to concentrate more while you listen.

While you listen,

- remember that the speakers may say the same things as in the questions, but using different words or expressions. Remember also that other speakers may use the actual words that come in the questions, but there is only one correct answer for each speaker.
- sometimes you have to identify the speaker's attitude. In this case you need to interpret not only what the person is saying but also why and how he/she is saying it.
- don't worry if you don't understand everything the first time you listen. Usually you listen twice. Use the second listening to find the answers you didn't hear the first time and to check the answers you already have.

After you listen,

- check that you have an answer for each question. Never leave answers blank in an exam.

SPEAKING: GIVING A PRESENTATION

In this type of activity, you have to talk about a topic which could appear in the form of a question, title, text or photo. Often the topic is a general one, but in some exams you need to talk about personal experiences. You usually have a fixed amount of time to prepare the presentation and to give it.

- Make notes with the information you want to give in your presentation and use them when you are giving it. *But* don't just read your notes aloud.
- Look at your audience. See if they understand you and are interested.
- Don't speak too fast. If you speak too quickly, people will not be able to follow you.
- Try to speak for exactly the right amount of time. The more you practise, the easier it will become.
- Often you will be asked further questions after your presentation. This is not because there was a problem with your presentation. It is usually to check that you can speak spontaneously on the topic, too.
- Use intonation to show that you are interested and to make others interested.
- Don't worry excessively about vocabulary. When you don't know a word, explain it or use a simpler word.
- Don't let mistakes stop you from speaking. Correct your own mistakes if possible, or start the sentence again, but don't stop completely.
- Remember that if you are talking about personal experiences, the examiner is less interested in the actual experiences than in the way you express yourself in English.

WRITING: REVIEWS

- The important thing in a review is to give a clear picture of the thing that you are reviewing and to make your own opinion and attitude clear. To do this, use a wide variety of adjectives and adverbs and use expressions of opinion.
- The style in a review should not be particularly formal or informal.
- For more information on writing reviews, see page 156 of the Writing bank.

Unit 4

READING: MISSING PARAGRAPHS

In this type of exercise you have to find the best place to put different paragraphs (or sentences) taken from a text. There are usually one or two more paragraphs than spaces.

Step 1: Read the text to get a general idea of the overall meaning.

Step 2: Read the missing paragraphs and identify the key information. What is the paragraph about? Do you remember any other paragraphs connected with this topic when you read the text for the first time? Look again at this part of the text in more detail.

Step 3: Look for words and phrases in the first or last sentences in the paragraph which connect with the information that comes in the text just before or after each gap.

Step 4: Try out each paragraph in the most probable space and continue reading. Is the meaning logical? Do pronouns like *this* or *it* make sense, or linking words like *and, but* or *although*? Look also for ideas that are repeated from one paragraph to the next by using synonyms.

Step 5: If there are gaps which you cannot complete, continue with other, easier gaps first and then go back later to the difficult ones.

Step 6: When you finish, read the completed text again to check that it makes sense. Check also that you have an answer for each question. Never leave answers blank in an exam.

USE OF ENGLISH: SENTENCE TRANSFORMATIONS (UNITS 4 AND 8)

In this type of activity you have a sentence and you must complete a second sentence so that it means the same as the original sentence. Usually you must use a word that they give. In this case, you cannot change the form of this word. In most exams, you can only use between two and six words, including the word they give you. Find out in your exam whether contractions such as *can't* or *don't* count as two words or one.

Step 1: Read the original sentence carefully. Think about the meaning of the sentence, the type of structure(s) used, the tense(s) used, etc.

Step 2: If they give you a word, think about its meaning. Think also about the grammatical function of the word. Does it always or usually go with another word or tense?

Step 3: Write your sentence. Do not add or change any other words unnecessarily. They may change the meaning of the sentence or make you write too many words.

Step 4: When you finish, check that you have:

a not changed the meaning from the original sentence.
b not changed the form of the word they gave you.
c not written more than the maximum number of words permitted.

SPEAKING: TALKING ABOUT STATISTICS

In this type of activity you have to talk about different things such as graphs, photos, charts, statistics, headlines and quotes. These things are all usually connected to one general topic.

Step 1: Look at all the stimuli and decide what the general topic is.

Step 2: Check that you understand the content of each different stimulus.

Step 3: Make notes with your ideas. Look at these notes and refer to them when you speak, but do not read them aloud. React to what the examiner asks you.

Remember:

- Give your opinion or interpretation of the topic and stimuli. There is not usually a right or wrong answer. The examiner wants to hear you speak English.
- Don't describe every detail of the information. Decide what you think are the most important and interesting facts.
- If you don't understand what the examiner says, ask them in English to repeat or to speak more slowly. Use expressions like: *Sorry, can you say that again?* or, *Sorry, could you speak more slowly?*
- Speak loudly and clearly so that the examiner can hear you.
- Don't worry excessively about vocabulary. When you don't know a word, explain it or use a simpler word.
- Don't let mistakes stop you from speaking. Correct your own mistakes if possible, or start the sentence again, but don't stop completely.
- Use *Well, Hmm* or *Let me think* to give you time to think of what you want to say next.

WRITING: FOR-AND-AGAINST ESSAYS

- In for-and-against essays you must present both sides of an argument.
- In for-and-against essays you should have a number of relevant points to make. Think about how to organise these points in a logical way. A common way of doing this is to have one main paragraph giving one side of the argument and another paragraph presenting the other side. In the conclusion, you can summarise both sides and give your own opinion.
- A typical way of beginning a for-and-against essay is by talking about the current situation and mentioning the fact that people have different opinions on the topic because it is complex or controversial.
- You must always justify the arguments you present.
- The style in for-and-against and opinion essays should be formal.
- Remember that there are no right or wrong answers. The examiner wants to see that you can write and express yourself clearly and effectively.
- For more information on writing for-and-against essays, see page 157 of the Writing bank.

Unit 5

READING: TRUE/FALSE/NOT GIVEN

In this type of activity you decide if statements are true, false or if the information is not stated according to the information in the text.

Step 1: Read the text quickly to get a general understanding.

Step 2: Read the sentences that you need to prove true, false or if the information is not stated.

Step 3: Find the parts of the text where you think the information comes. Read them again in more detail. Remember that the statements will probably not be expressed the same way as in the text. Decide what the key words are in each statement and try to find similar ideas in the text. Put *Not Given* if you can find no information in the text to prove or disprove the statements.

Step 4: When you finish, check that you have an answer for each question. Never leave answers blank in an exam.

USE OF ENGLISH: OPEN CLOZE (UNITS 5 AND 10)

In cloze activities you have a text with gaps. When there are no options given, we call them open cloze activities. You must fill in each gap by thinking of a word which is grammatically correct and is logical.

Step 1: Read the complete text or sentences without thinking about the gaps.

Step 2: Look again at the gaps and especially the words which come just before and after the gap. Do those words need a special preposition? Is an article or auxiliary verb missing? Think about the type of word you need (noun, verb, pronoun, article, etc.) and the general meaning. The spaces in cloze activities will often be for prepositions, articles, pronouns, auxiliary verbs, modal verbs and conjunctions (*and, but, although*, etc.). Also remember that some words typically go with other words. We call this collocation.

Step 3: Fill in the gap with the word that you think is best. Read again with your answer in the gap. Sometimes you will need to read a larger section of text to know what word is missing. If there is more than one possible answer, you only need to put one.

Step 4: When you finish, check that you have one answer for each question. Never leave answers blank in an exam.

SPEAKING: ROLE-PLAYS

In role-plays, you are given a situation and a task which take you 'outside' the classroom and into a possible real-life scenario. Usually the task will be done in pairs, with either another student or a teacher/examiner taking the other role.

- Before you begin, make sure you understand the situation and task that you are to discuss. If you aren't sure, ask for clarification before you begin. Above all, check that you know the relationship between the people in the role-play, e.g. parent-child, friend-friend, boss-employee, etc. This is important because it will have some effect on the level of formality of the language you use.
- Make sure you listen carefully to what your partner or partners say. In any conversation we speak, but we also listen and react to what others say. You can agree, disagree, make suggestions or ask questions.
- Make eye contact with the person you are speaking to and speak loudly and clearly.
- If you can prepare the role-play, make notes, but use them only for reference. Never read your notes aloud.
- If you are working with other students, be sensitive. Don't talk for too long without giving your partner a chance to speak.
- In some role-plays, you must come to an agreement, but in others it is not necessary. Make sure you know before you begin.
- There are no right or wrong answers in situational role-plays. The important thing is to talk, listen and respond.

WRITING: LETTERS AND TRANSACTIONAL TASKS (UNITS 5 AND 9)

- Remember that when you write letters, invitations, messages and notes, it is essential to write in the correct style. When you write to a friend, use contractions and informal expressions. When you write a formal or semi-formal letter, invitation, message or note, do not use contractions or informal language. Use words that are typical of a more formal register. If your letter is grammatically correct but not in the correct style, you lose marks.
- Transactional writing tasks are ones where the instructions tell you who you are writing to and what information to include. When a question asks you to put specific information in your text, you lose marks if you do not include the information.
- Sometimes the information you need to include is indicated in the form of notes written on the letter or email. Remember to expand the notes and give extra information. For example, if the note is 'Say when you can come', do not just say 'I can come in the summer.' Explain why the summer is the best/only option.
- For more information on writing letters and transactional tasks, see page 158 of the Writing bank.

Unit 6

USE OF ENGLISH: MULTIPLE-CHOICE CLOZE

In cloze activities you have a text with gaps. Sometimes there are different options and you must choose the best for each space. We call these multiple-choice cloze activities.

Step 1: Read the text or sentence to get a general idea of the overall meaning. Do not worry about the gaps at first. This is to get a general understanding.

Step 2: Read more carefully and try to predict which word comes in each gap. Look especially at the words which come just before and after the gap. Do those words need a special preposition? Is an article or auxiliary verb missing? Think about the type of word you need (noun, verb, pronoun, article, etc.) and the general meaning.

Step 3: Look at the alternatives. Is one of them the same as the word you thought of in Step 2? Be careful because often the meaning of the different options can be very similar, but the difference may be that each word goes with a different preposition or typically goes with another word (called collocation).

Step 4: If you aren't sure which answer is right, think about why other answers are definitely wrong and eliminate them.

Step 5: When you finish, check that you have an answer for each question. Never leave answers blank in an exam.

LISTENING: COMPLETING SENTENCES OR NOTES (UNITS 6 AND 10)

In this type of activity you listen to a text and complete sentences or notes with the correct information. Be careful, because in some cases there is a maximum number of words that you can use, and you may have to use exactly the same words that you hear.

- Always read the incomplete notes *before* you listen. This helps you to know what to listen for. Look carefully at the words that come just before or after each space and think about what *type* of word is missing (noun, verb, adjective, adverb, etc.). But be careful. If you know that you need a number, for example, do not simply write the first number that you hear.

- It is not usually necessary to understand every word that you hear. Listen out for the sections which correspond to the information in the notes. Then pay special attention to these sections. Remember that you may not hear the exact words that appear in the incomplete notes.
- For most spaces you need to write between one and three words. Usually it is a good idea to write the words you actually hear. Be careful with spelling and make sure that what you write fits in grammatically with the words that come before and after the space.
- Don't worry if you don't understand everything the first time you listen. Usually you listen twice. Use the second listening to find the answers you didn't hear the first time and to check the answers you already have.

WRITING: ARTICLES

- It can be a good idea for articles to have a title which grabs the reader's interest.
- Include expressions which speak directly to the reader in order to enage them and maintain their interest.
- Use a wide range of vocabulary in articles so that the reader gets a clear sense of what we are saying to him/her. This means going beyond vague or basic vocabulary (e.g. write *picturesque views* rather than *nice views*, *comprehensive facilities* rather than *good facilities*, etc.). Use synonyms to avoid repeating words in the article.
- Make sure you include all the information in your article that the magazine or newspaper asks for.
- The style in a report should usually be conversational and more or less informal so that you can connect with the reader. You can also include direct questions to communicate with the reader.
- For more information on writing articles, see page 159 of the Writing bank.

Unit 7

SPEAKING: NEGOTIATING AND COLLABORATING (UNITS 7 AND 9)

In speaking exams, there are sometimes collaborative tasks where you must work with one or more other speakers. You may be given a series of pictures or situations which you have to talk about and compare. You may have to rank them and choose the best/most suitable/most enjoyable option.

- Make sure you understand the topic that you are to discuss, and the concrete task(s). If you aren't sure, ask for clarification before you begin. Your mark will be calculated according to how successfully you complete all the tasks, or parts of the task.
- Make sure you listen carefully to what your partner or partners say. In a discussion we speak, but we also listen and react to what others say. You can agree, disagree, make suggestions or ask questions.
- If you are working with other students, be sensitive. Don't talk for too long without giving your partner a chance to speak.
- In some situations, you must come to an agreement or decision, but in others it is not necessary. Make sure you know before you begin. If you do have to come to an agreement or decision, don't do this until you have discussed most of the different options. If you can't come to an agreement, try to end in polite disagreement.
- Remember that there are not usually any right or wrong answers. The important thing is to have an opinion, to explain it clearly, to justify it (especially if somebody disagrees with it) and to give examples to support it.

WRITING: REPORTS

- Reports should have a title.
- Separate reports into sections and give each one a suitable heading.
- It is a good idea to outline what the report is about in the introduction. At the end of the report you should be ready to make recommendations or suggestions if they ask you to.
- Make sure you include all the different points of information that they ask for.
- The style in a report should usually be formal since you usually write a report for an organisation or people that you do not know personally. If you are writing for a group of your peers, it can be less formal but should still be informative.
- For more information on writing reports, see page 160 of the Writing bank.

Unit 8

SPEAKING: DISCUSSIONS BASED ON VISUAL STIMULI

In this type of activity you have different visual stimuli (photos, adverts, pieces of art, etc.) which you must talk about. You must then answer a question or questions related to the theme of the visual stimuli.

- Listen very carefully to the examiner's instructions. Your marks will depend on completing the whole task, so if you only complete one part, you will lose marks. If you aren't sure that you have understood what the examiner says, ask them to repeat.
- Do not describe the visual stimuli if you are not asked to.
- Try to dedicate the right amount of time to each different task. The more you practise, the easier it will become.
- Give your own opinion if the examiner asks for it and give reasons to justify your opinions. There is not usually a right or wrong answer. The examiner wants to hear you speak English.
- Try to use a wide range of grammar and vocabulary to show the examiners what you know.
- Speak loudly and clearly so that the examiner can hear you.
- Don't let mistakes stop you from speaking. Correct your own mistakes if possible, or start the sentence again, but don't stop completely.
- Use *Well*, *Hmm* or *Let me think* to give you time to think of what you want to say next.

WRITING: FOR-AND-AGAINST ESSAYS AND OPINION ESSAYS

- Remember that in for-and-against essays you must present both sides of the argument whereas in opinion essays you can just give your own side of the argument.
- In for-and-against essays and opinion essays, you should have a number of relevant points to make. Think about how to organise these points in a logical way.
- The style in for-and-against and opinion essays should be formal.
- Remember to justify the arguments you present in both types of essay.
- Remember that there are no right or wrong answers. The examiner wants to see that you can write and express yourself clearly and effectively.
- For more information on writing for-and-against essays and opinion essays, see page 157 of the Writing bank.

Unit 9

LISTENING: SHORT-ANSWER QUESTIONS

In this type of activity you have to answer comprehension questions, but there is a limit to the number of words that you can write.

- Always read the questions before you listen. They can give you clues about what is going to come and can help you to predict possible answers.
- The words that you write will actually appear in the text. It is not necessary to change them at all.
- Make sure that you do not write more than the number of words they tell you in the instructions or you will lose marks.
- Be careful with spelling.
- Don't worry if you don't understand everything the first time you listen. Usually you listen twice. Use the second listening to find the answers you didn't hear the first time and to check the answers you already have.

Unit 10

READING: COMPLETING TABLES, SUMMARIES OR SENTENCES

In this type of activity you complete a table, summary or sentences with information from a text. There is often a limit to the number of words that you can use in each space, and sometimes the words have to be taken straight from the text, in the same form. Sometimes you have a list of words which you must choose from.

Step 1: Read the text quickly to get a general understanding.

Step 2: Read the table, summary or sentences that you need to complete. Be aware that the summary or sentences will probably not use exactly the same words as in the text.

Step 3: Find the parts of the text where you think the information comes. Read them again in more detail. Remember that you will probably need to find the exact words that have to complete the gaps. When you have a list of words to choose from, these will probably not be exactly the same as the words used in the text.

Step 4: Try the words in the space and see if they make sense and follow the original meaning of the text. Make sure they fit grammatically, too. Check that you haven't repeated a word that comes just before or after the space.

Step 5: When you finish, check that you have an answer for each question. Check that you have not written too many words, or changed the form of the word if this was included in the instructions. Don't leave any answers blank in an exam.

WRITING: PROPOSALS

- Proposals should have a title.
- Separate reports into sections and give each on a suitable heading.
- It is a good idea to outline what the proposal is about in the introduction. At the end of the proposal you should be ready to make recommendations or suggestions if required.
- Make sure you include all the different points of information that were asked for.
- The style in a proposal should usually be formal since you usually write a report for an organisation or people that you do not know personally. If you are writing for a group of your peers it can be less formal but should still be informative.
- For more information on writing reports, see page 160 of the Writing bank.

Unit 1

STORIES, NARRATIVES, ANECDOTES

pp14–15

EXAMPLE QUESTION **You have decided to enter a short story competition in an international magazine. The competition rules say that the story must be about a lucky escape.**

Write your story.

MODEL TEXT

It had been snowing all week, so on Sunday my family decided to drive out into the country to find a beautiful spot to go for a walk and enjoy the **spectacular** winter landscape. **Having spotted a beautiful stream**, we got out of the car and put on our backpacks. I also picked up the walking pole that my father had given me as a present when I was just seven. I never went walking without it.

The landscape was breathtaking that day, with patches of ice on the ground reflecting the sun **like a mirror**. As we got to the stream, I was amazed to see that it was frozen in places. Curious, I used my pole to see how thick and hard the ice was. But **just as** I was doing so, the stick fell out of my hands into the ice-cold water. I went closer to the edge of the stream and bent over to see if I could reach it. As quick as a flash, I slipped on the icy rocks, straight into the freezing stream.

'Help!' I **shrieked**, but there was nothing really that my parents or sister could do. I gasped as the cold water penetrated my clothes. I would freeze to death if I didn't get out fast. With the shock, I managed to pull myself up out of the water, against the current.

I was standing, shivering in my wet clothes, when suddenly I felt a strange movement just next to my heart.

'That's it! I'm going to have a heart attack!' I groaned.

But then I realised that it wasn't my heart, it was my mobile phone which was vibrating wildly after getting soaking wet.

'Two lucky escapes in one day!' I sighed as we all headed back to the car.

Use a variety of adjectives and adverbs to make descriptions vivid.

Use participle clauses to talk about two actions happening at the same time, or in sequence.

Use similes to add drama and interest.

Say when or in what order things happened with expressions like *just as*, *suddenly*, *last week*, *then*, *finally*.

Use direct speech with a variety of reporting verbs such as *gasp*, *sigh*, *shriek*.

Useful grammar: Narrative tenses

- Past simple. We use it to tell the main events and actions in the story.
- Past continuous. We use it to describe scenes, to say what activity was in progress when another interrupted it.
- Past perfect. We use it for the background of the story, to talk about actions that happened before other actions in the past.
- Past perfect continuous. We use it for the background of a story, particularly when the duration of an activity is important.
- *used to*. We use it to talk about past habits.
- *must/may/might/can't have*. We use these to make speculations or deductions about what happened.
- *was going to*, *was doing*, *would*. We use these to talk about future activities in the past.
- Participle clauses. These describe two actions happening at the same time, or in sequence.

Suggested paragraph plan

First paragraph:	Explain where and when the story began. Introduce the characters.
Middle paragraph(s):	Explain the main events in the story, and the background to these events.
Final paragraph:	Explain how the story ended and what the consequences were.

OPINION ESSAYS

pp26–27 (Unit 2) and 104–105 (Unit 8)

EXAMPLE QUESTION **Some people think that school and university should teach the knowledge and skills needed in the world of work. Others say that schools and universities should teach knowledge for its own sake, without worrying about future professional needs. What do you think should be the main function of schools and universities?**

MODEL TEXT

Over the years, there has been much debate about the true aim of education. Should schools be preparing students for the workplace, or should the objective be something different? To my mind, the answer is clear. **I am** convinced that we should not be training students in professional skills. We should be preparing students for life itself.

First and foremost, in my opinion, the goal of education should be to help students to become independent thinkers and learners. The essential idea is to help young people to think creatively so that they can respond to future challenges and problems in a positive and constructive way.

Furthermore, if students are trained in professional skills at a very young age, we are limiting their future career possibilities. **To my mind**, it is far more worthwhile to give students general tools and strategies at school and university which they can apply to any job in any particular field. After all, companies can always train employees after school or university.

Some people claim that knowledge which is not directly relevant to the world of work serves no purpose. **I believe there is no evidence to support this view**. How can we know exactly which pieces of information any particular student will need in the future? By giving a broad education including elements of all types of arts and sciences, we are helping students to develop as complete human beings who can gradually start specialising in the subjects they are most interested in or best at.

To sum up, as far as I am concerned, schools and universities are not simply vocational colleges producing future bankers, mechanics or nurses. They are places where young people should be trained in life-long skills and strategies that help them to develop and bring something positive to society in general.

The style is formal. Do not use contractions.

Put opinions and ideas in sequence with linkers such as *First and foremost*, *Furthermore*, *Last but not least*.

Give your opinion with expressions like *Personally*, *To my mind*, *In my opinion*, *As far as I'm concerned*, *I believe*.

Express other people's opinions using expressions like *Some people claim/argue/maintain that …*, *It is often said that …*

Make contrasts and give counterarguments using expressions like *Whilst it is true that*, *However*, *Nevertheless*, *Despite*, *I believe there is no evidence to support …*

To give a conclusion, use *To sum up*, *In conclusion*, *All in all*.

Suggested paragraph plan

Paragraph 1: Introduction, including your opinion.
Paragraph 2: Main point(s) in support of your opinion.
Paragraph 3: Additional point(s) in support of your opinion.
Paragraph 4: Point(s) in support of a different opinion and your counterargument(s).
Paragraph 5: Conclusion, restating and possibly expanding your main point.

Unit 3

REVIEWS

pp40–41

EXAMPLE QUESTION **An international magazine wants reviews of recent box-office successes and failures. Write a review of a successful or unsuccessful film you have seen recently.**

MODEL TEXT

Continuing the success of superhero films such as *The Avengers*, *Thor* and the *Iron Man* films, the latest Marvel box-office smash is *Guardians of the Galaxy*. Starring the up-and-coming US actor Chris Pratt, *Guardians of the Galaxy* combines extra-terrestrials and a whole range of special effects to create a fast-moving film which is enjoyable, though not **particularly** memorable.

As always with adaptations of classic comics, the film has to condense years of stories into just two hours. **The plot is slightly disjointed** as the film begins with the hero Peter Quill's abduction from Earth by a group of space pirates but then goes forward in time to see how and why he escapes. Living on the planet Morag, Quill finds a mysterious orb, which he decides to sell. However, other people also want the orb so he has to escape Morag but then ends up in prison on the planet of Xandar with five other space creatures. They decide to sell the orb and split the money although they don't like each other initially. But then they find out that the orb can be used to destroy planets and they have to protect it. Quill has to learn to be less arrogant and impulsive and learn to work together with others before he can protect the orb and save the universe.

Central to any superhero films are the action scenes and special effects. Both are gripping in *Guardians of the Galaxy*. Whether you watch the 2D or 3D version, many scenes are **breathtaking**, thanks particularly to the epic scenery of the mythical planet of Xandar. What's more, incredibly realistic effects used to create the space creatures who become Quills friends lead to some light-hearted moments which help to vary the mood of the film.

Apart from the action scenes, in my opinion what makes the film really work is the relationship between the characters. Pratt's portrayal of Quill as he changes from a brash young man into a more mature, thoughtful character is particularly impressive.

All in all, *Guardians of the Galaxy* does exactly what you would expect from a big budget superhero movie. It's exciting, entertaining, and even funny at times. **But if what you're looking for is something deep and moving**, stay away!

Use modifying adverbs to make adjectives stronger or softer in order to give more accurate descriptions.

Explain and justify your opinions by giving specific details about the things you like or dislike.

Use a range of adjectives to make your review vivid.

Make it clear who you would/ wouldn't recommend sees the film/ reads the book.

Useful vocabulary

Nouns

adaptation • box-office • cliché • cliff-hanger • critic • masterpiece • portrayal • script • sequel
twists and turns (of a plot)

Adjectives

amazing • amusing • appealing • awful • brilliant • catchy • clever • (un)convincing • credible • deafening
deep • disappointing • disjointed • epic • far-fetched • fascinating • fast-moving • flawed • gripping • hilarious
incredible • (un)inspiring • intricate • intriguing • light-hearted • lively • loud • low-budget • memorable
mesmerising • mind-blowing • moving • mysterious • perceptive • realistic • relaxing • risqué • rousing • scary
sensitive • soothing • spectacular • stunning • stupid • terrible • thrilling • thought-provoking • up-and-coming
vivid • well-produced

Other expressions

(the film) bombed • (critics) panned (the film) • (the film) grossed ($10,000) • (the story) unfolds
deliver a great performance • (the film) received rave reviews • get a lukewarm reception • a box-office smash/flop
(the film) hit the big screen

Suggested paragraph plan

Paragraph 1: Basic information about what you are reviewing.
Paragraph 2: More detailed information.
Paragraph 3: Your opinion and justification(s) for it.
Paragraph 4: Your recommendation.

FOR-AND-AGAINST ESSAYS

pp52–53 (Unit 4) and 104–105 (Unit 8)

EXAMPLE QUESTION **Some people say that children are born with a special talent, for music or sport for example. But others argue that, with training, any child can learn to be a good musician or sportsperson. Discuss both views and then give your own opinion.**

MODEL TEXT

Are musicians or sportspeople born with special abilities, or can anybody learn them? The answer to this question is important since, if anybody can learn them, this could inspire us all to try our best to develop these talents. On the other hand, if these talents are purely natural, **it would** mean that it is pointless to train hard since we could never achieve much even if we practised for hours and hours.

Many experts claim that children are born with special aptitudes. This would explain why some young children seem to find some things really easy whilst others struggle to do or understand them. Some children can pick up a guitar or ball and soon find that they can do things with it without thinking or trying. This would suggest that we have natural skills that are part of us, the same as our physical features.

However, if we gave a guitar to a young child and gave him or her lessons every day, would that child not learn to be a good guitarist? Many people, especially teachers, would argue that, with instruction and practice, anybody can learn to do a particular task well. **Furthermore**, somebody with natural talent who never practised would find it very difficult to achieve a high level of ability in that task.

Personally, I believe that we can all learn to be good at something, whether it is sport or music, by learning about it and by practising. Nevertheless, to be truly great at something I believe that we need natural talent or aptitude, and we have to practise hard and often. **To sum up**, natural talent and hard work must go hand in hand.

The style is formal. Do not use contractions.

Express other people's opinions using expressions like *Some people claim/argue/ maintain that …, It is often said that …*

Make contrasts and give counterarguments using expressions like *However, Nevertheless, On the one hand, On the other hand…*

To add arguments, use *Furthermore, What's more, Not only … but also …*

Give your opinion with expressions like *Personally, To my mind, In my opinion, As far as I'm concerned, I believe that …*

To give a conclusion, use *To sum up, In conclusion, All in all.*

Suggested paragraph plan

Paragraph 1: State the topic of the composition using general statements.
Paragraph 2: Make points for (or against).
Paragraph 3: Make points against (or for).
Paragraph 4: Conclusion – restate the most important point(s) and give your opinion.

Unit 5

FORMAL LETTERS OF COMPLAINT

pp66–67

EXAMPLE QUESTION **Read this extract from a local newspaper.**

The town council has decided to close down the local library in Green Street. They say that nobody uses it to borrow books anymore, perhaps because of the influence of the Internet. They also say that the library has simply become a meeting place for young people who create a lot of noise and disturbance there.

You frequently use the local library. Write a letter of complaint to the local council about the closure of the library. Include the following points:

- **Nobody takes out books because they're all old.**
- **Why not install computers so that people can read things on the Internet?**
- **Young people meet there because there's nowhere else to meet.**
- **Young people don't disturb anyone there – they're busy studying.**

Use *Dear Sir/ Madam* when you do not know the name of the person that you are writing to. Otherwise, use *Dear Mr/Mrs/Ms.*

Give your opinion with expressions like *Personally, To my mind, In my opinion, As far as I'm concerned, I believe that …*

Use more formal vocabulary, eg, *numerous* instead of *a lot; believe* instead of *think.*

To give a conclusion, use *To sum up, In conclusion, All in all.*

MODEL TEXT

Dear Sir/Madam,

I am writing to protest about the imminent closure of the library in Green Street. **I believe that** closing the library will **not only** be unjustified but will also have a terrible impact on the neighbourhood.

Whilst it is probably true that fewer people borrow books from the library nowadays, I believe there are important reasons which explain why. Firstly, the books in the library are all old since no new books have been added in the last five years.

Secondly, the Internet has become more and more popular as you have stated. In that case, **may I suggest** you install computers with Internet access in the library? This step would encourage more people to use the library, and to read.

It has been stated that one of the reasons for closing the library is that it has become nothing more than a meeting place for young people. This is true in part, but the reason why young people meet there is that there are no alternative places where they can meet. If the library is closed, young people will have no alternative but to start meeting in the street.

Last but not least, I would like to state clearly that young people do not create any disturbance in the library. **The truth is** that **numerous** students from my school use the library to study as it is such a quiet place, and we can concentrate there.

In conclusion, what amazes me is that the local council are inventing any excuses they can to justify closing the library. This is scandalous since the library serves several vital functions in the local community. The consequences of shutting the library could have a highly negative impact on the neighbourhood as a whole. I urge you to reconsider your plan.

Yours faithfully,

Andy Powell

To add arguments, use *Furthermore, What's more, Not only … but also …*

Use more formal expressions, such as *May I suggest …?* instead of *Why don't you …?*

Use cleft sentences and other ways of adding emphasis such as *What amazes me is …, The truth is …*

When you do not know the name of the person you are writing to, use *Yours faithfully.* Otherwise, use *Yours sincerely.*

Suggested paragraph plan

First paragraph:	Explain why you are writing.
Middle paragraph(s):	Give details of the complaint (what, where, why, when …).
Final paragraph:	Summarise your opinion and ask for a solution.

ARTICLES AND COMPETITION ENTRIES

pp78–79

EXAMPLE QUESTION **You see the following announcement in an international magazine.**

We are preparing a special container to be buried and opened in 100 years' time. We want readers to write an article suggesting one album, one DVD and one book which represent life and culture today to put inside the time capsule. Explain why your choices would be of interest to people in the future.

Write your article.

Think of a title to grab the reader's attention or make him/her curious to read the article.

MODEL TEXT

1916, 2016, 2116: The more that things change, the more they stay the same

Think for a second about the year 1916. Do you know what music people were listening to? **Was it jazz or classical music?** Did records exist, or just the radio? And was the cinema already popular or could people only see plays? Now **imagine** opening a time capsule from 1916 and how it would help us to get a clearer picture of life then.

Use direct questions to involve the reader.

Use expressions such as *imagine, just think …*

When someone opens my time capsule in 2116, I would like them to find a Taylor Swift album inside. She may not have the best voice in the world, or be the best dancer, but her songs are all about problems that teenagers today are facing. And the music is **fun, catchy** and perfect for dancing and forgetting the world for a while. And that, **quite frankly**, says a lot about life today.

Use synonyms and a wide variety of vocabulary to avoid repetition.

Use comment adverbials such as *quite frankly* or *to be honest* to make your own opinion clear.

Meanwhile, if there's one thing that defines today's society it's the Internet and social networking sites. That's why I would choose to include the film *The Social Network*. The movie tells the story of Facebook and, in doing so, tells us a lot about human interaction and relationships in the 21st century.

As for my choice of book, over 32 million copies of the *Divergent* series have been sold over the world, and the young actors who appear in the film adaptations are adored by millions of fans. **What is intriguing** about the series and its success is that, despite being futuristic, it is all about old fashioned virtues, or factions, such as honesty, intelligence and bravery, which have appeared in old folk tales for centuries.

Try to create a positive impression by being enthusiastic and original, and justify your points by giving valid and convincing arguments.

Music, dance and celebrations. The search for friendship and company. Stories that reflect on our deepest fears and desires. Although we may think life was very different 100 or 200 years ago, personally I believe our time capsule will show future generations that, deep down, people haven't really changed that much.

Suggested paragraph plan

First paragraph:	Introduction – state the theme of the article.
Middle paragraph(s):	Have one paragraph for each major point you make, backed up with arguments and justifications.
Final paragraph:	Summarise your main point(s).

Units 7 and 10

REPORTS AND PROPOSALS

pp92–93 (Unit 7) and 130–131 (Unit 10)

EXAMPLE QUESTION **An international research group is investigating the teaching of sport in schools in different parts of the world. You have been asked to write a report on sports education in your country. Your report should look at the following questions:**

- What are the strengths and weaknesses of the way sport is taught in schools in your country?
- What changes would you like to see made in the way sport is taught in your country in the future?

Write your report.

MODEL TEXT

Report on the teaching of sport in schools in our country

Introduction

The purpose of this report is to outline the positive and negative aspects of the way sport is currently taught in schools in our country and to make recommendations for future improvements.

Strengths in the way sport is currently taught

Logically, at school most sport **is taught** in Physical Education lessons. Most students have three hours of P.E. a week, and some schools have an additional hour of swimming. On top of this, most schools offer extra-curricular sports activities, which often involve competing for a school team. **In my opinion**, the number of hours dedicated to sport is sufficient. Usually within the three hours of P.E. lessons, students are given practice in a wide variety of different sports and tasks, which is valued positively by most students. **Furthermore**, most lessons are very practical, and this helps students to maintain a certain degree of fitness.

Possible weaknesses

Despite the fact that practical lessons are popular, very little theory is taught, so, **for instance**, students know very little about preventing or overcoming injuries, or the best way to stay in shape. Another problem is that nearly all games and activities are highly competitive, and I believe that this has a negative influence on some students, reinforcing the idea that sport is always a question of winning or losing, but not something valuable in itself.

Recommendations for the future teaching of sport

Having taken everything into consideration, I recommend that all schools add occasional lessons in sports theory so that students know more about the science of fitness. This will help students to know more about their bodies, something which will help them to lead healthy lives in the future. I also suggest varying sports practice so that not every activity is competitive. I feel that this would encourage every student to enjoy doing sport, not just the students who are good at it.

Give your report/proposal a title.

Reports and proposals are formal when you write them for an organisation or people that you do not know personally. Do not use contractions or informal language in these cases.

Use linkers of addition, contrast, consequence, etc. to structure your arguments.

Explain and justify your opinions with phrases like *for instance, this is because …*

To give a conclusion, use *To sum up, Having taken everything into consideration, All in all.*

Separate the report/proposal into sections and give each one a suitable heading.

Use passive and impersonal structures to convey a more serious, formal style.

Give your opinion with phrases like *In my opinion, Personally, I think, As far as I'm concerned …*

Make recommendations with phrases like *I (strongly) recommend that* in formal reports, or *Why don't you …?* in less formal reports.

Suggested paragraph plan

Paragraph 1: Introduction – state the aim of the report/proposal.
Paragraph 2: Main point(s), e.g. strengths, advantages, etc.
Paragraph 3: Main point(s), e.g. weaknesses, disadvantages, etc.
Paragraph 4: Conclusion, making a recommendation if required.

Unit 9

COVERING LETTERS

pp118–119

EXAMPLE QUESTION **Look at this job advertisement.**

Seymour Castle is situated on the north-west coast of Scotland. We require a kitchen assistant for the summer. The role involves not only cleaning but also applicants should be prepared to assist chefs with food preparation. The position has an immediate start and will run to the end of September. Please send a CV and covering letter, complete with referee details, to PO Box 368, Sandy Beach, Scotland.

You are interested in the job. Write a covering letter including this information:

- **You speak English and French.**
- **You worked as a kitchen assistant in a busy restaurant last summer.**
- **You love cooking and cook at home.**
- **You are free to start immediately.**

Use *Dear Sir/Madam* when you do not know the name of the person that you are writing to. Otherwise, use *Dear Mr/Mrs/Ms.*

MODEL TEXT

Dear Sir/Madam,

I am writing in response to your advertisement offering the post of kitchen assistant, which appeared in last Wednesday's edition of the Daily Post.

I am seventeen years old and have just begun my summer holidays, for the duration of which I am intending to work. Ideally, I am looking for a job in which I can perfect my English. This makes the job at Seymour Castle particularly attractive to me.

I believe that I am well suited for this job since last summer I had experience of working in the kitchen of a busy restaurant in my home town. I think it is also worth mentioning that I love cooking and often cook dishes for my family at home. Therefore, I would be more than happy to help the chefs with any food preparation that they should need doing.

In terms of personal qualities, I believe I am hard-working, sociable and very willing to learn new skills. I can also speak French, which may be an advantage in an international hotel such as yours. Since I am already on holiday, I could begin work immediately.

I would be **delighted** to attend an interview at your earliest convenience. As requested, I enclose my curriculum vitae and the contact details of my referee, Ms Gabriela Portman, **in whose restaurant I worked** last summer.

Yours faithfully,

Gabriel Ivanov

Use more formal vocabulary, e.g. *delighted* instead of *very happy*.

Use more formal expressions, eg, *in whose restaurant I worked* instead of *whose restaurant I worked in.*

When you do not know the name of the person you are writing to, use *Yours faithfully*. Otherwise, use *Yours sincerely*.

Suggested paragraph plan

Paragraph 1: Say what job you are applying for.
Paragraph 2: Give basic information about yourself and why you are applying for the job.
Paragraph 3: State any relevant experience.
Paragraph 4: Give information about your character and any other relevant skills.
Paragraph 5: Give information so that the company can continue further with the application.

Unit 2

DEVELOPING SPEAKING

Exercise 6, p25

Unit 4

GATEWAY TO LIFE SKILLS

21st century task, p49

IS TOO MUCH FRUIT BAD FOR YOU?

Many of us believe that fruit can only be healthy and so make an effort to eat five portions a day. We have grapes or bananas as a snack, and stick to fruit for dessert. But what happens if we eat more than five portions?

According to some experts, people may actually be eating too much fruit, leading to health problems, such as obesity and tooth decay.

There's no denying fruit has health benefits – it contains vitamins, fibre and antioxidants, which protect again disease. But people forget that fruit – like all food – contains calories. The calories in fruit can lead to weight problems, just as much as those in chocolate, explains Dr Carel Le Roux, consultant in metabolic medicine at Imperial College London. Health-conscious people sometimes drink several fruit smoothies a day, and each of these may contain several hundred calories.

What's more, fruit contains fructose (fruit sugar), which doesn't make you feel full. When we eat sugar, our body releases the hormone insulin, explains Ursula Arens, a dietician with the British Diabetic Association. This hormone tells the brain when we've had enough to eat. The problem with fructose is that it doesn't trigger this response, so the brain doesn't get the message that you are no longer hungry, and so you continue to eat.

Weight gain isn't the only health problem associated with too much fructose. It can increase levels of triglycerides, a type of blood fat that is linked to heart disease. In a recent study at Colorado University, scientists looked at 4,500 people with no history of high blood pressure, and discovered that those who ate more than 74 grams of fructose a day increased their risk of the condition by up to 87 per cent.

Then there's the damage fruit can cause to teeth. Eating fruit releases sugar in the mouth, where it attacks teeth and causes cavities. Fruit juice and smoothies in particular are harmful as the process of juicing breaks down the fruit and releases more sugar into the mouth.

So while fruit should be part of a healthy diet, the key is not to eat too much. As Glenys Jones, a nutritionist at the Medical Research Council of Human Nutrition says: 'Everything in moderation. Just as you make a decision not to eat a packet of biscuits, you should think about portion control when it comes to fruit.'

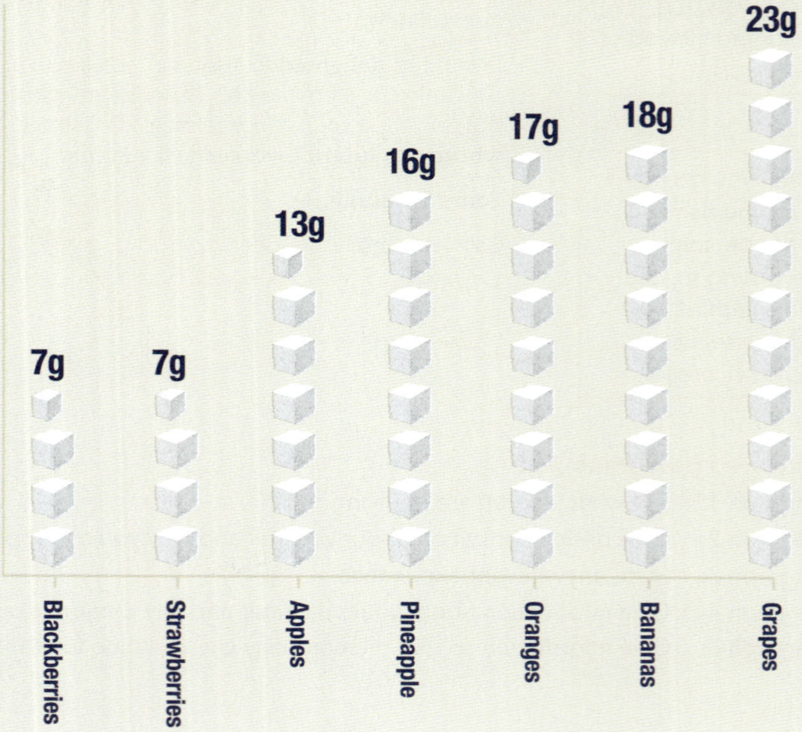

Is milk really good for us?

How many of us have grown up drinking milk every day? We're told it contains calcium, which helps to build strong teeth and bones. Children in particular are encouraged to drink at least two glasses a day. But is milk really good for us?

According to a study carried out by Dr David Ludwig and Dr Walter Willett from Harvard, there is no evidence to support the claim that the consumption of dairy products leads to better bones or improved health. In fact, the scientists found that milk may actually increase the risk of bone fractures.

Another study in Sweden produced similar results. More than 100,000 people were observed over a period of between 11 and 20 years. The study found that there was a correlation between how much milk people drank and the number of bone fractures they suffered.

One possible reason for the connection between milk and bone fragility may be the production of D-galactose, a type of sugar which is produced by the body when it processes high levels of lactose. Galactose has been shown to have harmful effects such as inflammation and chemical imbalances in studies of animals.

Another problem with milk is that it is high in calories. One glass of whole milk contains nearly 150 calories, with around 70 of those calories coming from fat. Although many people choose to drink low-fat milk, according to the Harvard scientists, this may do more harm than good. In studies in children and adults, those who consumed low-fat milk products gained more weight than those who consumed full-fat milk products. This may be because they increased the amount of food they consumed since the low-fat milk products weren't as satisfying.

The consumption of milk has also been linked to other health issues such as diabetes, allergies, asthma, eczema and acne. What's more, it causes millions around the world to suffer from digestive problems because of lactose intolerance. That's a startling 75 per cent of the global population.

So while milk is a convenient source of calcium as well as many other vitamins and minerals, it seems that we should probably all limit the amount of milk we drink.

Unit 4

DEVELOPING SPEAKING

Exercise 6, p51

A People feel informed about science

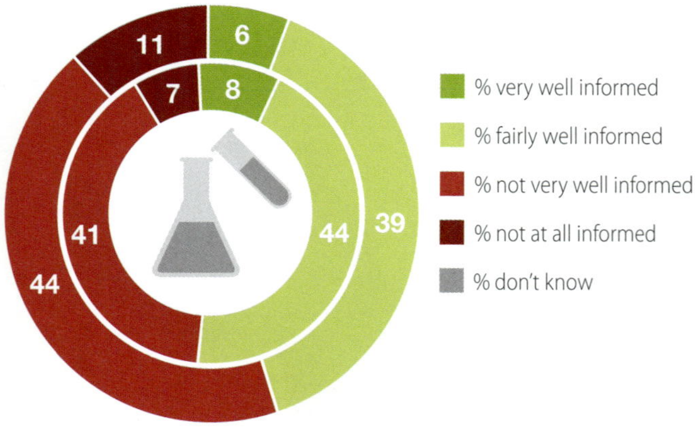

C Hopes and concerns about science over time

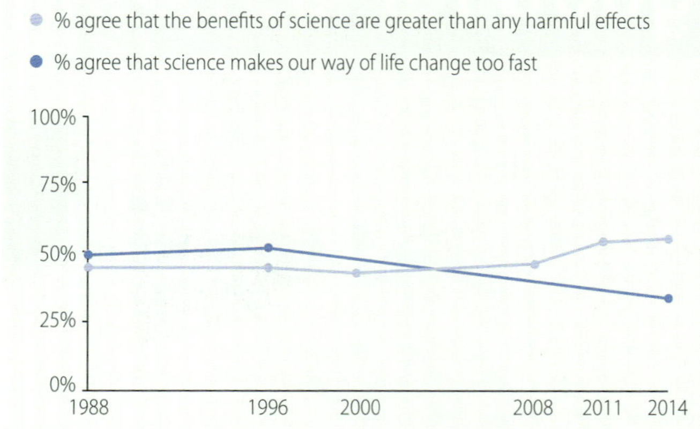

B Overall hopes and concerns about science

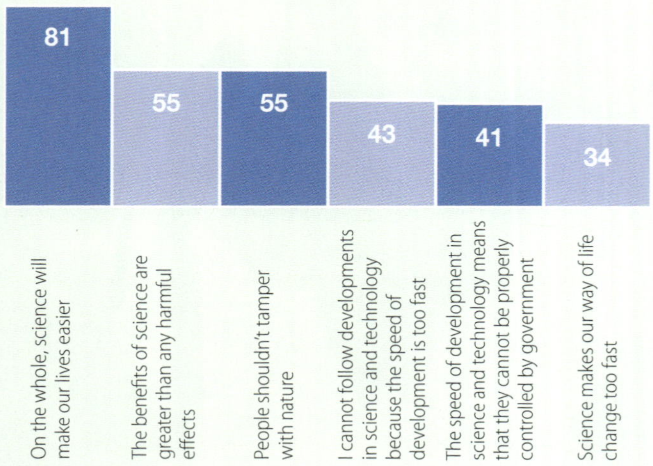

D Risks versus benefits

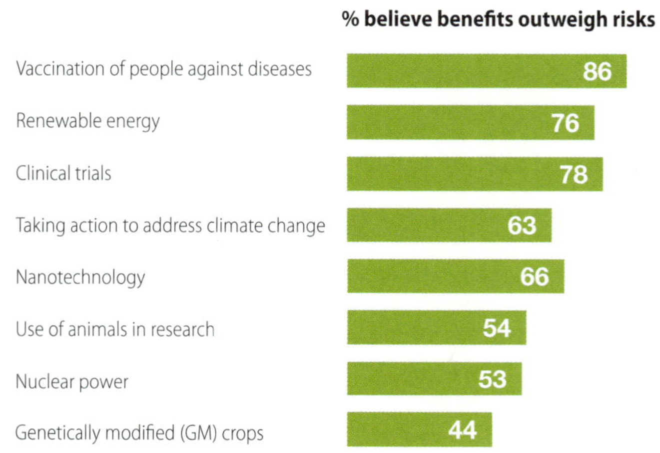

Unit 8

DEVELOPING SPEAKING

Exercise 8, p103

Unit 9

DEVELOPING SPEAKING

Exercise 5, p117

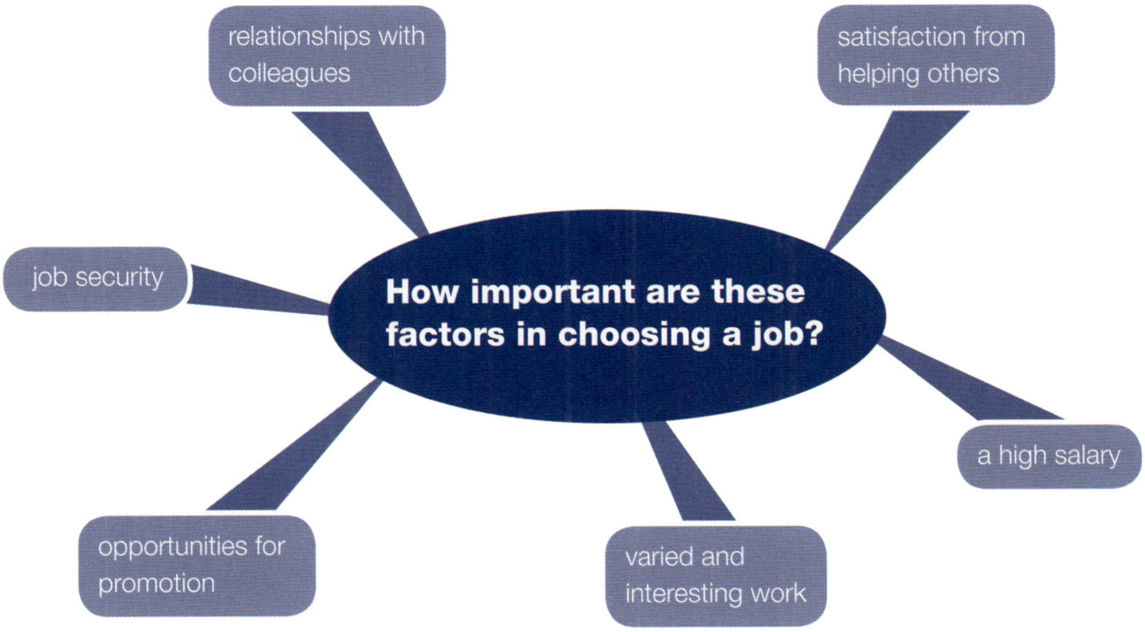

Unit 10

DEVELOPING SPEAKING

Exercises 8a–b, p129

You will have to talk about this topic for one to two minutes.

You have one minute to think about what you are going to say.

You can make some notes to help you.

Describe a positive learning experience that you have had, either in or out of school.

You should say:

- *where and when it was.*
- *what the experience was.*
- *who was to thank for the experience.*

Also, explain why the experience was so positive and what the outcome was.

Student A:

1 Do you think technology will replace teachers in the future? Why/Why not?

2 What do you think is necessary for a positive learning environment?

3 In the past people stopped learning when they finished school or university, but now people talk about 'lifelong learning'. Why do you think this is?

Student B:

1 Why is education so important to society as a whole?

2 Do you think that education's main goal is to prepare people for the world of work? Why/Why not?

3 Until which age do you think education should be compulsory and why?

Unit 1

Past simple

We use the **past simple** to:

1 describe finished actions or situations in the past.

2 say that one thing happened after another.

Past continuous

We use the **past continuous** to:

1 talk about activities in progress at a moment in the past.

2 describe scenes in a story or description.

3 talk about an activity in progress when another, shorter activity happened or interrupted it. It tells us that an action was in progress, but not that it was finished.

Present perfect simple

We use the **present perfect simple** to talk about:

1 an experience in someone's lifetime, without saying the exact time when the event occurred.

*I've **seen** Coldplay in concert.*

2 recent events which have a result in the present.

*She's **lost** her bag. (= She hasn't got her bag right now.)*

3 actions or situations that began in the past but continue in the present.

*Mark's **lived** here for ten years.*

4 actions finished very recently.

*They've just **had** an accident.*

Unit 4

Zero conditional

FORM

If + **present simple**, … **present simple**

If you don't water plants, they die.

USE

We use the zero conditional to talk about situations that are generally or always true.

First conditional

FORM

If + **present simple**, … ***will*** + infinitive

If you eat junk food, you will put on weight.

USE

We use the first conditional to talk about possible and probable situations in the future, and their consequences.

Second conditional

FORM

If + **past simple**, … ***would/wouldn't*** + infinitive

If I had a beard, I'd look older.

USE

We use the second conditional to talk about imaginary or improbable situations and their consequences. The imaginary or improbable sentences are in the present or future, not in the past.

Unit 6

Reported speech – Statements

FORM

The tense of the verb in reported speech usually changes, going one tense 'back'. The past perfect stays the same.

Direct speech tenses	Reported speech tenses
present simple	past simple
present continuous	past continuous
present/past perfect	past perfect
past simple	past perfect
will	*would*
can	*could*
may	*might*
must/have to	*had to*

Could, ***would***, ***should*** and ***might*** do not change.

When the statement is something which is still true, or is and will always be true, the tense of the verb in reported speech usually stays the same.

'I'm American.' ➤ *Hayden said he's American.*

Pronouns and possessive adjectives also change.

'I love your smile.' ➤ *Brad said he loved her smile.*

Here are some other words which change from direct to reported speech.

With **say** you do not need to use a personal object.

He said it was going to be a great film.

~~*He said me it was going to be a great film.*~~

With **tell** you must use a personal object.

He told me it was going to be a great film.

~~*He told that it was going to be a great film.*~~

Direct speech	Reported speech
this/these	that/those
here	there
today	that day
yesterday	the day before
tomorrow	the next/following day
last night	that night
next (week/year)	the following (week/year)
last (week/year)	the previous (week/year)
a (week/year) ago	a (week/year) before

Unit 7

The passive

FORM

subject + **be** + **past participle** (**+ by + agent**)

*Smoking **is forbidden**.*(present simple)

*The prize **has been awarded by the committee**.* (present perfect)

*This speech **is being listened to by millions of people**.* (present continuous)

*Lots of new technology **will be invented** in the future.* (will)

We make the passive with the appropriate tense and form of the verb *to be* and the past participle of the verb.

To make questions in the passive, we put the first auxiliary verb before the subject.

*Is the concert **being shown** on TV?*

*Has the film **been finished**?*

We use the preposition *by* to introduce the agent, that is, the person or thing which does the action.

USE

We use the passive when:

1. we are more interested in the action than the people who do the action.
   *A suspicious bag **has been found** in the station.*
2. we do not know who exactly does the action.
   *The bank **has** just **been robbed**.*
3. it is obvious or understood who did the action.
   *The suspect **was arrested**.*

In some languages, reflexive or impersonal forms are used instead of the passive.

Macmillan Education
4 Crinan Street
London N1 9XW
A division of Springer Nature Limited

Companies and representatives throughout the world

ISBN 978-0-230-47099-6

This edition published 2016
First edition entitled *Gateway B2+ Student's Book* published in 2011

Designed by emc design ltd
Illustrated by A Corazón Abierto (Sylvie Poggio Artists) pp9, 10, 11, 28, 29(r) 32, 36, 73, 95, 115, 125, 136(r), 137; Kathy Baxendale p26; Tim Bradford (Illustration Ltd) pp13(br), 80, 92, 130, 136(l); Janos Jantner (Beehive Illustration) p89(tr); Mark Ruffle pp6, 13(c), 14, 25, 29(l), 33, 37, 51, 81, 85, 89(b), 103, 129, 155, 156; Norbert Sipos (Beehive Illustration) p134.

Cover design by emc design ltd and Springer Nature Ltd
Cover photographs by **Getty Images**/Dougal Waters(friends); **Thinkstock**/Zoonar/N.Okhitin(mountains).
Picture research by Emily Taylor

Author's acknowledgements – David Spencer
I would like to give a big thank you to the whole Macmillan team in the UK for their dedication, hard work, and enthusiasm throughout the writing of this course. Thanks also to all the other Macmillan teams around the world for their help, encouragement and always making me feel welcome. Very special thanks to Colegio Europeo Aristos in Getafe, Spain. The daily contact with my students there continues to be a main source of inspiration and I am sincerely grateful to every one of my students, past and present. Massive thanks, as always, to Gemma, Jamie and Becky for their unending love and support.

This book is dedicated to Emily Rosser.

The publishers would like to thank staff and pupils at the following schools in Mexico and Spain for helping us so enthusiastically with our research for the course: Concha Campos, IES Burgo de Las Rozas, Las Rozas, Madrid; Félix Gaspar, IES Las Encinas; Villanueva de la Cañada, Madrid; Cristina Moisen, IES Joaquín Turina, Madrid; Colegio Montessori Cuautitlán; Colegio Conrad Gessner; Colegio Erasmo de Rotterdam; Colegio Kanic, Centro Educativo Erich Fromm; Universidad Franco Mexicana; Centro Pedagógico María Montessori de Ecatepec; Instituto Cultural; Escuela Maestro Manuel Acosta; Liceo Sakbé De México.

The publishers would also like to thank all those who reviewed or piloted the first edition of Gateway: Benjamin Affolter, Evelyn Andorfer, Anna Ciereszynska, Regina Culver, Anna Dabrowska, Justyna Deja, Ondrej Dosedel, Lisa Durham, Dagmar Eder, Eva Ellederovan, H Fouad, Sabrina Funes, Luiza Gervescu, Isabel Gonzalez Bueno, Jutta Habringer, Stela Halmageanu, Marta Hilgier, Andrea Hutterer, Nicole Ioakimidis, Mag. Annemarie Kammerhofer, Irina Kondrasheva, Sonja Lengauer, Gabriela Liptakova, Andrea Littlewood, Maria Cristina Maggi, Silvia Miranda Barbara Nowak, Agnieska Orlińska, Anna Orlowska, Maria Paula Palou, Marta Piotrowska, N Reda, Katharina Schatz, Roswitha Schwarz, Barbara Ścibor, Katarzyna Sochacka, Joanna Spoz, Monica Srtygner, Marisol Suppan, Stephanie Sutter, Halina Tyliba, Prilipko, Maria Vizgina, Vladyko, Pia Wimmer, Katarzyna Zadrożna-Attia and Katarzyna Zaremba-Jaworska.

The author and publishers would like to thank the following for permission to reproduce their photographs:

Alamy/AF archive p34, Alamy/Backyard Productions p38(tl), Alamy/Bildagentur-online p56(cr), Alamy/BSIP SA p52, Alamy/BUILT Images p70(bl), Alamy/Bill Cheyrou p66(bl), Alamy/Robert Churchill p130-131, Alamy/Cultura Creative p71(bl), Alamy/Cultura RM p102(tl), Alamy/Dinodia Photos p76, Alamy/EPA european pressphoto agency p33(cr), Alamy/Antonio Guillem Fernandez p11(bm), Alamy/Anthony Hatley p77(tl), Alamy/Steve Hellerstein p56(tr), Alamy/Elizabeth Livermore p71(br), Alamy/Erik Reis p66(tl), Alamy/Andres Rodriguez p110(stepping feet), Alamy/The Art Archive p57, Alamy/Marco Varrone p47, Alamy/Zoonar GmbH p164(bl); **BananaStock** p70(cm); **BrandX** p36(clock); **ComStock** p36(razor); **Corbis**/Gardel Bertrand/Hemis p162(tml), Corbis/Mara Brandl/imagebroker p14(bl), Corbis/Cadalpe p91(tl), Corbis/Kai Chiang/Golden Pixels LLC p71(tr), Corbis/J. Glueck/F1 Online p49(tl), Corbis/Ted Horowitz p50, Corbis/JGI/Jamie Grill p77(cr), Corbis/Iryna Hramavataya p90(br), Corbis/See Li/Demotix p36(cr), Corbis/Ian Lishman/Juice Images p19(bottom), Corbis/Macduff Everton p83(bl), Corbis/Mango Productions p74(drummer), Corbis/Simon Marcus p165(bl) Corbis/Philipp Nemenz p59(tl), Corbis/Hugh Sitton p45(cr), Corbis/Tim Tadder p90(cr), Corbis/Wolfgang Weinhupl/Westend61 p67; **Eyewire**/Getty Images p19(cr); **Getty Images** p36(bulb, remote), Getty Images/AFP pp24(bl), 165(cl), Getty Images/Altrendo p102(br), Getty Images/James Ambler/Barcroft USA p33(br), Getty Images/Xavier Arnau p78(br), Getty Images/AWL Images RM p24(tl), Getty Images/Thomas Barwick p59(cr), Getty Images/Blend Images pp13, 63(tl), 127(bm), Getty Images/Lionel Bonaventure/AFP p33(tl), Getty Images/Brand X pp32, 75(tm), 101(br), Getty Images/Peter Cade p165(cr), Getty Images/Nick Clements p117(bl), Getty Images/Cultura Exclusive p116(bl), Getty Images/Cultura RF pp22–23(background), 102(tr), Getty Images/Robert Deutschman p18(tr), Getty Images/Claudia Dewald p74(br), Getty Images/DigitalVision Vectors p84(background header), Getty Images/DRB Images, LLC p10(br), Getty Images/Flickr State p164(br), Getty Images/Fuse p10(cl), Getty Images/Franckreporter pp26, 89(br), Getty Images/Gallo Images p97(bm), Getty Images/Gallo Images Roots Collection p162(tr), Getty Images/Hemera Thinkstock/Images p85(mouse), Getty Images/Noel Hendrickson p87, Getty Images/Hero Images pp74(studying), 135 Getty Images/Imagesource pp10(tr), 84(tr), Getty Images/ISC Archives p21, Getty Images/iStockphoto pp36(ring), 126(highlighters) Getty Images/iStockphoto/Thinkstock pp36(phone), 45(cl), 48(bl), 49(br), 56(cm), 85(phone), Getty Images/Chris Jackson p65(cl), Getty Images/Jupiterimages p162(cr), Getty Images/Sean Justice p30, Getty Images/Maskot p12, Getty Images/Nikola Miljkovic p25(tm), Getty Images/Marek Mnich p14(cm), Getty Images/Buero Monaco p7(4), Getty Images/National Geographic Creative p25(tl), Getty Images/OJO Images RF p25(tr), Getty Images/Paper Boat Creative p85(br), Getty Images/PeopleImages.com p37(br), Getty Images/David Sacks p118, Getty Images/Kristian Sekulic p35, Getty Images/Jordan Siemens p91(cl), Getty Images/Stephen Simpson p130(cl), Getty Images/Gary K Smith p53, Getty Images/Cameron Spencer p65(tl), Getty Images/Sturti p115(cr), Getty Images/TongRo Image Stock RF p36(tap), Getty Images/Dimitri Vervitsiotis p6, Getty Images/Vetta pp162(tmr),163, Getty Images/Vladimir Rys Photography p108(cm), Getty Images/Westend61 p11(yawning), Getty Images/James Woodson p70(cl); **Image100** p18(top); **ImageSource** pp7(1), 36(comb), 93(tm), 119; **Anjana Iyer** used with permission p123; **Macmillan Publishers Ltd** p36(iron), Macmillan Publishers Ltd/Macmillan Australia p36(fork); **Photodisc**/Getty Images pp19(top, cl), 36(mirror, vase), 56(br, bl, cl), 99, 103, Photodisc/Ryan McVay p9(baby); **Plainpicture**/Caiaimages pp27(cr), 164(bm), PlainPicture/Robert Harding p39, PlainPicture/Frank Herfort p117(tcm), Plainpicture/Maskot p90(tr), PlainPicture/OJO p59(bl), Plainpicture/Kniel Synnatzschke p85(tr); **Joe Plimmer** p111(tm, cr); **Rex Features**/Everett/REX_Shutterstock p128, Rex Features/Jason Rasgon/REX Shutterstock p45(tr), Rex Features/REX_Shutterstock p40, Rex Features/SIPA/REX Shutterstock p108(br); **Shutterstock**/Ammak p85(tripod), Shutterstock/Gumpanat p88(header), Shutterstock/Jacob Lund p111(br); **Stockbyte/PunchStock/Getty Images** p134; **SuperStock** p56(tm); **Thinkstock** pp10-11(speech bubbles), 11(people with speech bubbles), 62(tr header, emojis), 62-63(background), 74(tr), 74-75(background), 100-101(background), 110(header background), 114-115(emojis), 114-115(illustrations), 122(map), Thinkstock/Digital Vision p96(tm), Thinkstock/Getty Images/Dorling Kindersley RF p22(cm), Thinkstock/Getty Images/Ingram Publishing p36-37(background), Thinkstock/Getty Images/iStockphoto pp7(2,3), 9(wallet), 14(br), 19(cm), 22(bm), 23(bm), 27(bl), 36(tl, br, tr, key), 44(tr, tm), 61, 64, 48-49(background), 48(tr), 48-49(chocolates), 49(chocolate swirl), 58(tm), 62(br), 70(tm, header, hands), 70(bm), 71(cm), 73, 74(messy kitchen), 77(br), 78(tl, tm, tr), 82, 83(tl, cl), 88(dollar plane), 88-89(euro planes), 88(br,bl), 88-89(background), 93(tr), 97(cr), 100-101(ereader), 101(grass and sky), 104, 110(arrows), 113, 114(br), 116(tl), 117(tm, tr), 122(tr), 126-127(background), 126-127(screwed up paper), 162(tl), Thinkstock/View Stock RF p125; **Truro and Penwith College** used with permission p111(cl); **Ross Wallace**/Copyright Guardian News & Media Ltd 2015 p97(tl).

The author and publishers are grateful for permission to reprint the following copyright material:
Graphs taken from 'Public Attitudes to Science 2014' © Ipsos MORI & BIS. Reprinted with permission.
Extract from 'Feet on the seat could land Wrexham passenger in court' by Claire Gallagher. Originally published in The Leader on 30 June 2010 © NWN Media Ltd, 2010. Reprinted with permission. www.nwnmedia.co.uk
Material adapted from 'Caught speeding? Well it's cheaper than skateboarding' © Courtney Trenwith, 2010. Originally published by Fairfax Media at http://www.brisbanetimes.com.au Reprinted with permission.
Material adapted from 'Roommate Conflict for Students and Families' © Westminster College. Reprinted with permission.
Extracts taken and material adapted from 'Seven decks of cards memorised each day, 1,500 digits recited aloud and 4.5 years of training' by Lucy Waterlow and 'Uni degree vs apprentice' by Ruth Tierney © Associated Newspapers Ltd., 2014. First published online at www.thedailymail.com Reprinted with permission.
Extracts and material adapted from 'Malaria-carrying mosquitoes wiped out in lab with genetic method that creates male-only offspring' © Imperial College London, 2014. Published at www.sciencedaily.com Reprinted with permission.
Material Adapted from 'Apprentice Case Studies' © Truro and Penwith College, 2015. First published at http://www.truro-penwith.ac.uk/business/case-studies Reprinted with permission.
Extracts and material adapted from 'A Genius Explains' by Richard Johnson and 'Experience: my bungee cord snapped' by Eric Langworthy © 2015 Guardian News and Media Limited. First published online at www.theguardian.com Reprinted with permission.

Book covers reproduced by permission:
Egmont UK Ltd/War Horse, published by Egmont UK Ltd, cover image used with permission p67
Hachette Childrens Publishers/Skellig by David Almond published by Hatchett Childrens, cover image used with permission p67

Printed and bound in Great Britain by Bell and Bain Ltd, Glasgow

2021 2020 2019
20 18 17